NEIL AND HARRIET PIKE met trekking in Chilean Patagonia in 2002 and together discovered a love for exploring the natural world on foot. They hiked extensively in Europe and Asia before buying bikes in Istanbul and cycling home to Oxford. An 18-month bike tour through the Andes followed, which ignited a passion for cycling high roads and climbing 6000m volcanoes. After a traverse of the Himalaya they were again drawn back by the majesty of the Andes to hike and bike some of the world's most spectacular mountain trails. They know of no better place for this than the Cordillera Blanca and the Cordillera Huayhuash, the ranges on the doorstep of Huaraz. Blog posts about their trips can be found at 🖥 pikesonbikes.com and information on thousands of kilometres of Andean dirt roads at 🖥 andesbybike.com.

CASS GILBERT wrote the mountain biking section for this book. Cass has been wandering the world on his bicycle for the last 15 years. He's traversed Asia and the Middle East, run a guiding business in the Indian Himalaya, bikepacked his way around the American South West, and ridden dirt from Alaska to Ushuaia. Catch up with his travels at 🖥 whileoutriding.com.

Authors

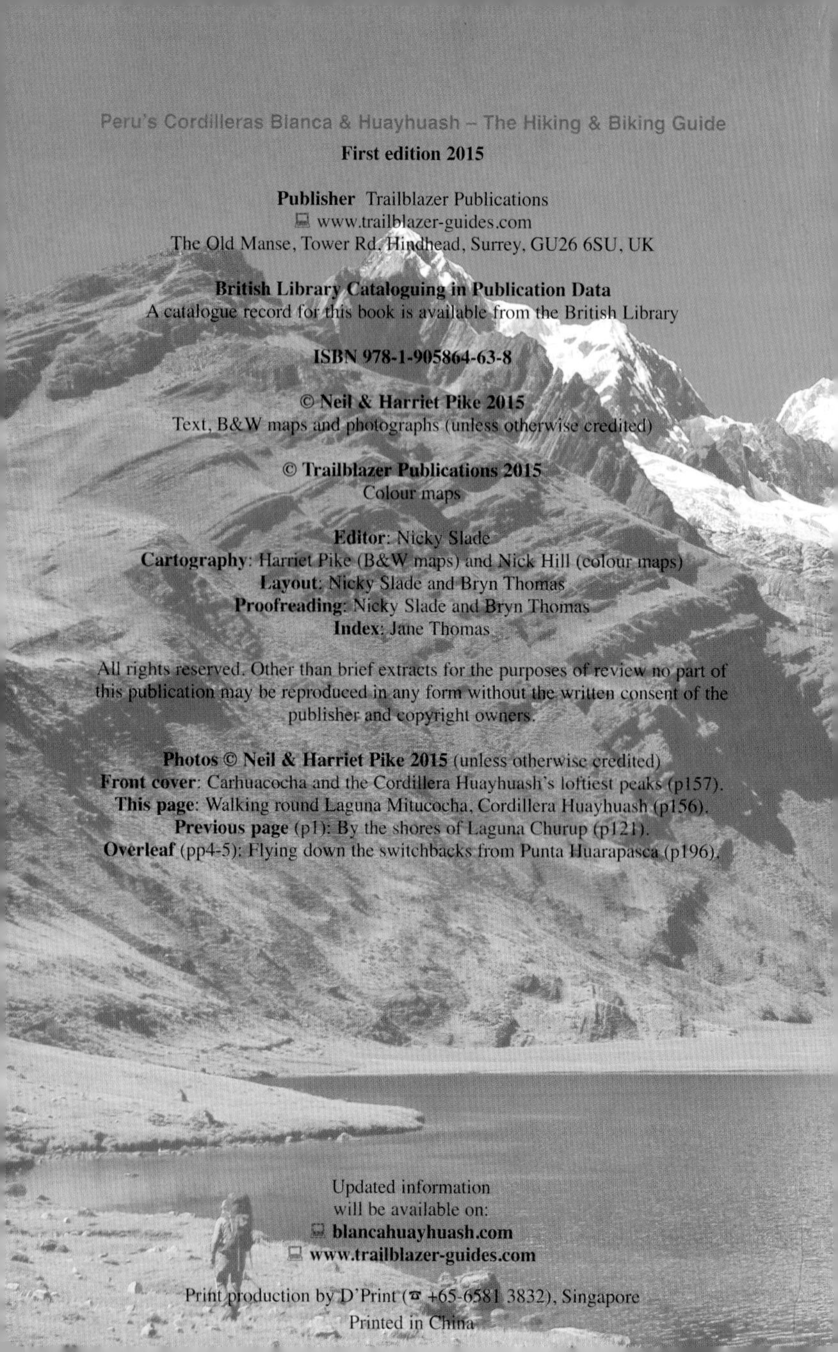

Peru's Cordilleras Blanca & Huayhuash – The Hiking & Biking Guide
First edition 2015

Publisher Trailblazer Publications
www.trailblazer-guides.com
The Old Manse, Tower Rd, Hindhead, Surrey, GU26 6SU, UK

British Library Cataloguing in Publication Data
A catalogue record for this book is available from the British Library

ISBN 978-1-905864-63-8

© **Neil & Harriet Pike 2015**
Text, B&W maps and photographs (unless otherwise credited)

© **Trailblazer Publications 2015**
Colour maps

Editor: Nicky Slade
Cartography: Harriet Pike (B&W maps) and Nick Hill (colour maps)
Layout: Nicky Slade and Bryn Thomas
Proofreading: Nicky Slade and Bryn Thomas
Index: Jane Thomas

Photos © Neil & Harriet Pike 2015 (unless otherwise credited)
Front cover: Carhuacocha and the Cordillera Huayhuash's loftiest peaks (p157).
This page: Walking round Laguna Mitucocha, Cordillera Huayhuash (p156).
Previous page (p1): By the shores of Laguna Churup (p121).
Overleaf (pp4-5): Flying down the switchbacks from Punta Huarapasca (p196).

Updated information
will be available on:
blancahuayhuash.com
www.trailblazer-guides.com

Print production by D'Print (☎ +65-6581 3832), Singapore
Printed in China

PERU'S
Cordilleras Blanca &
Huayhuash

THE HIKING & BIKING GUIDE

NEIL & HARRIET PIKE

Mountain biking section researched and written by
CASS GILBERT

TRAILBLAZER PUBLICATIONS

Contents

Contents

ABOUT THIS BOOK

The aim of this guide is to give the information needed to hike and bike a multitude of routes in the Cordilleras Blanca and Huayhuash, from the well-known circuits to valleys which rarely see a tourist. Virtually all the multi-day trips described require camping, often at sites which come with great views but no facilities. We hope the book helps promote this beautiful area and encourages more responsible trekking practices in the region, for the benefit of all: local people, visitors and the remarkable mountain environment.

ACKNOWLEDGEMENTS

This guide could not have happened without the help of many people in Peru and the UK. Special thanks to Cass Gilbert for his unflagging Andes enthusiasm and willingness to go swimming in the pursuit of virgin biking trails; to Marie Timmermans and David Lazo, Charlie Good, Julio Olaza, Antonio Paredes, Clodoaldo Figueroa, Edson Ramírez, Philip Bennie, Sandra Aquino, Dmitri Antonio, Jo Haines, Benjamin Webb, Parker Kempf, John Biggar and the Pike clan for their help in making the information more accurate than it would otherwise have been.

Thanks to the Trailblazer crew for making it all come about: Bryn Thomas for believing in the project, Nicky Slade for turning the text into a book, and Nick Hill for magicking kmz files into colour maps. Thanks also for the use of material in the Lima and Minimum Impact sections.

Lastly gracias to biking friends Anna Kortschak, James Butcher, Sarah Bedford, Alex Messner Krauss and Nathan Jesus Haley, without whom the research wouldn't have been nearly so much fun.

A REQUEST

The authors and publisher have tried to ensure that this guide is as accurate as possible. Nevertheless, things change. If you notice any changes or omissions, please write to Trailblazer (address on p2) or email us at 🖳 pikes@trailblazer-guides.com. A free copy of the next edition will be sent to persons making a significant contribution.

INTRODUCTION

As mountain adventure destinations, the Cordilleras Blanca and Huayhuash are unrivalled in South America. Well known amongst mountaineers, the unique landscape of sheer valleys, colourful alpine lakes, ice falls and giant glaciated peaks also offer some of the best hiking and biking on Earth. These ranges form the snowy highlights of Peru's 2000km Andean spine, and routes that wind their way through dramatic alpine scenery have attracted trekkers for decades.

> **What really distinguishes the area from other great ranges is the accessibility of high trails and peaks**

What really distinguishes the area from other great ranges is the accessibility of high trails and peaks. There are no Himalayan walk-ins: you'll be near a glacier by the second day of almost every multi-day hike in this book. This brings with it the risk of going too high too fast, so spend time acclimatizing in the lively regional capital Huaraz beforehand – the city makes an excellent base for day hikes and rides.

Situated in the department of Ancash, the Cordillera Blanca is sandwiched between the populated Callejón de Huaylas (the Río Santa valley to the west of the range, which houses Huaraz) and Callejón de Conchucos – the series of river valleys to the east of the mountains. The Cordillera Blanca is protected by Parque Nacional Huascarán, and treks within this park and in the Cordillera

(Above): Early morning cloud on 6094m Jirishanca (see p156).

Huayhuash are in wilderness areas with sparse, but friendly, local populations. Lower down, expect a more colourful scene; it's not unusual to happen upon a

Some walking trails were laid down by ancient civilizations millennia ago

village fiesta with live music, traditional clothing, dancing, and of course a little drinking.

Some walking trails were laid down by ancient civilizations millennia ago, but more recently audacious Peruvian road builders have chiselled ways through the heart of the Blanca – ribbons of dirt and tarmac which crawl up precipitous hillsides and drift within a stone's throw of glaciers. Cycle tourers are drawn by the most thrilling high passes in the Andes – it won't just be the altitude taking your breath away. Cycling allows

Cycle tourers are drawn by the most thrilling high passes in the Andes

an authentic insight into Peruvian mountain life, the chance to pedal past *campesinos* out tending crops of quinoa and potato, and visit bucolic

villages which are a world away from our fast-paced digital media age.

Mountain biking is beginning to blossom in the region too. In a country known for its verticality, word is getting out about the extraordinary possibili-

ties for cross-country riding or gnarly singletrack descents that shoot hundreds of metres down hillsides.

In a country known for its verticality, word is getting out about the extraordinary possibilities for cross-country riding

The majority of outdoor-loving visitors to Peru make a beeline for the Inca trails near Cusco, but for those after magnificent mountainscapes and less crowded paths, these more northerly Cordilleras are the place to come.

ITINERARIES   [for overview see overleaf]

Good trekking options in this area are almost unlimited, and there are many exciting roads to cycle, so time rather than a lack of ideas is likely to be the constraining factor on any trip. It is important to factor in time to reach the region, and allow a couple of days at the beginning in Huaraz or another mountain town, to aid acclimatization. Starting with some of the easier day trips, before setting out on a longer, more strenuous hike/ride, will not only improve your chances of enjoying your time in the mountains but will also reduce the risk of suffering from Acute Mountain Sickness (AMS, see p26). *(continued on p13)*

INTRODUCTION

(**Below**): Panoramic views of the Cordillera Huayhuash, from near Mojón (p195).

TREKKING & CYCLING ROUTES

	Trekking route	Start	Finish	Days*
1	Alpamayo Basecamp	Pomabamba	Hualcayán ,	5-9
2	Santa Cruz	Vaquería	Cashapampa	4
3	Santa Cruz – Alpamayo Circuit	Cashapampa/ Vaquería	Hualcayán/ Cashapampa	7-14
4	Ulta – Yanama	Quebrada Ulta	Yanama	2
5	Laguna 69	Cebollapampa	Cebollapampa	1
6	Artesonraju Basecamp	Pueblo Parón	Pueblo Parón	2
7	Laguna Lejiacocha	Vicos	Vicos	1-2
8	Akilpo – Ishinca	San Miguel de Aco	Collón/Pashpa	3-4
9	Quebrada & Laguna Ishinca	Pashpa	Collón	3
10	Laguna Wilcacocha	Chihuipampa	Chihuipampa	0.5
11	Laguna Churup	Pitec	Pitec	0.5
12	Laguna Shallap	Pitec	Pitec	1
13	Quilcayhuanca – Cojup	Llupa	Marian	3-4
14	Chacas – Huari	Chacas	Huari	2-3
15	Quebrada Rurichinchay	Huari	Huari	3
16	Quebrada Rurec (Conchucos)	Huántar	Huántar	2
17	Quebrada Carhuascancha	Chavín	San Marcos	4-5
18	Olleros – Chavín	Olleros	Chavín	3
19	Quebrada Rurec (Huaylas)	Olleros	Olleros	3
20	Quebrada Raria	Carpa	Machac	3
21	Huayhuash Circuit	Quartelhuain	Llamac	7-14
	Cycling route	**Start**	**Finish**	**Days***
1.1	Huaraz Ruins Loop	Huaraz	Huaraz	0.5
1.2	Negra Acclimatization Loop	Huaraz	Huaraz	0.5
1.3	Blanca Acclimatization Loop	Huaraz	Huaraz	1
1.4	Santo Toribio Circuit	Huaraz	Huaraz	1
1.5	Laguna Llaca	Huaraz	Huaraz	1
2	Huascarán Circuit	Huaraz	Huaraz	6-7
3	Huayhuash & Puya Raimondii Loop	Huaraz	Huaraz	6-7
4	Cordillera Blanca Circuit	Huaraz	Huaraz	10-14
5	Laguna Parón	Caraz	Caraz	2
6	Winchus Loop	Caraz	Caraz	2

¶ Navigation
1 **Easy** – Routes are on clear paths; there may even be occasional signposting.
2 **Some navigation skills** – Sections with only faint trails, or short stretches with no path.
3 **Challenging** – Sections with no trail, where route finding is tricky.

† Terrain
1 **Easy** – Walking on paths which are in decent condition and not overly steep.
2 **Moderate** – Trails which may be on rough or loose ground, including scree and boulders. Some steep inclines – trekking poles are helpful.
3 **Hard** – Route includes some short, steep sections where hands will be needed to ascend/descend and care needs to be taken; or, walking on very rough ground.

OVERVIEW TABLES

Distance	Max Alt	Daily Climb	Navigation¶	Terrain†	Popularity§	Page No
68km+	4860m+	800m	2	2	2	p74
55km	4780m	450m	1	1	3	p88
93km+	4860m+	700m	2	2	2/3	p99
20km	4840m	450m	2	2	1	p104
13km	4600m	700m	1	1	3	p107
32km	4770m	800m	1	2	2	p109
23km	4640m	1700m	2	1	2	p111
38km+	5060m	750m	3	3	1/3	p112
38km+	4980m	500m	1	1	3	p116
7km	3720m	600m	1	1	2	p119
6km	4470m	650m	1	3	3	p121
23km	4280m	550m	1	1	1	p121
47km+	5080m	600m	3	2	2	p123
39km	4520m	750m	1	1	1	p128
56km	4560m	1000m	2	2	1	p132
32km	4220m	600m	2	1	1	p133
55km	4780m	600m	3	3	1	p137
44km	4680m	450m	1	1	2	p143
48km	4490m	400m	1	1	1	p146
39km	4800m	300m	2	2	1	p148
110km+	5060m	650m	2	2	3	p152

Distance	Max Alt	Daily Climb	Paved/Unpaved	Page No
23km	3660m	650m	20%/80%	p178
29km	3280m	650m	40%/60%	p179
39km	3870m	900m	10%/90%	p183
47km	4040m	1100m	50%/50%	p184
47km	4450m	1400m	15%/85%	p185
299km	4890m	1050m	60%/40%	p186
315km	4880m	900m	55%/45%	p192
589km	4470m	1100m	30%/70%	p197
67km	4200m	1000m	5%/95%	p209
90km	4380m	1250m	55%/45%	p210

§ Popularity

You'll never find yourself in a 'tourist crocodile', and even on the Santa Cruz trek or Huayhuash Circuit it's possible to spend hours alone on the trail; however, some routes are more popular than others. The ratings below refer to high season – in rainy season it would be a surprise to meet anyone other than a local *campesino* (peasant farmer) on any trail.

1 Quiet – Unlikely to meet other hikers.

2 Moderate – Expect occasional meetings with other hikers or groups, but not uncommon to have an official campsite to yourself.

3 Popular – Expect to meet other hikers during the day and have company at campsites.

* Actual walking/cycling days. Does not include rest days or acclimatization days.

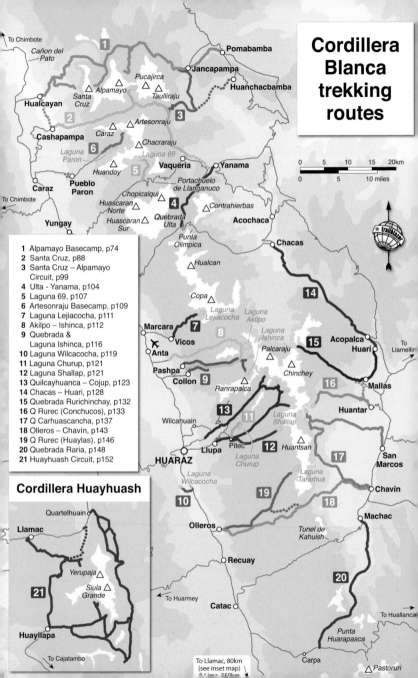

Cordillera Blanca trekking routes

0	5	10	15	20km
0		5		10 miles

1 Alpamayo Basecamp, p74
2 Santa Cruz, p88
3 Santa Cruz – Alpamayo Circuit, p99
4 Ulta - Yanama, p104
5 Laguna 69, p107
6 Artesonraju Basecamp, p109
7 Laguna Lejiacocha, p111
8 Akilpo – Ishinca, p112
9 Quebrada & Laguna Ishinca, p116
10 Laguna Wilcacocha, p119
11 Laguna Churup, p121
12 Laguna Shallap, p121
13 Quilcayhuanca – Cojup, p123
14 Chacas – Huari, p128
15 Quebrada Rurichinchay, p132
16 Q Rurec (Conchucos), p133
17 Q Carhuascancha, p137
18 Olleros – Chavín, p143
19 Q Rurec (Huaylas), p146
20 Quebrada Raria, p148
21 Huayhuash Circuit, p152

Cordillera Huayhuash

The suggested itineraries below and on p14 are for those arriving unacclimatized. If you're coming from Cusco or another high altitude area see the table (preceding pages) for actual walking or cycling days.

TREKKING ITINERARIES

● **7-10 days** Do some day hikes near Huaraz before a short multi-day trek such as Santa Cruz, Laguna Ishinca or Quilcayhuanca – Cojup.

● **2-3 weeks** After some acclimatization, tackle one of the classic longer treks in the region – the Huayhuash Circuit or Santa Cruz – Alpamayo.

● **1 month** Do the above, adding in a trip to the quiet Callejón de Conchucos; or, walk both the Huayhuash Circuit and Santa Cruz – Alpamayo.

● **Off the beaten track** Try a trek in or to Conchucos, like Carhuascancha or Raria. Closer to Huaraz, explore Quebradas Akilpo or Rurec.

● **To see ruins** Head to Yayno on the Santa Cruz – Alpamayo Circuit, or spend a day in Chavín before or after one of the many routes near the town. Closer to Huaraz, visit Wilcahuaín or Honcopampa.

● **To avoid camping** Stay at the refugios in Quebrada Ishinca, or explore the quebradas above Huaraz or Yungay from the comfort of a luxurious lodge.

(**Below**): Looking down over Laguna Churup (p121).

INTRODUCTION

INTRODUCTION

CYCLING ITINERARIES

● **10 days to 2 weeks**   Warm up with day rides near Huaraz, then spend your time pedalling the Cordillera Blanca's classic route, the Huascarán Circuit.

● **3 weeks**   Cycle the Huascarán Circuit before heading off for the Huayhuash Loop or trips into the hills above Caraz.

● **1 month**   This is enough time to cycle the Huayhuash Loop, then a circuit of the whole Blanca, including crossings of Punta Olímpica and Llanganuco.

SUGGESTED ITINERARIES (see also p10)

Huascarán Circuit
Day 1. Carhuaz
Day 2. Quebrada Ulta
Day 3. Chacas
Day 4. Yanama
Day 5. Quebrada
        Llanganuco
Day 6. Huaraz

Huayhuash and Puya Raimondii Loop
Day 1. Catac
Day 2. Chiquián
Day 3. Llamac/
        Quartelhuain
Day 4. Huallanca
Day 5. Near Huarapasca
Day 6. Huaraz

Cordillera Blanca Circuit
Day 1. Recuay/Catac/
        Querococha
Day 2. Chavín
Day 3. Huari
Day 4. San Luis
Day 5. Llumpa
Day 6. Pomabamba
Day 7. Andaymayo
Day 8. Yanac
Day 9. Caraz
Day 10. Huaraz

(Below): On the lower slopes of the Cordillera Blanca, with the Cordillera Negra in the background. (Photo © Cass Gilbert).

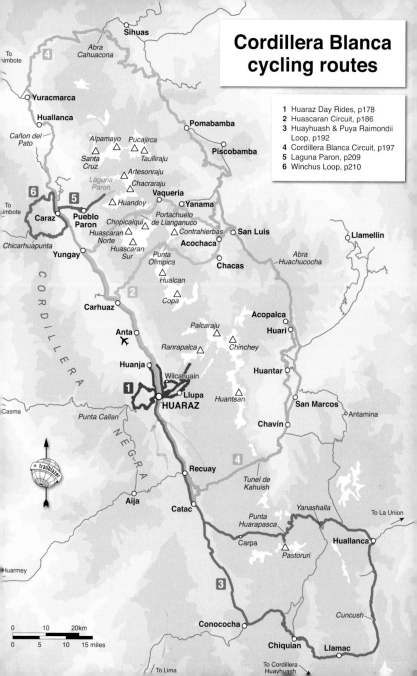

INTRODUCTION

When to go

WEATHER

The best time for outdoor enthusiasts to visit the region is between May and September, the **dry season** in the Peruvian Cordillera. Though weather patterns in the Andes are no longer as stable and predictable as previously, July and August are still the most popular months as the skies are generally at their clearest, and you're most likely to get the best mountain views.

The best time for outdoor enthusiasts to visit is between May and September

The **wet season** runs from November to March, and though it doesn't rain all the time, or even every day, the peaks can be enshrouded in cloud for long

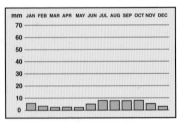

Average rainfall (mm)

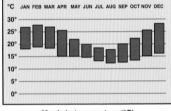

Max/min temperature (°C)

LIMA – CLIMATE CHARTS

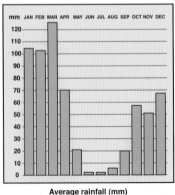

Average rainfall (mm)

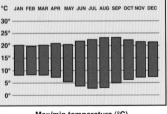

Max/min temperature (°C)

HUARAZ
CLIMATE CHARTS

(Opposite): The reward for reaching Paso Jurau (5060m) on the Huayhuash Circuit: superb views of Siula Grande and Yerupajá.

periods; January to March is wettest. It is still possible to visit the area for day walks and rides from towns, but any multi-day trips mean soggy camps, extremely boggy pampas, snow on high passes and usually only fleeting peak views.

The shoulder months of April and October can be nice and they're certainly quieter than the busiest months, but you're more likely to encounter rain. The beginning of the dry season is often a lovely time to visit as trails are quiet, and there is a profusion of colourful wild flowers in the valleys.

Being in the tropics, temperatures vary little throughout the year – in Huaraz expect temperatures of around 20°C (70°F) during the day and 5-10°C (40-50°F) at night. At the highest trekking camps temperatures are often below freezing at night, though it's rare for them to fall much below -5°C (23°F).

The eastern side of the mountains is noticeably wetter (and consequently greener and with a lower snowline) – it is not unusual to leave the Callejón de Huaylas in the sun, only to arrive in Conchucos in rain!

❏ **FIESTAS AND FESTIVALS**
Important festivals during the year include: Semana Santa (Holy Week), Señor de la Soledad (Huaraz, early May) and Fiestas Patrias (Independence celebrations, 28th July). There are numerous smaller festivals throughout the year and also various adventure festivals which take place in and around Huaraz, including the Festival del Andinismo in late July.

Following pages

● **C1 (opposite)**: Negotiating the traffic on the cruise down from Punta Olímpica (p186).

● **C2** On the Huascarán Circuit (pp186-191), Chopicalqui (6345m) towering above.

● **C3 (clockwise from top left): a)** Tocllaraju from the shores of Laguna Akilpo (p114). **b)** Laguna Mitucocha from above, on alternative Day 2 of the Huayhuash Circuit (p159). **c)** Chiquián (p68), gateway to the Cordillera Huayhuash. **d)** The grassy plaza in Chacas (p71), in the Callejón de Conchucos. **e)** Descending from Gara Gara (p82) towards Laguna Jancarurish and Alpamayo. **f)** The impressive ruins of Yayno (p102), on the alternative route to Huanchacbamba on the Santa Cruz-Alpamayo Circuit. **g)** Bucolic scene only an hour out of Huaraz, on the climb from Llupa to Pitec (p120).

● **C4 (Main picture)**: Dwarfed by Ranrapalca (6162m) on the 5080m Paso Huapi (p126). **(Bottom, from left)**: Hummingbird and *Puya raimondii*, © Cass Gilbert; Zapatito de Diablo (*Calceolaria sp.* © Anna Kortschak); Devil's Fig (*Solanum hispidum)*; Lupin; Gentian; Rima Rima (*Krapfia weberbauerii,* buttercup family, © Anna Kortschak).

● **C5 (clockwise from top left): a)** The multiple peaks of Huandoy, from Portachuelo de Llanganuco (p191, © Jo Haines). **b)** The road to Punta Huarapasca (p196). **c)** *Chakinani* ('singletrack', perfect for mountain biking) in the Cordillera Blanca, © Cass Gilbert. **d)** On a day ride above Huaraz and the Río Santa valley, © Cass Gilbert. **e)** A break on the trail, Quebrada Ishinca (p220, © Cass Gilbert). **f)** Admiring the *Puya raimondii* near Carpa (p197), © Cass Gilbert. **g)** Rattling down from the Portachuelo de Llanganuco (p191, © James Butcher).

● **C6** Local cyclists and other amiable Ancashinos.

C1

C2

C3

C4

C5

PLANNING YOUR TRIP

Guided or independent?

All treks in this book can be undertaken independently (though see p31). On multi-day routes this means lugging supplies along with camping equipment in a backpack on high altitude trails, which is not everyone's cup of tea.

Choosing to go on a guided trip means not only a lighter pack and more comfortable trek, but also, if you go with a reputable agency, your experience will be greatly enhanced by your guide's knowledge of local flora, fauna, history and the peaks, and you will be providing employment for local people. Note that while it isn't difficult finding tours in Huaraz for the more popular treks, a few of the treks in this book are not well known, so it won't be easy finding a guide who's familiar with the route. Before employing a guide, always check their ID and guiding qualifications.

ARRIEROS

Those preferring to trek with just an *arriero* (muleteer) and mules will find it's possible to hire them at some trailheads. The daily amount charged by an arriero is about S/.30 and each animal is around S/.15 (minimum two animals). If your trek is not a circuit, you must also pay for the days it will take the arriero to return to his village/the start point. Trekkers must provide the arriero with all food and a tent and shouldn't expect him to act like a guide. His main duty will be to transfer mules and luggage between campsites, not show you the way. Organizing on arrival is likely to take at least a few hours, and in many places there's no guarantee that you'll actually find anyone available. A good option is to make arrangements through a respectable local agency beforehand – they'll be able to put you in contact with a reliable arriero and will charge you a fee for this service.

AGENCIES

Booking directly with a local agency is the cheapest way of organizing a guided trek – see City & town guides for recommended agencies in Huaraz/Caraz/Chiquián. Booking with a company from your home country can buy you additional peace of mind and get you a more comprehensive package that includes flights and transfers, albeit at a much higher price.

Some of the international agencies which offer Cordillera Blanca and/or Huayhuash tours include:

• **Europe** Allibert Trekking (🖳 allibert-trekking.com), Andean Trails (🖳 and eantrails.co.uk), Exodus (🖳 exodus.co.uk), High Places (🖳 highplaces.co.uk), Jagged Globe (🖳 jagged-globe.co.uk), Journey Latin America (🖳 journey latinamerica.co.uk), KE Adventure Travel (🖳 keadventure.com), and Last Frontiers (🖳 lastfrontiers.com), as well as the social enterprise Project Cordillera (🖳 projectcordillera.org).

• **North America** Adventure Center (🖳 adventurecenter.com), Adventure Life (🖳 adventure-life.com), Andean Treks (🖳 andeantreks.com), G Adventures (🖳 gadventures.com), Wilderness Travel (🖳 wildernesstravel.com) and World Expeditions (🖳 worldexpeditions.com).

Getting there

TO PERU

It is easier and cheaper to reach Peru from North America than Europe.

A number of cities in the USA have direct flights to Lima, including New York, Miami, Los Angeles, Atlanta, Houston and Dallas. These flights take between 5h30 and 9h and return tickets in dry season cost US$800-1200. Often, cheaper flights with a stopover in Central America can be found, though they take a couple of hours longer.

From Europe there are direct Lima flights from Paris, Madrid and Amsterdam. These take 12-13h and a return ticket usually costs over US$1500 in dry season.

There are no direct flights from the UK or Ireland – connections must be made in mainland Europe, South America or the US. Journey times are usually 16-20h each way and prices will be around US$1500. Flights are significantly cheaper outside of the July/August peak.

Those travelling with bicycles need to factor the price charged by the air-line to carry a bike into the total cost. Some companies (including LAN, the largest Peruvian carrier) currently take bikes for free, while others (including most airlines from the US) charge substantial fees.

FROM LIMA TO THE TRAILS

The airport at Anta is 1h15 by direct flight from Lima's Jorge Chávez International Airport; by road it's 8 hours from Lima to Huaraz by comfortable, modern bus – numerous companies make the journey by day and night (p52). All but a few trailheads can be reached by vehicle in half a day from Huaraz.

Budgeting

For independent travellers, the major expenses of any trip to Peru will be the airfare to get there and insurance to cover your activities. Those going with a group will find the trek itself is also a/the major cost, particularly if you choose to go with an operator from your home country. In Lima and to a lesser extent Huaraz, there's the option to splash out on expensive hotels and eat out at pricey restaurants. In non-touristy towns and small villages, it's usually hard to find a meal costing more than S/.5, or accommodation for more than S/.10 per person. Once in Peru, if you are willing to forego tourist restaurants and smart hotels and travel independently, surviving on S/.50 per day is not difficult.

ACCOMMODATION

Lima is more expensive than Ancash, and though you can find a bed in a dorm for S/.15, a comfortable double room will set you back S/.70-200. For a luxury room the sky's the limit. For a double room in Huaraz, decent budget options are priced at around S/.40; in a nice mid-range option expect to pay S/.80-120, while the plushest hotels charge as much as S/.550 a night. In small villages where the only lodging options are very basic, a bed usually costs S/.10 a night, while at the other end of the spectrum there are lodges in the Callejón de Huaylas charging US$200 or more.

Prices for tourist accommodation are usually seasonal. High season (Apr/May – Sep/Oct) prices are included in town chapters – expect as much as 30% lower in wet season.

FOOD

Those on a shoe-string budget can eat well at the numerous menu restaurants, *pollerías* (chicken and chips) and *chifas* (Peruvian-Chinese) which offer large meals for about S/.5-12 (see p34). Though hygiene standards at these aren't normally that bad, they're not always of the highest. In a good, clean tourist restaurant in Huaraz you'll be able to find a main course for S/.15-25. To experience *novoandina* cuisine, at one of Lima's world-renowned restaurants, will set you back a good deal more.

TRANSPORT

Though rising with the cost of petrol, transport in Peru is still cheap. Bus and *combi* (minibus) journeys cost the equivalent of about S/.5 an hour, slightly more if you're lucky enough to be on a route with the option of a comfortable vehicle. In a private taxi, as a general rule of thumb a journey of half an hour costs around S/.40; however, the price will be higher to book a more reliable driver with a newer vehicle.

What to take

CLOTHING

Daytime temperatures are often quite warm, but as soon as the sun passes behind a cloud or sets it rapidly gets chilly due to the high altitude; a layering system will allow for these different temperatures. A couple of fast drying **base-layer tops** made from synthetic material are preferable to cotton or wool t-shirts and while you wear one you can wash the other, which will dry quickly in the hot Andean sun. For a **mid-layer**, take either a mid-weight fleece or a synthetic insulation jacket (e.g. Primaloft) as well as a full set **of thermal underwear** to wear in the evening.

On the higher routes described, a **down jacket** is nice to have but isn't absolutely necessary unless you particularly feel the cold – a **micro-down jacket** may be more appropriate. A woolly **hat and thermal gloves** are needed in the evenings and for early starts and, as it can rain at any time of year, it's important to have a good breathable **waterproof jacket** – Gore-Tex or eVent come recommended. Lightweight **waterproof over-trousers** are advisable, particularly if you come in the rainy season. A pair of high quality **sunglasses** is essential.

The terrain in the Cordillera Blanca and Huayhuash can be challenging and it's advisable to wear a pair of **hiking boots** which cover the ankles and have a sturdy sole. Valley floors are often boggy, particularly during the wet season, so make sure your boots are waterproof (either with a Gore-Tex lining or a waxed leather boot) to avoid having continually-damp feet. For the treks with a terrain rating of 1 (see p11), a stiff pair of trail running or walking shoes should suffice, especially if you are not carrying your own camping equipment. Bring at least three pairs of good quality **hiking socks**, and on multi-day treks it is also a good idea to take a pair of **sandals** to wear around camp.

Wear light/medium-weight **hiking trousers** that allow for free movement and will dry quickly if there is a sudden downpour. Rural Peru is reasonably conservative so you should not wear very short shorts or sleeveless tops. A good **sun hat** is essential: you will never see a Peruvian campesino out without a hat for good reason. Bring a change of clothing to wear in towns; these can be left at your hotel while trekking.

For **cyclists**, pack a couple of pairs of **padded shorts**, and to be culturally sensitive it's wise to take a pair of **over shorts** too. Wear either quick drying base layers or a **cycle jersey** on your top half. Descents from any of the high passes can be bitterly cold on the bike, so bring a pair of warm **waterproof over gloves**. Don't forget your **helmet** and **cycling gloves**.

It's a good idea to use a stiff pair of hiking **shoes**, or cycling shoes that are grippy and comfortable to walk in, so that you can manage with only one pair of shoes and some sandals or flip flops. Fast-drying **socks** are also recommended.

EQUIPMENT

For multi-day trips, a 3-season **tent** is ideal. The most important consideration is to ensure it is waterproof and lightweight, as very high winds, heavy snow or extreme cold are rarely problems on trekking routes in this area. For most people a 4-season **sleeping bag** is recommended, particularly for the Huayhuash Circuit trek, though warmer sleepers usually find a 3-season bag is adequate. Cheap foam **sleeping mats** do the job, but go for something like a Therm-a-Rest ProLite or NeoAir for a better night's sleep.

You can get fuel for gas, alcohol and multi-fuel **stoves** in Huaraz (see table p58). Bring lightweight aluminium or titanium **pans**, and to save weight eat out of the pan, or else bring a plastic bowl. A **spoon** and a **penknife** are sufficient cutlery for most meals.

A 1-litre **water bottle or hydration bladder** should be sufficient as there are frequent mountain springs on most trekking and cycling routes. Whether you are going independently or in a group you should carry some sort of **water treatment**. Chlorine dioxide tablets, a LifeStraw or a SteriPEN (bring spare batteries) are the best lightweight and user-friendly products currently available. The sun is super strong in the Cordilleras so bring (or buy in Huaraz) a good quality **sun cream** with an SPF of at least 30, and reapply it regularly.

Bring a **headtorch** with spare batteries for using around camp and for night loo visits. For navigation equipment see p43.

Your **first-aid kit** should include plasters, antiseptic cream, sterile gauze and a bandage, rehydration sachets, zinc oxide tape and anti-inflammatory painkillers such as ibuprofen. Bring paracetamol and acetazolamide for treating mild symptoms of AMS (see p43). Having loperamide is a good idea in case you get the runs, and consider speaking to your doctor about being prescribed an antibiotic such as ciprofloxacin for bacterial stomach bugs.

Trekking-specific equipment

On most of the treks **trekking poles** are useful, particularly if you are carrying a large pack. It's worth investing in a good telescopic pair such as Leki or Black Diamond as they are lighter and more durable.

If you're going on an organized tour or hiring mules, take a **duffle bag** (around 70 litres) with padlock, so you can put all equipment that you won't require during the day on the mule. Check with your agency whether you need to bring your own sleeping bag and sleeping mat, or if they are supplied. You'll need a 30-40 litre **daypack** to carry spare clothing, snacks and a drink. If you are hiring an arriero, remember you need to provide him with a tent.

If you are trekking independently, make sure you have a comfortable **ruck-sack** of around 70 litres. Try out several to find the most comfortable, getting a competent shop assistant to help fit it, as you would with a pair of boots.

Cycle touring-specific equipment

Bike A hardtail mountain bike is the best steed to take on the dirt roads in the Cordilleras; run either with a bikepacking setup, or with a rear rack and panniers. The next best thing is a sturdy touring bike fitted with a rear rack and panniers.

Front suspension will make unpaved descents swifter and more comfortable. The long climbs mean that you want to keep weight to a minimum, so it is inexpedient to bring front panniers, especially as you never need to carry that much food. It's also a good idea to have a handlebar bag or another way of storing your camera and other essentials close to hand.

For mountain biking see p215.

Tools and Spares Your toolkit should include: a good **pump, tyre levers, Allen key set, small screwdrivers** (one flat, one Phillips), small **pliers** with a good wire cutting tool, small **adjustable spanner** (preferably slim enough to remove pedals), **chain tool, puncture patches, rubber solution**, small bottle of **lubricant**, small roll of duct tape, a spare **PowerLink, gear and brake cables**, spare **brake pads**, two **spokes** of each size and an **inner tube**. If you're using 700c or 29" tyres, carry an extra inner tube on your bike and leave a spare **tyre** in Huaraz just in case. Don't forget a bike **lock**.

Note that Schrader valves are more commonly found in Peru, so it's advisable to have a pump and rims which are compatible with this, or bring more spare tubes from home. Also be aware that it's possible to wear out a new set of rim brake pads on a single dirt-road Peruvian descent in the rain.

Gear rental
Sleeping bags, sleeping mats, tents, multi-fuel or gas stoves, rucksacks and down jackets can all be rented in Huaraz (see p59). For information on bike rental, see p214.

MAPS
We highly recommend you trek with a topographical map, the most useful of which are the Austrian *Alpenvereinskarte*. They come in three sheets: 0/3a Cordillera Blanca Nord (1:100k), 0/3b Cordillera Blanca Sud (1:100k) and 0/3c Cordillera Huayhuash (1:50k). Trails are not always marked correctly, but they cover all treks in this book, except Chacas – Huari. There are also more recent 1:75k *Aoneker* maps which cover the Huayhuash and a smaller area of the Blanca. These are all available locally, but are cheaper in Europe or North America.

Carhuaz mapmaker Felipe Díaz produces a helpful overview map of the Cordilleras Blanca & Huayhuash, which can be bought locally for S/.20.

RECOMMENDED READING
Guides
Classic Climbs of the Cordillera Blanca by Brad Johnson is a comprehensive guide to mountaineering in the area, featuring beautiful photography. *Huaraz – Peru – The Climbing Guide* by David Lazo and Marie Timmermans provides a lifetime of bouldering and rock-climbing problems, from the owners of Quechuandes travel agency.

Jan Sevink's *The Cordillera Blanca Guide – A Unique Landscape Explained*, describes the geology and geography of the range. Available locally are the *Inca Guide to Ancash*, published by Peisa, and Felipe Díaz's *Cordilleras Blanca and Huayhuash*.

Literature
Dervla Murphy's journey through Peru in the late '70s, described in *Eight Feet in the Andes*, gives a fascinating account of the Callejón de Conchucos (she avoided the Callejón de Huaylas and Huaraz, having heard there was a nascent tourist scene there!). *Touching the Void* is Joe Simpson's epic account of his escape from a mountaineering accident on Siula Grande in the Huayhuash.

In *Andes,* Michael Jacobs travels to the Callejón de Huaylas and Conchucos as part of a longer journey in the range. *Cochineal Red* by Hugh Thomson is a fascinating historical travelogue about early Peruvian civilizations, including the Chavín and Wari.

Death in the Andes by Mario Vargas Llosa and *Broad and Alien is the World* by Ciro Alegria both give interesting insights into Andean life.

Field guides
Flores Silvestres de la Cordillera Blanca by Helen and Kees Kolff is a comprehensive guide to the wild flowers in the region, but it's tricky to track down these days. *Birds of Peru* by Thomas Schulenberg is a guide to all of Peru's 1800+ bird species; the *Travellers' Wildlife Guide Peru* by David Pearson and Les Beletsky is also recommended.

Health precautions, inoculations and insurance

Any form of outdoor physical activity carries with it the possibility of accidents and trekking in the Andes is no exception. However, there are certain golden rules to follow on the trail that will help minimize the risk of accidents or getting lost. To avoid unpleasant or unwanted surprises, always plan each day's walk carefully, study a map and familiarize yourself with the route, the type of terrain and the length of time you expect to be trekking.

FITNESS

It's a good idea to have a reasonable level of fitness before beginning a trek and for independent trekkers to have done some training with a rucksack – you'll enjoy the treks a lot more if you are fitter and stronger. Cycle tourers will find the going much easier in the Cordillera if they have improved fitness and stamina by practising hill climbs on their loaded bike beforehand.

HEALTH

The Andean **sun** is strong, so bring sunglasses and a hat, and wear sunscreen even on cloudy days. Moisturizer and lip balm come in handy for combating dry skin. The cold can be equally hazardous when trekking. Weather in the mountains is highly changeable and you should be prepared for cold, wet and windy conditions at any time, and know what to do if a member of your group begins to develop **hypothermia**.

INOCULATIONS

Before travelling to Peru, make sure you are up to date with the following inoculations: tetanus, polio, diphtheria, tuberculosis, hepatitis A and typhoid. Malaria tablets and a yellow fever injection are recommended for some areas of Peru, but not currently for those covered by this guidebook.

It's advisable (especially for cyclists) to have rabies injections before arriving in Peru, as you may be travelling in areas which are several days from the nearest doctor. The inoculation won't stop you getting the disease, but will buy you time to get to a hospital, and mean far less disruption to your trip if you are bitten (see p44).

Prior to departure it is always a good idea to: check the full list of current requirements and recommended injections at the US Centers for Disease Control and Prevention (🖥 cdc.gov) or at the Fit For Travel website (🖥 fitfor travel.scot.nhs.uk); ask a doctor; or visit a travel clinic.

HIGH ALTITUDE TRAVEL

One of the most common complaints on treks and bike rides in this book is Altitude Sickness/Acute Mountain Sickness (AMS). Huaraz lies at 3060m above sea level and the highest trekking pass described is nearly 5100m. At these altitudes, air pressure is substantially lower than at sea level. AMS is caused by the inability of the body to get enough oxygen and it can be fatal; however, it's also very common and entirely preventable. See p43 for symptoms.

Before you go, if you suffer from heart or lung problems, high blood pressure or are pregnant, you must visit your doctor to get advice on the wisdom of a trip to the Andes.

Acclimatization
The safest way to avoid problems with altitude is to acclimatize properly. We would recommend spending at least the first day in Huaraz relaxing, then doing a couple of easy day hikes/rides before heading out on higher multi-day routes. Note there is no correlation between a person's fitness and their speed of acclimatization.

INSURANCE

Before leaving your home country, make sure you have insurance (be it travel insurance or a domestic policy) that covers you for all activities you will be undertaking on your trip. Read the small print carefully, as some providers have altitude limits on cover, or limit the number of cycling days permitted.

PERU & THE CORDILLERAS BLANCA & HUAYHUASH

Facts about the region

HISTORY OF THE CORDILLERAS

The colonization of South America began about 15,000 years ago and reached the Andes and the Callejón de Huaylas around 10,000 BCE. Excavations of the **Guitarrero Cave** in the province of Yungay, north of Huaraz, have found proof of advanced hunter-gatherers. The cave's occupants practised one of the earliest cultivations of tubers, beans and chilli in the Americas and consumed wild guinea pigs. Fragments of woven textiles and rope made from agave found at the cave date back 12,100 years and are the oldest discovered in South America. The domestication of camelids and guinea pigs occurred between 6000 and 3000 years ago. From then until the Spanish conquest, the Andean people became gradually more dependent on domestic animals rather than hunting wild game, transforming from foragers into subsistence farmers.

Meanwhile on the coast, the first Peruvian civilizations were evolving. The oldest of these, the **Norte Chico** civilization 200km north of modern-day Lima, developed between 3500 and 1800 BCE. Their success is credited to the fact that there was an abundance of fish and because they managed to develop irrigation channels to supply water from nearby rivers. After the Norte Chico civilization fizzled out, a number of smaller cultures developed along the coast, including the **Sechín** culture, in the Casma valley to the west of the Cordillera Blanca, around 1500 BCE.

The **Chavín** culture was the first highland civilization in Peru and dates from 1000 BCE; at its centre was the pilgrimage site of Chavín de Huántar (see p67) in the Río Mosna valley to the east of the Cordillera Blanca. Chavín was a hierarchical society led by priests and a political elite. The ordinary people were llama herders, hunters and farmers who cultivated potato, quinoa and maize. The cult of Chavín spread over an enormous area, for the first time unifying unrelated groups with a common ideology. As the religion spread, people were drawn to the temples, bringing offerings which enriched the city and funded advances in metallurgy, textiles and water irrigation. Traders from Chavín also started to travel, taking goods and ideas with them, and the people of Chavín began to specialize as stone carvers, metal workers, weavers and potters, fuelling demand for their goods. Chavín artefacts have been found throughout northern and central Peru. For unknown reasons, around 200 BCE the Andean people turned their backs on the Chavín cult, returning to their disparate groups.

The **Recuay** culture began to prosper at the foot of the Cordillera Blanca in around 200 CE as the Nazca, Moche and Pukara cultures developed elsewhere. They built large settlements with temples, stone defences and irrigation systems. Previously there had been little animosity between neighbouring groups in the Andes, but at this time societies all over Peru were being militarized, and the Recuay culture developed fortified towns in strategic military locations to combat this increased external threat. The most impressive Recuay ruins are the fortified citadel of Yayno, which sits atop a hill to the west of Pomabamba and can only be visited on foot (see p102). The Recuay people developed a unique art style, including their iconic monolithic statues, carved from tall cylindrical chunks of rock. There is a collection of these monoliths and other examples of Recuay lithic art at the Ancash Archaeological Museum in Huaraz (see p52).

The Recuay culture was absorbed into the **Wari** civilization as they pushed up from Ayacucho in around 600 CE. Susan E. Bergh, (curator of the Arts of the Ancient Americas at the Cleveland Museum of Art) describes the Wari as being 'to the Inca as the Greeks were to the Romans'. They ruled the highlands and coast of modern-day Peru until collapse around 800 CE, introducing terraced field technology, *quipus* for keeping numerical records and an extensive road network, all of which went on to be further developed by the Incas. The Wari were an agricultural society, fond of a *chicha* (corn beer) and *pachamanca* (see p61). **Wilcahuaín** (see p178), an archaeological site 7km from Huaraz, was originally a Recuay administrative centre and important funerary site, which the Wari later made their regional capital and mausoleums were built on top of the Recuay underground tombs. Other notable Wari sites in the region are Honcopampa and Huaullac.

The areas around present day Huaraz were assimilated into the **Inca Empire** in the mid-15th century during Pachacutec's reign. They didn't play an important part in the Inca Empire, continuing to subsist and paying their dues to the Inca overlords. The Cordilleras were then colonized, with little resistance, in 1533 by the Spanish who immediately recognized and began to

❏ **Qhapaq Ñan**
The fabled Inca road network, the Qhapaq Ñan, was made a UNESCO World Heritage Site in 2014. Its main axis, the *Camino Real* (Royal Road), passed through the Callejón de Conchucos. The section from Pomachaca (near Huari) to the extensive ruins of Huánuco Pampa (near Huallanca) is one of the better preserved and can be walked in about six days.

exploit the region's mineral wealth. The *encomienda* system was introduced whereby *conquistadores* were entrusted with a number of indigenous peoples who were to be converted to Christianity and to work for them as forced labour in mines. In January 1574 the town of Huaraz was founded as part of the Indian Reductions, during which indigenous populations were gathered up and moved to towns so they could better be converted, controlled and taxed by the Spanish.

The troops of **Simón Bolívar** and **José de San Martín** converged on Peru and declared it independent of Spain in July 1821; however, this independence did little to change the disparity between the wealthy Europeans and the native Andean people.

MODERN PERU

Since 1930 a series of democratic and military governments have ruled the country. **Agrarian reform** in 1963 took land from wealthy landowners and divided it between communities (*comunidades campesinas*), allowing *campesinos* to work the land for themselves. Trekkers are most likely to notice these today in the Cordillera Huayhuash, where communities charge tourists to pass through their lands.

Both the Callejón de Huaylas and Conchucos have been hit by tragic disasters caused by earthquakes throughout recorded history. The Ancash earthquake of 1970, in which the town of Yungay was wiped out by an *aluvión* (see box p104), was the most deadly with estimates of up to 100,000 people killed in the region.

In 1973 a number of social reforms saw rural schools being built, cooperatives formed and women gaining equality, but the economy was in a downward spiral and inflation through the roof. Peru was further hit by the rise of the Maoist **Sendero Luminoso** (Shining Path) terrorist organization. Between 1976 and 1992 armed conflict raged throughout Peru, and in rural communities the Sendero Luminoso attacked those who didn't conform to their ideology. Over 70,000 people, mostly *campesinos*, were victims of these atrocities.

Alberto Fujimori was elected President in 1990 amid economic and political chaos. He introduced a series of drastic economic measures, privatized numerous state-owned businesses and controversially rewrote the constitution; his authoritarian acts stabilized the economy and opened Peru up to international investment. He resigned in 2000 and currently languishes in prison, locked up for human rights abuses carried out during his presidency.

Since Fujimori's resignation, Peru has undergone a period of ongoing democratisation and economic growth. Ancash in particular has benefitted from heavy foreign investment in mineral extraction projects, though not all see it this way. Protests by rural communities over the foreign exploitation of Peru's mineral wealth are commonplace, with accusations of water sources being polluted and ancestral lands destroyed without local people seeing any of the economic benefits. The manifesto of Ollanta Humala (the current president, elected in 2011) includes a promise to spread the benefits of the economic boom to the poor.

FLORA

The routes described in this book travel through an incredibly biologically diverse region. The altitude range from the summit of Huascarán to the depths of the Río Santa valley near Yuracmarca is a whopping 5500m, which creates many different microclimates and habitats suitable for a broad variety of species. Particularly between April and mid-June, the wild flowers adorning the slopes are a highlight of any visit to the area.

Trees
Generally found between 3500m and 4500m, the endemic **polylepis** forests (*bosques de queñuales*) guard the entrances to many quebradas. Trees are characterized by their warped trunks and flaky orange bark. At lower altitudes, imported **eucalyptus** predominates.

Flowers
Lupins (*Lupinus sp.*), shrubs with bluish-lavender flowers, are commonly found in grasslands at about 4000m. The *Lupinus weberbauerii* variety is frequently seen at 4000-4500m and has an inflorescence of lavender flowers over 50cm long. **Anqush** (*Senecio canescens*) is a herbaceous plant, 50cm tall, with drooping yellow flowers and very soft, long leaves, which is found at 4100m-4400m. **Werneria nubigena**'s daisy-like flowers have petals which are white on top and magenta underneath. They're often seen at ground level on high pampas (3900-4900m). The herb **Lycopodium crassum** (in Quechua it's *jacapa pishqun*, meaning 'guinea-pig penis') grows in groups of reddish stems up to 50cm high, on the high puna between 4000m and 4500m.

Found at altitudes of 3400-4300m, **zapatito de diablo** (*Calceolaria* sp., 'Devil's Slippers') has yellow, slipper-like flowers. **Snapdragons** (*Alonsoa linearis*) grow at 3500-4100m and have orange flowers and a black centre with long yellow anthers. From the **wild potato** family, *Solanum hispidum*, with its violet five-point flowers and green marble-like buds, is encountered at 3000-3800m. **Amor Seco** (*Bidens andicola*) is found at 3100-3300m and has dark yellow flowers which are 5cm in diameter. **Gentians**, **orchids** and **buttercups** are also prevalent.

Other plants
See box below about the incredible bromeliad *Puya raimondii*. **Agave** (*Agave americana*) is common in the lower main valleys – its rosette of sharp-tipped greyish-green leaves can reach up to four metres across and ancient civilizations

> ❏ *Puya raimondii*
> The endangered *Puya raimondii* is the largest bromeliad in the world, with an inflorescence that can reach 10m in height, with 20,000 green-white flowers and six million seeds. They can live for up to 100 years before flowering, after which they soon die. The best places to admire these conspicuous giants are near Carpa on the Huayhuash cycle loop and on the Winchus cycle above Caraz.

❑ PARQUE NACIONAL HUASCARÁN

Parque Nacional Huascarán (PNH) was created in 1975 to protect the largest and highest tropical mountain range in the world. With an area of 343,000ha, the park encompasses all but the most-northerly peaks in the Cordillera Blanca, including Huascarán, Peru's highest mountain. PNH was declared a UNESCO Biosphere in 1977 and a World Heritage Site in 1985.

The park is home to over 900 species of flora, 210 species of birds and 25 different mammals. Vegetated areas are characterized by beautiful, gnarled polylepis forests (all of which are strictly protected), ichu grasslands and *bofedales* (marshy wetlands).

Threats

There are various threats to the ecosystems in the park, from both local and global sources. It is anticipated that Peru will be affected by climate change more than almost any other country on Earth, and this is strikingly evident within PNH with the retreat of the glaciers. Though the latest surveys show glaciers still cover over 500 square km of the Cordillera Blanca, this is a reduction of nearly 30% since 1970. The number of lakes in the park is increasing – forming in the moraine debris the glaciers are leaving behind. There are an astonishing 400 lakes in the Blanca and a further few hundred in the neighbouring Negra and Huayhuash ranges.

Overgrazing by cattle affects almost every quebrada in the park, while litter on popular trekking routes and felling of trees for firewood are also issues. Both legal and illegal mining are also a threat to local ecosystems and water courses in some valleys.

Ticketing

Peru is one of the world's most geographically diverse countries, and PNH is one of its most important national parks and among the biggest money earners. Tourists are charged S/.10 for 1-day tickets and S/.20 for 3-day tickets which cover 'conventional tourism' (day trips, no overnighting allowed). For 'adventure tourism' (multi-day trips, overnighting allowed) you must purchase a 21-day ticket for S/.65. A passport (original or copy) is needed to purchase all tickets.

At the PNH office in Huaraz, staff toe the official line from Lima and only sell 21-day tickets to tourists who are going hiking with a registered guide, or who can show some kind of affiliation to an alpine club back home. This rule is not adhered to by *guardaparques* (park wardens) at most park entry checkposts however, meaning it is much easier for independent trekkers to simply buy their ticket as they enter the park.

Though the park is under-manned and it's common to encounter unattended guardaparque posts on quieter routes, tickets can always be bought (without a guide or alpine club affiliation) at Huaripampa (Santa Cruz trek), Pitec and at the PNH offices in Llanganuco and Carpa. Note that while there's a guardaparque post at Cashapampa (Santa Cruz trek), the wardens there have been known to refuse to sell tickets to mountaineers and very occasionally to independent trekkers. We have never heard of independent trekkers being refused tickets at the other posts.

If you stick to less popular routes and don't see a guardaparque within the park, please purchase a ticket at the Huaraz office at the end of your trip. The ticket is exceptional value, and the money is much needed to protect the park and improve facilities in it.

PERU & THE CORDILLERAS

once made ropes from the leaf fibres. **Ichu grass** (*Stipa ichu*) is spiky, golden brown and grows in tussocks on the puna above 3000m. It's used to make the roofs on *chozas* and as animal feed. *Plantago rigida* grows in round, hard cushions in high swampy areas (4500m-4800m); on a number of treks it acts like handy stepping stones. Red-leafed **bromeliads** are frequently seen clinging to steep rock faces.

FAUNA

Mammals

Pumas (*Felis concolor*) and **Andean** or **spectacled bears** (*Tremarctos ornatus*) reside in the park, but sightings are extremely rare. Mammals which are more commonly spotted include **vicuñas** (*Vicugna vicugna*), a wild relative of the llama, **Andean foxes** (*Lycalopex culpaeus*), **white-tailed deer** (*Odocoileus virginianus*) and **viscachas** (*Lagidium peruanum*), which resemble rabbits with long, bushy tails.

All are more commonly seen in the wilder, southern end of the Cordillera Blanca and in the Huayhuash. Domesticated animals are found in many valleys in the form of cows, horses and sheep; it's much more unusual to happen upon **llamas** and **alpacas**.

Birds

The region is home to an impressive number of bird species, ranging in size from the hulking Andean **condor** (*Vultur gryphus*), with its white collar and three metre wingspan, to the most delicate of **hummingbirds**. Piebald, red-faced **mountain caracara** (*Phalcoboenus megalopterus*) are often seen on high altitude routes, as are pairs of **Andean geese** (*chloephaga melanoptera*), which have tiny pink bills and black and white plumage. Polylepis forests are one of the best places for spotting smaller avifauna.

ANDEAN CONDOR

MOUNTAIN CARACARA

❑ Peaks in the Cordilleras Blanca and Huayhuash

Huascarán Sur	6746m	22,133ft	Ranrapalca	6162m	20,217ft
Huascarán Norte	6655m	21,834ft	Hualcán	6160m	20,210ft
Yerupajá	6617m	21,709ft	Pucaranra	6156m	20,197ft
Huandoy	6395m	20,981ft	Chacraraju	6108m	20,039ft
Huantsan	6369m	20,896ft	Jirishanca	6094m	19,993ft
Chopicalqui	6345m	20,817ft	Pucajirca	6046m	19,836ft
Siula Grande	6344m	20,814ft	Quitaraju	6036m	19,803ft
Santa Cruz	6241m	20,476ft	Tocllaraju	6034m	19,797ft
Chinchey	6222m	20,413ft	Caraz	6025m	19,767ft
Palcaraju	6200m	20,341ft	Artesonraju	5999m	19,682ft
Copa	6188m	20,302ft	(from John Biggar: 🖥 andes.org.uk)		

Practical information for the visitor

DOCUMENTS AND VISAS

Citizens of the USA, Canada and EU countries do not currently need a visa to enter Peru, and are entitled to stay as tourists for up to 183 days; ask for the length of time you need when your passport is being stamped. Regulations change, so always ensure you check detailed passport and entry requirements with your local Peruvian embassy well before travelling. On arrival you will be given a Tarjeta Andina de Migración (TAM, tourist card); keep the copy you're given safe so you can hand it back to immigration officials on leaving the country.

MONEY

Peru's currency is the nuevo sol (S/.); each sol is composed of 100 centimos. Notes in circulation are: S/.200 (rare), S/.100, S/.50, S/.20, S/.10; coins come in denominations of S/.5, S/.2, S/.1, S/.0.50, S/.0.20 and S/.0.10. At the time of writing, £1 = S/.4.6, US$1 = S/.2.90. Peru currently has the dubious distinction of being the world's counterfeit capital for dollars, and many fake soles are also produced. Though nothing to be paranoid about (the vast majority of tourists leave without seeing one), it's still a good idea to check notes, as the local people do. See the money guide at 💻 limaeasy.com for details of security features.

There are plenty of ATMs in Lima and Huaraz from which to withdraw cash (soles, but often dollars too) using Visa or MasterCard. BCP machines usually allow the largest single withdrawals. Many of the pricier hotels and restaurants accept payment by credit card, as do supermarkets.

LOCAL TRANSPORT

Buses are the best way of travelling long distances between Peruvian towns. On paved routes such as Huaraz/Caraz to Lima, most buses are modern and comfortable. Journeys on unpaved roads to smaller mountain towns are considerably less luxurious, in dilapidated old vehicles with little leg room.

Combis (minibuses) are the most common form of transport for shorter trips – they ply fixed routes within towns as well as between towns and can be a fun, though cramped, way of getting from A to B. They have a *cobrador* (conductor) – pay (by hollering *'cóbrase'* to catch his/her attention) a minute before you need to get off (*'bajo'*). Many small mountain villages are connected to the outside world by a combi; more journeys are made on market days.

Bigger towns have *colectivos* (shared taxis) which also run on fixed routes and are slightly quicker and more expensive than combis. It's often impossible to distinguish between a taxi and a colectivo without asking the driver

('*¿colectivo?*'). In many towns, *mototaxis* (auto-rickshaws) offer a cheaper alternative to taxis.

FOOD

Eating out in Peru
Peruvians eat out regularly, and joining them in local restaurants or at street stalls makes for an authentic and entertaining experience. With it comes the chance of picking up some kind of food poisoning, but try and go for food which is being cooked on the spot and also scout out the places that are popular with local people. Though their stomachs may be stronger than yours, they're also unlikely to frequent places with a poor reputation for hygiene.

This section is designed to assist you at the main types of eatery you'll encounter.

Set menu restaurants
● **How to spot** *Desayuno/Almuerzo/Cena* (Breakfast/Lunch/Dinner) written on a chalk board with a list of menu options.

Breakfast comes with a hot drink (*agüita/matecito*), bread (*panes*) and main course (*segundo*). At lunch you get a soup (*sopa*) or occasionally a starter (*entrada*), main course, drink (*refresco*) and sometimes a dessert (*postre*). Dinner consists of soup or bread, a main course and a hot drink. *Ají de gallina* and *lomo saltado* are particularly good mains.
● **Useful tips & words** You'll never be given a knife. To ask for one say: *un cuchillo por favor*. You may want to avoid any side salads and the *refresco*, although this is usually made with boiled water. To check it has been, say: *¿el refresco esta hecho con agua hervida?* Alternatively just opt for the Inca Kola.
● **Price** S/.5-10. In general the more expensive, the higher the menu quality and often the more hygienically it is prepared.

Chicken restaurants
● **How to spot** *Pollería/Pollo a la Brasa*' sign, often full of large families. Rotisserie chicken is immensely popular and chicken restaurants are found even in small towns. Allow a quarter of a chicken (*un cuarto de pollo*) per person which will come with a mountain of chips and salad.
● **Useful words** Breast (*pecho*), wing (*alita*), condiments (*cremas*).
● **Price** S/.6-10 for a quarter.

❏ **Vegetarians beware!**
Vegetarians should note that almost everything comes with meat; your only safe bet is *Arroz a la Cubana* (rice topped with fried egg and fried banana). *Tortilla de verduras* (vegetable omelette on a bed of rice) may come without meat, but you need to stress that you want it thus (*sin carne o pollo*). Even if these two dishes are not on the menu, they are often available, and restaurants will normally also whip up an egg sandwich (*sándwich de huevo*) at any time of day, making a great second breakfast for cyclists.

❏ Menu and street snack decoder

Aeropuerto	Chinese mixed fried rice and noodles.
Ají de Gallina	Creamy, slightly spicy sauce with strips of chicken.
Alfajor	Manjar caramel sandwiched between shortbread pieces.
Arroz a la Cubana	Rice topped with fried egg and fried banana.
Asado de Pollo/Chancho	Roast chicken/pork.
Caldo de Cabeza	Ram's head soup.
Caldo de Gallina	Chicken soup with a chunk of chicken, an egg and a potato.
Cau cau	Intestine stew with cubed potato, carrot and peas.
Chaufa	Chinese fried rice (with meat).
Chicha de Jora	Slightly alcoholic corn beer.
Chicha Morada	Non-alcoholic purple maize drink, flavoured with cinnamon & citrus fruits.
Chocho	Lupin seeds in a salsa of onion, coriander, tomato and lime.
Choclo y queso	Boiled corn on the cob with cheese.
Churros	Deep fried batter with caramel filling; served late afternoon.
Combinado	Half plate of fried rice, half plate of noodles.
Empanadas	Pastry parcels stuffed with chicken or meat, egg and olive.
Ensalada	Salad.
Escabeche de Pollo/ Pescado	Stew of chicken/fish with sweet potato (camote), mild chillies and olive.
Locro de Zapallo	Pumpkin stew.
Lomo Saltado	Stir fried beef, onion, tomato and chips on a bed of rice.
Marciano	Frozen fruit juice.
Menestra	Lentil or bean stew served as a side dish.
Milanesa de Pollo	Breaded chicken.
Mondonguito	Tripe stew with tomato, carrot, potato and peas.
Papa a la Huancaína	Potatoes with a cheesy white sauce (starter or side dish).
Papa Rellena	Ball of mashed potato stuffed with meat and onion and then deep fried.
Papas Fritas	Chips (fries).
Picante de Cuy/ Carne/Pollo	Mildly spicy sauce with guinea pig/meat/chicken, served with potato.
Picarones	Deep fried pumpkin and sweet potato doughnuts covered in honey syrup; served in the late afternoon.
Pollo a la Brasa	Roast chicken.
Pollo Broaster	Deep fried chicken.
Quinoa	A thick hot drink made with quinoa.
Seco de Pollo/Ternera	Chicken/veal stew with carrot, potato & peas in coriander sauce.
Sudado de Trucha	Trout steamed in tomatoes and chillies. Literally 'sweated trout'.
Tallarín de Pollo	Spaghetti and chicken with a tomato sauce.
Tamales	Steamed maize parcels stuffed with chicken, egg, olive and a spicy sauce wrapped in maize husks.
Tamarindo	Sweet, fruity Chinese sauce.
Tipakay	Chinese sweet and sour battered chicken.
Tortilla de Verduras	Vegetable omelette on a bed of rice.
Trucha Frita	Fried trout.

Chinese
● **How to spot** *Chifa* sign/Chinese lanterns
It may come as a surprise, but Chinese restaurants are to be found in every corner of Peru. Cantonese contracted labourers were brought to the country to work on sugar plantations and guano mines in the 19th century, and when their contracts ended many stayed on and set up Chifas.
● **Useful tips & words** The portions are normally enormous. If you have a small appetite, a plate of fried rice (*chaufa*) is enough for two or you can ask for a doggy bag (*una bolsa*) and scoff it the next day.
● **Price** S/.7-15.

Street snacking
● **How to spot** A cart with vendor yelling about whatever they are selling.
There are some real treats to look out for in terms of street food, though be wary about hygiene, particularly in relation to cheese, sandwiches, salads and meat. Whilst almost certainly tasty, these bring the risk of a stomach bug ruining your trip. It's usually safer to go for items sold from municipal carts rather than by ladies with buckets. For pastries, cakes and *empanadas*, pop into one of the numerous bakeries.
● **Price** S/.1 for most things.

Other restaurants
Other types of restaurants include *cevicherias* (raw seafood), *parrilladas* (barbecued meat) and tourist restaurants – for specific recommendations, see City & town guides (p45).

SUPPLIES

Most of the treks in this book do not have places to resupply en route, so you will need to buy everything before beginning. There is a basic shop at least every couple of days on cycling routes.

Dehydrated food is the lightest and easiest option, however it's not available in Huaraz; if desired, bring meals from your home country. In Huaraz, the Novaplaza or Trujillo supermarkets provide the best one-stop shops. Shopping in the market and other *tiendas* (shops) in that area is cheaper and can be great fun.

If you are going on an organized tour, consider taking chocolate, dried fruit or nuts to keep you going during the day.

Independent travellers should be aware that cooking time (and therefore the amount of fuel you need) is increased at altitude.

❏ **Food flags**
In more-remote villages you may see small flags outside houses. A white flag, flour sack on a chair or even just a white plastic bag on a stick means there is bread for sale. Red flags or a bunch of maize indicates *chicha de jora* is available.

❏ **Maca**
Maca is an unassuming radish-like plant with high nutritional content which was tra-
ditionally used by warriors before heading into battle in order to increase stamina and
strength. You can buy maca flour or oats with maca in many shops to help fuel your
mountain adventures.

Breakfast

Porridge made with oats and powdered milk is a nutritious and easy breakfast –
oats (*avenas* or *quaker*) are available in all towns and villages. **Granola** and
expanded or **popped rice, kiwicha** *(achis pop)* or **wheat** cereals are cheap and
available at the Huaraz market or supermarkets. Instant coffee, black and herbal
tea and hot chocolate are readily available in all towns.

Lunch

For a short trek, or the first days of a long trek, **bread** is a good option. **Wraps**
(*tortillas*), which are sold in supermarkets and at the central market, are pricier
but don't take up much pack space. The best **crackers** are '*Field*' cream crackers or '*Costa Integral*' wholemeal crackers. The supermarkets have a good
selection of **salami, paté, dried meats** and **parmesan cheese** (which keeps
much better than the local cheese). Local cheese sold by ladies on the street is
not always made or stored hygienically – it's safer to purchase from one of
Huaraz's cheese shops such as 'Don Queso' near the market. **Avocados** (*palta*)
are available in most towns and make a nutritious cracker topping; **manjar** (a
thick caramel-like spread) can be smeared on bread/crackers or squeezed
straight down your throat. Peanut butter and jam are available in Huaraz supermarkets.

Dinner

Pasta, **rice**, a wide variety of flavours of **instant noodles** (*fideos instantáneos*),
quinoa, couscous, polenta, bulgur wheat and **instant mash** are all available
in Huaraz. Only rice, pasta, quinoa and chicken or beef instant noodles are
available in smaller towns, but be warned that rice cooked at altitude often turns
out a mushy mess. Sachets of concentrated tomato (*pasta de tomate*) with added
garlic, carrot and onion make a good pasta sauce. Sachets of *Huancaína* sauce
can be stirred into pasta, polenta or mash. Powdered soups can be found in
Huaraz and can either be made into soup or used to make a sauce. Instant potato with lashings of olive oil, garlic and salami is a calorie-filled personal
favourite. Kraft Macaroni and Cheese is also available.

Snacks

Entering the main, east, door of the market in Huaraz, by the huge bread bas-
kets, turn right and the first aisle on the left has the best dried fruit (raisins –
pasas de uvas), nuts (peanuts – *maní*) and trekking food. *Alfajores* (caramel
sandwiched between shortbread) also make excellent trekking snacks; chocolate (*Sublimes* and *Triángulos* are recommended) is available in towns.

SAFETY

Peru doesn't have the best reputation abroad when it comes to safety, but this is largely unfounded in Huaraz and the Cordilleras. Safety in Lima has improved markedly in the past decade, and the parts frequented by tourists are no more dangerous than many European cities – see p47. Lima and Huaraz have tourist police; elsewhere, to call the police dial ☎ 105.

Occasionally there's a night bus hold-up reported on a remote mountain road; try and travel during the day for this reason, but more so because of the views and the fact that fewer accidents happen in the light. Pickpocketing and opportunist theft occasionally occur; but keeping your wits about you in public places, not flaunting valuables and asking locally for information about areas you're unsure of should mean that you, like most visitors to the area, don't have any trouble.

Traffic is more of a danger, particularly for cyclists – pay attention and ride (or walk) defensively at all times. Many streets in Peruvian towns are one-way, so look both directions before crossing, and beware of turning vehicles when crossing at a green pedestrian light.

When camping, remove temptation by ensuring all your belongings are stored inside your tent, and on popular treks only camp at official campsites. Cyclists who wild camp should ensure they are not visible from the road and should ask permission if camping near someone's home. We wouldn't recommend independent trekkers leaving a tent up and unattended while out on day walks on more popular routes – it's better to pack up and stash your gear if you can't find a reliable person to look after camp.

OTHER INFORMATION

● **Telephone** Land lines have 7 digits in Lima and 6 in the rest of the country; all mobile/cell phones have 9 digits. The area code for Lima is (1) and for Ancash it's (43). To call a mobile from another mobile or a land line, just dial the 9 digit number. To call a land line from a mobile or a land line in a different area, dial (0 + area code + number). The code for Peru when calling from abroad is +51.

● **Haggling** isn't that common, as most items or services have fixed prices. You're most likely to need to haggle when buying souvenirs, getting a taxi, or for certain items in markets. The vast majority of Ancashinos aren't out to rip you off, but it does sometimes occur in touristy areas, so try and find out what the usual price is beforehand.

● **Tipping** Also not normally expected, though it will always be appreciated. It is usual to tip trekking staff and at tourist restaurants; expensive restaurants may even add a 10% service charge. It is not customary to tip staff at cheap local restaurants, or taxi drivers.

● **Electricity** 220V, 60Hz AC. Type A (North American, twin flat prongs) and C (European, twin round prongs) plugs are both common. Power cuts and surges are not unusual and Peruvian wiring can be a bit dodgy – see box p212.

● **Time** – Peru is five hours behind GMT, in line with Eastern Standard Time.

MINIMUM IMPACT, HEALTH & SAFETY

3

Minimum impact hiking and biking

Tourism is a vital source of income for Peru and, directly or indirectly, a great many Peruvians benefit from the increasing numbers of adventure tourists flocking to the country. However, there are undoubtedly problems, including those of litter and pollution, along the popular trekking routes in the Cordilleras Blanca and Huayhuash that are caused by visiting trekkers and their crews.

Guardaparques from PNH, some agencies and organizations in Huaraz, and local communities in the Huayhuash arrange periodic clean-ups; however, these are not currently enough to keep some trails spick and span. Whilst it's easy to blame the authorities for the decline of the pristine wilderness, many trekkers are equally at fault. On the trails, people must take responsibility for their own litter and actions; each individual should remember that their thoughtlessness and selfishness has consequences for everyone else.

ENVIRONMENTAL IMPACT

Damaged vegetation, litter, human excrement at campsites, polluted waterways, deteriorating facilities and an increase in erosion are all indications that trekkers have had a negative impact on the landscape. Fortunately, most people are now much more conscious of the potential impact that they have on the environment and are more likely to adopt a considerate, responsible attitude whilst trekking or cycling. It's important that we all maintain this newfound responsibility.

Pack it in, pack it out

All waste must be carried out of the hills. Unsightly and unhealthy, accumulated rubbish is one of the most significant threats to the natural environment. If you are with an agency, in theory trekking staff and clients should, between them, ensure all rubbish is removed from the trail. Unfortunately some unscrupulous trekkers, guides and arrieros dump or drop rubbish along the route. Keep an eye on your team and make sure they understand that it is important to you that they adhere to the 'pack it out' rule.

MINIMUM IMPACT

If you are trekking independently, bring rubbish bags to carry all waste, and be conscious, when preparing to trek, of the amount of litter you are likely to generate. If you come across litter along the trail consider picking it up and removing it, in order to set a good example.

Bury your excrement

Where possible, always use the purpose-built toilet blocks at official campsites in PNH or the Huayhuash. If you are trekking on a route that doesn't have facilities, or are caught short on the trail, stick to the following rules: make sure you're at least 20m away (the further the better) from both the path and any water source or stream; take a trowel with you so that you can dig a hole to squat over and cover the hole with plenty of soil once you're done; dispose of your toilet paper properly either by carefully burning it or burying it deeply in the same hole. Better still, pack it out along with everything else, having taken the precaution of double-bagging the offending article. All female sanitary products should also be packed out, or use a (far more eco-friendly) menstrual cup.

Don't pollute water

The Andean waterways and lakes are fragile ecosystems and contamination can easily lead to deterioration in water quality. If you are going to wash yourself, clothes or dishes, carry water well away from streams or lakes and, if necessary, use small amounts of biodegradable soap.

Erosion

Wherever possible, stick to existing paths. The continued use of shortcuts, particularly on steeper sections of trail, erodes the slopes and causes irreparable damage.

Camping

On popular trails in PNH and the Huayhuash, always camp at official sites. When wild camping on quiet routes, try to have as little impact as possible on the countryside. Always ask permission if wishing to camp near a farm or smallholding – a particularly relevant consideration for cycle tourers. Take the usual precautions of camping out of sight of a road, avoiding exposed sites if there's a risk of thunderstorms and staying clear of sites at risk of flash floods. When you strike camp make sure you tidy everything up and leave the site as you found it, undisturbed.

Do not light campfires

Whilst a campfire sounds appealing and the stuff of true camping expeditions, the local ecosystems have already been damaged by people chopping down rare and scarce trees for firewood. Lighting fires is outlawed in PNH and in the Huayhuash and there's no excuse for lighting a fire on any of the routes described here: for cooking use a portable stove, whilst for warmth put on another layer of clothes.

Don't pick flowers or disturb fauna

The Blanca and Huayhuash are full of stunning flowers and contain some extraordinary bird and animal life. Leave all flora and fauna alone, in the natural habitat where they belong.

ECONOMIC IMPACT

The economic importance of tourism to Ancash is undeniable, however, not everyone benefits equally. If you book an organized trek through a foreign operator, the bulk of your money stays outside the country. Book a trek through an agency in Huaraz, and a far greater proportion of the money remains in the city. Although the arrieros and trek team may not be from the city, they'll benefit from the opportunity to work. If you find a local arriero at the trailhead, you'll contribute more to that village's economy. By all means trek independently if you wish, but it's far more useful to the region if you hire help and can also be a surprisingly simple and cheap way of giving something back, as well as making your trip more enjoyable.

Pay a fair price for a fair service

Unfortunately competition and hard and aggressive bargaining by some backpackers has led to some agencies in Huaraz offering treks for less than it's actually possible to run a responsible tour. These agencies try and turn over high volumes of business with small margins, to the detriment of good service, trekking staff and the natural environment. At the time of research, it was possible to book on a Santa Cruz trek for as little as US$100 and a Huayhuash Circuit trek for US$150 – neither of which is a fair amount to pay. This leads to trekking staff being underpaid and under-trained, pack animals being overloaded, trekkers not being given enough food and the environment suffering.

Please don't make price your only consideration when choosing an agency; instead, recognize the worth of a service to you and pay a reasonable rate for it. Do not attempt to bargain arrieros right down – they are paid poorly, yet are worth every sol to the success of a trek.

❑ **Protecting the Huayhuash**

The Huayhuash range's remoteness is one of its attractions, but when it comes to protecting and respecting this incredible mountain environment, it becomes an Achilles' heel. Straddling the Departments of Ancash, Huánuco and Lima and nine communities' land, the Huayhuash is in theory protected as a 'Zona Reservada'. In practice, despite strong calls from many in the area for something to be done, little in the way of protecting the local landscapes or ecology occurs. The current system for managing the area is far from ideal in this respect; local communities do not want to lose their lands and are at present the ones charging the fees. However, lacking the necessary knowledge and resources, they are ill-equipped to protect this wonderful area from the negative effects of tourism. In future, more needs to be done to reduce the impact and improve the sustainability of trekking in the region.

CULTURAL IMPACT

Whilst you're trekking, be considerate to local people and other visitors. Try to be selfless, keep noise to a minimum and remember that you are only visiting.

Encourage local pride

Encourage local pride by giving Peruvians a balanced view of life in your home country. In answer to queries about how much you earn, reply honestly but put the figures into context. Tell them what you think is good about their lifestyle – the extraordinary natural surroundings, the lack of real crime, the clean air. If you particularly enjoyed your stay or tour, be sure to let people know.

To give or not to give?

Giving to beggars can perpetrate an attitude of dependency; don't load up with sweets or other gifts to answer begging requests. Although handing things out might make you feel good in the short term, it can lead to a detrimental effect on the recipient, resulting in low self-esteem and an associated idea that the West and tourists, rather than their own culture, hold the answer. Additionally, there are no dentists in the rural communities.

If someone has done something helpful, consider rewarding them, but be careful how you do it. You should also be wary of handing out medicines along the trails: strong or prescription drugs may be taken incorrectly and do more harm than good.

Ask permission before taking a person's photograph

Respect people's privacy and if they aren't comfortable or happy with being snapped then leave them alone. Ideally you should not pay anyone for posing. If you offer to send someone a copy of the photo you've taken, make sure you follow through with your promise.

Don't flaunt your wealth

Your wealth, however poor you may be by the standards of your home country, is far in excess of that of most Peruvians, so don't make a big issue of it and certainly don't flaunt it. Consider carefully what valuables you actually need to take with you to Peru.

Don't lose your temper

Peruvians rarely lose their rag, and you should work hard to control your temper as well. Be polite and the chances are the courtesy will be returned.

Health and safety in the mountains

SAFETY WHILE TREKKING

Although there are hazards in the mountains, a properly prepared expedition with the right equipment and a bit of common sense should not be troubled by them.

Weather

The weather in the Andes is very changeable. You should expect rain whatever the season and ought to carry warm clothing at all times, since temperatures can plummet and conditions can deteriorate extremely quickly. Check the weather forecast online (🖥 mountain-forecast.com is recommended) before setting out.

Keeping on course

Although some routes in the region are well trodden, there are others where you'll come across very few people and where there's no trail. Bad weather and diverging cow-paths can also make any route harder to trace. A topographic map (see p24) and compass are helpful, as long as you know how to use them, but beware that even the best topo maps of the area show some trails incorrectly. A GPS used in conjunction with waypoints (see 🖥 blancahuayhuash.com) should help you to find your way.

Tell someone where you're going

Before setting off to trek independently, tell someone responsible (at your guesthouse, for example) where you're going and when you expect to return. They should be aware of what to do if you fail to come back and how long to wait before raising the alarm.

HEALTH IN THE MOUNTAINS

Whilst Peru does have a handful of serious health problems, you are very unlikely to be affected by them in the mountains of Ancash, and if you follow simple guidelines you'll minimize the risk to yourself.

Altitude sickness/Acute mountain sickness (AMS)

It is recommended for all members of your group to have some knowledge of symptoms and treatment of AMS. See 🖥 altitude.org or the Mountain Medicine section at the International Climbing and Mountaineering Federation website (🖥 theuiaa.org) for detailed and up-to-date information.

AMS is a potentially fatal condition which generally occurs above 3000m and must not be underestimated. At the altitudes covered by this book, it can be prevented with adequate acclimatization. However, there is no hard and fast rule as to how long it takes to acclimatize to increases in altitude, as individuals are affected differently.

AMS and High Altitude Pulmonary Oedema (HAPE) and High Altitude Cerebral Oedema (HACE), the serious, life-threatening conditions that can occur as a result of it, are entirely preventable, if certain precautions are taken:
• Don't exceed the recommended rate of ascent (once you are above 2500-3000m you should not sleep more than 300-500m higher than the previous night)
• Keep hydrated by drinking plenty of liquid and avoiding alcohol
• Avoid overexertion by climbing slowly and steadily
• Look out for early symptoms of AMS and react to them.

Mild symptoms are uncomfortable, but not dangerous, and will pass in a couple of days. They include a headache and nausea on top of breathlessness and an irritating dry cough. In more serious conditions vomiting begins to occur. Increasing tiredness, confusion and a reduction in coordination are more severe symptoms.

With light to moderate symptoms you should remain at the same altitude, avoiding workloads, until symptoms disappear. Treat nausea with antiemetics and headaches with paracetamol or ibuprofen (if these fail, consider taking acetazolamide), and try and drink enough to avoid dehydration. Descend if symptoms don't improve, or if they worsen.

If symptoms become severe you must descend at once (with company), even during the night, to the last camp where you felt well, as dropping even small vertical amounts can have a beneficial effect.

Food
To improve your chances of not getting sick, maintain a high standard of hygiene. If you can't cook it, peel it or wash it in clean water you should be wary of it.

Water purification
There are cattle in almost every valley of PNH and the Huayhuash, so you should always boil, filter or purify your drinking water. This will help to reduce the risk of picking up a water-borne illness such as giardia, but will also eliminate the need to use very environmentally-unfriendly plastic mineral water bottles. A LifeStraw or SteriPEN are good solutions; purification tablets can be tricky to find in Huaraz, so bring them from home.

Beware of taking water downstream from a mine – some larger watercourses are polluted with heavy metals – and also avoid drinking from rust-orange coloured streams, which are occasionally seen in the mountains and which may be contaminated with lead-oxide.

Dog bites
In the unlikely event of being bitten, rinse (don't scrub) the wound thoroughly for 15 minutes with soap and water, and clean with iodine if available. If the dog has an owner, ask if the animal has had rabies injections (*¿Su perro ha sido vacunado contra la rabia?*). Get to the Emergency Department at the public hospital in Huaraz (p53) where they'll clean the wound and give you further instructions. After some form-filling, the two (assuming you've had a course pre-travel) post-bite injections are given free of charge a few days apart. Those who haven't had the pre-travel course will need five injections over a period of a month.

Room prices for Lima and Huaraz are split into budget, mid-range and expensive categories. These prices are particularly changeable, but you will be able to make comparisons between the relative price brackets. Prices are quoted for single, double and (where different) twin rooms (**sgl/dbl/twin**), and descriptions include whether they have attached bathrooms (**AB**) or shared bathroom (**SB**). Expensive hotels may add a 10% service charge and 18% IGV tax (the tax does not need to be paid by visiting tourists who can show proof of a passport stamp and TAM card; it has not been included in prices). Be warned that hotels get booked up well in advance for Semana Santa (holy week) and other large festivals.

The abbreviations Jr = *Jirón* (street) and Av = *Avenida* (avenue) are used throughout.

Lima
Altitude: 160m

For many lovers of the great outdoors who are itching to get into the Andes, Lima will be a stepping-stone, a place to pass through en route to the snowy peaks. The city lies below a shroud of sea cloud for many months of the year and has also been subject to years of negative press, with reports of it being shabby and unsafe, or simply boring. Peru's capital has another side to it though; the former Spanish capital of South America, originally christened Ciudad de los Reyes (City of Kings), was once one of the continent's most alluring and impressive cities.

These days, it is in fact hugely underrated and a wonderful introduction to what you'll see and find elsewhere. Archaeological sites stand amidst residential neighbourhoods whose architecture spans styles from the last 500 years. There are good museums, world-class restaurants and a burgeoning food scene, lively night spots and an irresistible energy and edge borne out of the multicultural mix found here. What's more, a resurgent local middle class are taking pride in their city and pioneering a renaissance that should ensure Lima's reputation is restored.

PRACTICAL INFORMATION
Arrival

All flights arrive at **Aeropuerto Internacional Jorge Chávez** (💻 www.lap.com.pe) in Callao, 16km north-west of the city centre. Inside the arrivals hall are exchange bureaux (rates are better in town) and ATMs that accept all major cards. There are also car-hire desks, an iPerú information desk (☎ 574-8000, open 24 hrs), public telephones and internet access.

There are **taxi** desks outside the arrivals hall; touts and drivers for official firms, wearing ID badges, will accost you the moment you emerge. Fares cost around S/.50-60 depending on whether you go to the centre, Miraflores or Barranco. Going past these desks into the main building and turning right towards the exit, you'll find a small desk for Taxi Green (💻 taxigreen.com.pe); these are recommended. Cheaper, unlicensed cars can be hailed outside, opposite the terminal, but you'll have to haggle hard for a good fare.

Those wishing to bypass central Lima and head straight for the mountains should catch a ride to Plaza Norte bus terminal. Taxi Green charges S/.60 to Plaza Norte in a car and S/.90 for a van which accommodate bikes. There is no extra charge for baggage or bikes.

Orientation

Lima is built on a flat plain above a large arc of a bay. A sprawling city, it has many different neighbourhoods and districts (see map opposite), which are often too far apart to walk between.

Lima Centro is the original heart of the city and now a UNESCO World Heritage Site. Amidst the chaotic centre is a host of colonial sights, museums and excellent restaurants to discover.

To the south-east is the industrial-commercial area of **La Victoria**. West of the centre is **Bellavista**, the coast and the port of

Callao. Along the coast south of Callao lies affluent **San Isidro**, where several good hotels and upmarket restaurants are located.

Beyond is the well-to-do residential neighbourhood and shopping area of **Miraflores**, and then the more bohemian district of **Barranco**, a one-time coastal retreat that has been absorbed into the city and which boasts hip bars, a lively night scene and a number of workshops that double as art galleries.

Getting around

Taxis There are countless cabs on Lima's streets. For the safest ride and fairest fare, hail a yellow cab with a number painted on the door, as these are more likely to be reputable. From Miraflores to the city centre is about S/.12-15 and to Barranco around S/.6. Always agree the fare before you set off.

El Metropolitano A Bus Rapid Transit system that was opened in 2010, this is the easiest way of travelling between the centre and Miraflores/Barranco on public transport. First purchase an electronic prepaid card (S/.4.50, available at all stations), then top it up to travel. There's a flat fee of S/.2 per journey.

Combis and colectivos Lima's bus network of combis and colectivos is pretty efficient, far-reaching and surprisingly cheap. Destinations are written on cards in the window; you can flag them down or ask them to stop anywhere along this route. Beware though, buses can be crowded and are often targeted by pickpockets.

Services

Tourist information As well as at the airport, there's an **iPerú office** in Larcomar (see Miraflores map; ☎ 445-9400; Mon-Fri 11:00-13:00 & 14:00-20:00) and a more substantial **Municipal tourist office** on Pasaje Ribera el Viejo in Lima Centro.

Books El Virrey (Calle Bolognesi 510, see Miraflores map) is one of Lima's lead-

The area code for Lima is ☎ 1 and for Ancash it's ☎ 43. To call a land line from a mobile or a land line in a different area, dial (0 + area code + number). Phone numbers are given as 6 digits (Ancash), 7 digits (Lima) or 9 digits (mobile/cell phone).

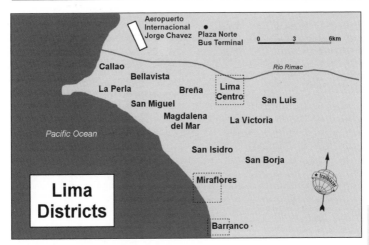

CITY & TOWN GUIDES

ing **bookshops** (*librerías*) and has a number of branches. SBS (off Miraflores map; Av Angamos Oeste 301, 🖥 sbs.com.pe) sells a good collection of guidebooks.

Banks & casas de cambio There are 24-hour **ATMs** throughout Lima as well as at the airport. Several **banks** have branches all across the city, and although they exchange currency, **casas de cambio** give a better rate. *Cambistas* (street changers identified by the green bibs they wear and the wads of notes they clutch) may offer an even better rate but beware, there are plenty of scams associated with changing money this way.

Communications

Internet There are internet cafés across Lima, all charging similar rates of around S/.2 per hour. Most hostels and hotels also have free internet access or wi-fi.

Telephone You can make calls using coin-operated phone booths coloured blue or green and marked Telefónica. Alternatively, buy a pre-paid telephone card or a SIM card from a kiosk or shop. See box opposite for calling instructions.

Emergencies

Police Lima is a big city in a less developed country. Crime happens, but is not

something to be paranoid about, especially if you take the same sensible precautions you would in any city. Don't flash your wealth, don't carry valuables, be on your guard in crowded places and at ATMs and don't walk in unlit, unfamiliar places at night. If you are a victim of crime, contact the tourist police (☎ 243-2190; 24 hours) at Jr Colón 246 in Miraflores.

Pharmacies such as Inka Farma are open 24 hours, well stocked and found throughout the city. In many cases you won't need a prescription to buy medicines. If you need **medical help**, try Clínica Anglo Americano (Av Salazar 350, San Isidro, ☎ 616-8900, 🖥 angloamericana.com.pe) or Clínica Internacional (☎ 619-6161, 🖥 clinicainternacional.com.pe) at Av Garcilazo de la Vega 1420.

Information sources The website 🖥 **limaeasy.com** is a fantastic fount of knowledge about the city, covering everything from historical sights and food guides, to social projects and tips on tipping. **South American Explorers** (Miraflores Clubhouse: Enrique Palacios 956); Mon-Fri 09:30-17:00, Sat 09:30-13:00, 🖥 saexplorers.org) provide a wide range of assistance to members.

WHERE TO STAY

There is a huge range of accommodation options in Lima, befitting a city of its size.

Airport *Ramada Costa del Sol* (Av Elmer Faucett, ☎ 711-2000, 🖳 www.costadelsol peru.com, rooms from US$300).

Lima Centro

Budget *Hostal Roma* (Jr Ica 326, ☎ 427-7572, 🖳 hostalroma.8m.com, sgl/dbl S/.40-50/60-75). *Hotel España* (Jr Azangaro 105, ☎ 428-5546, 🖳 hotelespanaperu.com, dorm/sgl/dbl S/.22/50-60/55-65). *Inka Path* (Jr de la Unión 654, ☎ 426-9302, 🖳 hotelinkapath.com, sgl/dbl S/.130/155-170).

Mid-range *Gran Hotel Bolívar* (Jr de la Unión 958, ☎ 619-7171, 🖳 granhotelboli var.com, dbl from US$85).

Expensive *Sheraton Lima* (Av Paseo de la República 170, T315-5000, 🖳 shera ton.com, rooms US$180-500).

Miraflores

Budget *Hitchhikers* (Calle Bolognesi 400, ☎ 242-3008, 🖳 hhikersperu.com, dorm/sgl/dbl S/.28/65-70/70-84). *K'usillu's Hostel* (Av Larco 655, ☎ 444-0817, 🖳 kusillushostel.com, per person US$9-12). *Flying Dog Hostel* (Martir Olaya 280, ☎ 447-0673, 🖳 flyingdogperu.com, dorm/dbl S/.33/100-120). *Friend's House* (Manco Capac 368, ☎ 446-6248, sgl/dbl S/.35-40/48-70).

Mid-range *Hostal El Patio* (Diez Canseco 341, ☎ 444-2107, 🖳 hostalelpatio.net, sgl/dbl S/.126-201/156-231). *Bayview Hotel* (Las Dalias 276, ☎ 519-0770, 🖳

bayviewhotel.com.pe, sgl/dbl/twin US$65/80/130). *Hotel Antigua* (Av Grau 350, ☎ 201-2060, 💻 antiguamiraflores.com, sgl/dbl US$92-122/106-142). The **Casa Andina chain** (💻 casa-andina.com) has a few options, including *Miraflores San Antonio* (Av 28 de Julio 1088, ☎ 241-4050, rooms from US$70).

Expensive *Sonesta Posadas del Inca Miraflores* (Alcanfores 329, ☎ 241-7688, 💻 sonesta.com/miraflores, sgl/dbl US$248/263). *Casa Andina Private Collection Miraflores* (Av La Paz 463, ☎ 213-4300, 💻 casa-andina.com, standard rooms US$320).

Barranco [see map p50]
Budget *The Point Hostel* (Malecón Junín 300, ☎ 247-7997, 💻 thepointhostels.com, dorm/dbl/twin S/.27-35/100/70).

Barranco's Backpacker Inn (Malecón Castilla 260, ☎ 247-1326, 💻 barrancobackpackersperu.com, dorm/dbl US$11/35). *Kaminu* (Bajada de Baños 342, ☎ 252-8680, 💻 kaminu.com, dorm/dbl S/.30-35/78).

Mid-range *La Quinta de Allison* (Av 28 de Julio 281, ☎ 247-1515, 💻 hotelbarranco.com, sgl/dbl S/.50/70).

Expensive *Second Home Peru* (Domeyer 366, ☎ 247-5522, 💻 secondhomeperu.com, rooms US$115-150).

San Isidro
Budget *Malka Youth Hostel* (Los Lirios 165, ☎ 442-0162, 💻 youthhostelperu.com, dorm/dbl/twin S/.33/90-100/75-90) is run by a climber.

Mid-range *Casa Bella Peru* (Las Flores 459, ☎ 421-7354, 💻 casabellaperu.net/

Miraflores

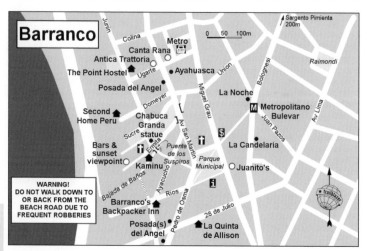

Barranco

Sargento Pimienta
200m

0   50   100m

Junin
Colina
Metro
Canta Rana
Antica Trattoria
The Point Hostel   Ugarte   • Ayahuasca   Union
Posada del Angel
Domeyer
Second
Home Peru   Chabuca
Granda
Sucre   statue
Bars &   Ermita
sunset   Puente
viewpoint   Kaminu   de los
Suspiros
Balada de Baños
WARNING!
DO NOT WALK DOWN TO
OR BACK FROM THE
BEACH ROAD DUE TO
FREQUENT ROBBERIES   Barranco's
Backpacker Inn
Posada(s)
del Angel

Raimondi

Miguel Grau
La Noche
Metropolitano
Bulevar

Bolognesi

Juan Pazos
Av Lima

Av San Martin
La Candelaria
Parque
Municipal   Juanito's
Ayacucho
Rios
Pedro de Osma
28 de Julio   La Quinta
de Allison

Trailblazer

sanisidro, dbl US$79). ***Libertador Lima*** (Los Eucaliptos 550, ☎ 518-6300, 🖥 liber tador.com.pe, rooms from US$132). **Expensive** *Country Club Lima* (Los Eucaliptos 590, ☎ 611-9000, 🖥 hotelcoun try.com, rooms from US$239). ***Sonesta Hotel El Olivar*** (Pancho Fierro 194, ☎ 712-6000, 🖥 sonesta.com/lima, rooms from US$450).

WHERE TO EAT

Whilst in Lima, make sure you discover the food scene; it's a chance to sample an emerging world cuisine in its original location. Countless eateries can rustle up versions of Peru's fusion food, but look out in particular for ceviche, nutty stews, anticuchos and *causas*.

Eating in Lima is surprisingly affordable, especially if you stick to restaurants popular with local people (see p34). The eateries below are more upmarket.

Cafés

Miraflores area   For a treat, head to *Xocolatl* (Manuel Bonilla 111; Mon-Sat 11:00-20:00, 🖥 xocolatl.pe), a specialist shop focusing on Peruvian sweets. *Haiti* (Diagonal 160, 🖥 haitimiraflores.pe) is stuck in a time warp, but serves up tasty

sandwiches and pastries in an ideal spot for people watching.

Lima centro   A bit more classy, *T'anta* (Pasaje Nicolas de Ribera El Viejo 142; Mon-Sat 09:00-22:00, Sun 09:00-18:00), is part of celebrity-chef Gastón Acurio's stable of restaurants. There are also branches in **San Isidro** (Pancho Fierro 115) and **Miraflores** (Av 28 de Julio 888).

Cevicherias and seafood

There are plenty of authentic neighbourhood *cevicherías* to sample Peru's national dish, ceviche, but also a number of more sophisticated joints where it is given the fine dining treatment. In line with cevichería tradition, most restaurants only open till about 17:00.

Miraflores area (all off-map) Celebrated chef Gastón Acurio's stylish *La Mar* (Av La Mar 770; Mon-Thur 12:00-17:00, Fri-Sun to 17:30, 🖥 lamarcebicheria.com/lima) is a high-end ceviche restaurant, popular with wealthy locals and visitors alike. *La Rosa Nautica* (Espigon 4, Costa Verde; daily 12:00-00:00, 🖥 larosanautica.com) is superbly sited in a Victorian-style end-of-pier restaurant. Far better in terms of the food is *Pescados Capitales* (Av La Mar 1337; daily 12:30-17:00 & 20:00-

23:00, ⌨ pescadoscapitales.com).

Barranco The locals flock to *Canta Rana* (Génova 101) to sample the 17 types of ceviche for which the place is renowned. Informal and simply decorated, it is quite expensive, but justifies it by being the epitome of the local *cevichería*.

Peruvian

Miraflores area *Central* (Santa Isabel 376, Mon-Fri 13:00-15:30 and 20:00-23:30, only evenings Sat, ⌨ centralrestaurante.com.pe) is ranked 15th in the 2014 World's 50 Best Restaurants list; chef Virgilio Martínez offers a modern take on Peruvian cuisine, with regularly changing menus incorporating ingredients from across the country.

Panchita (Av 2 de Mayo 298), focuses on street food and captures authentic flavours such as flame-grilled anticuchos and *tamales*. It's not possible to book a table so queues can be long.

Restaurant Huaca Pucllana (General Borgoño cuadra 8, 12:00-16:00 and from 19:00, ⌨ resthuacapucllana.com) is a smart restaurant alongside the Huaca Pucllana ruins serving contemporary Peruvian cuisine.

San Isidro Now housed in Casa Hacienda Moreyra, *Astrid y Gastón* (Av Paz Soldan 290; Tue-Sat 13.00-15:00 & 19:30-21:30, ⌨ astridygaston.com) is where the Peruvian food renaissance began. Chef Gastón Acurio and his wife Astrid pioneered novoandina cuisine, fusing traditional foodstuffs with Asian, African and Spanish flavours to startling effect. Book well in advance.

At *Malabar*, (Camino Real 101, Mon-Sat 12:30-16:00, 19:30-23:30, ⌨ malabar.com.pe) up-and-coming chef Pedro Miguel Schiaffino is influenced by Amazonian foodstuffs and cooking techniques and prepares a seasonal menu that draws on these.

International

Lima Centro For a slightly special chifa, seek out *Wa Lok* (Jr Paruro 878, daily 09:00-23:00, walok.com.pe) in *Barrio*

Chino (Chinatown). French-influenced food with a Peruvian twist is available at *L'Eau Vive* (Ucayali 370), opposite Torre Tagle Palace. Run by an order of nuns, there's a rendition of *Ave Maria* every evening at 21:00. Proceeds are donated to charity.

Barranco **Antica Trattoria** (Av San Martín 201, 12:00-0:00 daily) is a rustic style pizzeria with a firewood oven and choice of fresh pastas.

BARS AND NIGHTLIFE

Lima has a more contemporary and happening nightlife than almost any other city in Peru. Barranco in particular has a lively atmosphere and a wide range of places in which to hang out.

Lima Centro For old-world elegance head to the *Gran Hotel Bolívar* bar (Plaza San Martín), to sip a Pisco Sour. The best **folklórica show** in Lima is at *Las Brisas del Titicaca* (off map; Jr Heroes de Tarapaca 168, ⌨ brisasdeltiticaca.com).

Miraflores Miraflores has a number of expat-style bars, including *Old Pub* (San Ramón 295). Alternatively, try artsy hangout *Bar Habana* (Manuel Bonilla 107), *Media Naranja* (Schell 130), which has a Brazilian vibe, or *Huaringas* (Bolognesi 460), a busy lounge bar.

Barranco First try *Ayahuasca* (San Martín 130), a fashionable bar; *Juanito's* (Av Grau 270), where a bohemian crowd congregates, or one of the *Posadas del Angel* (Pedro de Osma 164 & 218 and Av San Martín 157). After, head to *tabernas* including *La Noche* (Bolognesi 307) in search of live Andean music, criolla or Latin jazz. Finally, hit the *peñas* such as *La Candelaria* (Bolognesi 292) or clubs including *Sargento Pimienta* (Bolognesi 757).

BIKE AND OUTDOOR SHOPS

Miraflores has the widest selection of good bike shops. **BiciCentro** (Paseo de la República 4986, ⌨ bicicentro.com.pe) comes recommended; other options include **Specialized Peru** (Av Reducto 1017) and **Best Bikes** (off map; Av Santa Cruz 535, ⌨ best.com.pe).

CITY & TOWN GUIDES

There are numerous small bike shops on Av Emancipación in central Lima, many of which don't open till mid-morning. Parts for sale here are often fakes and you'll need reasonable Spanish to get by.

Tatoo Adventure Gear (Larcomar 123-125B, 🖥 pe.tatoo.ws) in the Larcomar shopping centre south of Miraflores has a good selection of outdoor hiking gear.

Huaraz
Altitude: 3060m

Huaraz is a bustling city of over 100,000 inhabitants that is the pulsating heart of the Callejón de Huaylas. Almost totally destroyed in the devastating Ancash earthquake of 1970, the modern city that rose from the ruins is a sprawling mess of unplanned brick and concrete eyesores. But raise your gaze a few degrees for the real attraction of the place: its sensational location. Eight snow-capped 6000ers adorn the eastern skyline.

The town is a comfortable and fun place to hang out (see box p61): there are accommodation options in all categories, good restaurants for both Andean and Western cuisine, chilled-out cafés and convivial drinking establishments serving craft beer. As a result, the majority of visitors to the area base themselves in and around the Ancash capital.

WHAT TO DO

Though most visitors' time in Huaraz revolves around acclimatizing or planning and resupplying for the next foray into the Cordillera, the city is an engaging place that makes for an interesting introduction to Andean life. The **Centro Cultural** has free exhibitions about the local area and the **Ancash Archaeological Museum** (S/.5, 08:30-17:15, Tue-Sat, 09:00-14:00 Sun) displays artefacts from the region, including a vast outdoor lithic art collection. Both are on the Plaza de Armas. The **central market** makes for an eye-opening wander, and numerous street vendors mean that a walk round town is rarely dull. Slightly further afield are the **archaeological ruins** at Wilcahuaín (p178) and Honcopampa (p113).

On Sunday lunchtimes, Jr José Olaya hosts a **food fair** where it's possible to feast on many local specialities. Arrive before 14:00 to avoid missing out on some succulent pachamanca (see box p61), or thirst-quenching chicha de jora.

GETTING TO THE CORDILLERA
To reach Huaraz from Lima, you can either fly or journey by bus – sit on the right for best peak views.

Air
LCPerú (Av José Pardo 269, Miraflores, ☎ 204-1313, 🖥 lcperu.pe) has three flights a week (Tue/Thur/Sat) from Lima to Anta (near Huaraz). It's usually possible to get a one-way ticket for around US$120, but planes are small, so book early. The check-in baggage allowance is only 15kg, so those wishing to travel with a bike need to contact the airline before purchasing a ticket.

Bus
Lima doesn't have a central bus terminal,

so each operator manages its own departure points. However, except where stated, all companies below stop at the Plaza Norte terminal (Av Túpac Amaru, Cuadra 39), which is easily reached from the airport. There are numerous buses to Huaraz (7-9h) – more expensive companies make fewer intermediate stops and are thus quicker. *Bus cama* services are the most comfortable, followed by *semi-cama* then *económico*. Prices to take a bike are negotiable if not given.

Movil Tours: Paseo de la República 749, La Victoria; ☎ 716-8000; 🖳 moviltours.com.pe; 7 daily; S/.40-110; bikes S/.40; don't stop at Plaza Norte. **Cruz del Sur**: Av Javier Prado Este 1109, La Victoria; ☎ 311-5050; 🖳 cruzdelsur.com.pe; 09:30/22:30; S/.66-86; bikes S/.20. **Z Buss**: Jr Julián Piñeiro 440 (map p48); ☎ 381-2919; 🖳 zbussperu.com; 9 daily; S/.30-50. **Oltursa**: Av Aramburú 1160, San Isidro; ☎ 708-5000; 🖳 oltursa.pe; 12:15/ 22:15; S/.40-75. **Linea**: Paseo de la República 941, La Victoria; ☎ 424-0836; 🖳 linea.pe; 22:15; S/.40-60; bikes S/.20. **Turismo Cavassa**: Jr Raimondi 129, La Victoria; ☎ 431-3200; 🖳 turismocavassa.com.pe; 4 daily; S/.30-60.

Movil, Z Buss and Cavassa all have services that continue through Huaraz to **Caraz**. Cavassa also has direct daily buses to **Chiquián** and **Huallanca**. Many other small towns in the Cordillera Blanca and Huayhuash are serviced by direct buses from Lima, however these are uncomfortable and you could spend your entire holiday just in Lima trying to find where they leave from. It's best to use one of the above companies, then change in Huaraz (or Catac). For **Cajatambo** (see Huayhuash Circuit p154), go to Barranca, 200km north of Lima, and try and find the daily early morning bus there.

PRACTICAL INFORMATION

There are ATMs which accept foreign cards, pharmacies, internet cafés and wi-fi at every turn. For **medical** needs try Clínica San Pablo (Jr Inés Huaylas 172, ☎ 428811) – or for treatment of dog bites (see p44), the public Hospital Víctor Ramos Guardia (Av Luzuriaga, ☎ 424146).

The helpful crew at **iPerú** (09:00-18:00, to 13:00 Sun), just off the Plaza de Armas, can lay their hands on stacks of useful information about fiestas and sights. Trekking info isn't their strong point.

The **Parque Nacional Huascarán office** (08:30-13:00, 14:30-18:00 Mon-Fri, closes 12:00 on Sat) is just off Plaza Belen. There are informative displays, and PNH staff are usually available to answer questions (in Spanish). For ticketing see p31.

Safety issues

Huaraz is a safe place; as long as you steer clear of the following two trouble spots you'd be extremely unlucky to become the victim of crime.

Avoid walking in the vicinity of Rataquena, a mirador above town where robberies of tourists at gun point have occurred for years; and stay clear of the walking route from Wilcahuaín to Monterrey for the same reason (though both Wilcahuaín and Monterrey themselves are fine). If something untoward does happen, contact the Tourist Police (Plaza de Armas, 07:45-21:00, ☎ 421351).

In the event of an **accident in the mountains**, you should contact the Departamento de Salvamento de Alta Montaña (DEPSAM, ☎ 493327) who are based in Yungay. We would recommend contacting the Casa de Guías (☎ 421811, see p60) at the same time, as they can often organize a better and faster rescue.

Ancashinos are a friendly bunch, and visiting the area is normally hassle-free.

CITY & TOWN GUIDES

❏ **The Huaraz Telegraph**
It may come as a surprise to know that Huaraz has its very own English-language paper. Dutch editor Rex Broekman provides an interesting and useful insight into local life and events, pulling no punches when it comes to some of the more pressing issues in the area. The paper can be read online at 🖳 thehuaraztelegraph.com.

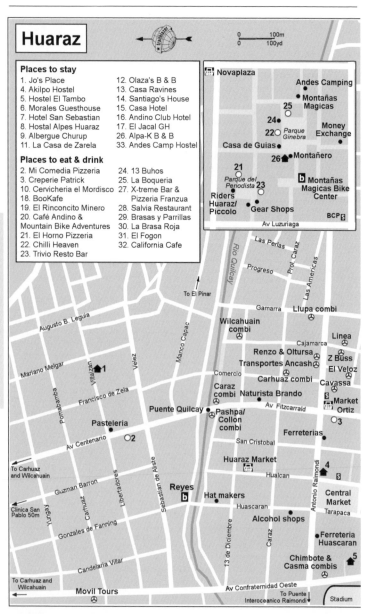

Huaraz

0   100m
0   100yd

Places to stay
1. Jo's Place
4. Akilpo Hostel
5. Hostel El Tambo
6. Morales Guesthouse
7. Hotel San Sebastian
8. Hostal Alpes Huaraz
9. Albergue Churup
11. La Casa de Zarela
12. Olaza's B & B
13. Casa Ravines
14. Santiago's House
15. Casa Hotel
16. Andino Club Hotel
17. El Jacal GH
26. Alpa-K B & B
33. Andes Camp Hostel

Places to eat & drink
2. Mi Comedia Pizzeria
3. Creperie Patrick
10. Cervicheria el Mordisco
18. BooKafe
19. El Rinconcito Minero
20. Café Andino &
Mountain Bike Adventures
21. El Horno Pizzeria
22. Chilli Heaven
23. Trivio Resto Bar
24. 13 Buhos
25. La Boqueria
27. X-treme Bar &
Pizzeria Franzua
28. Salvia Restaurant
29. Brasas y Parrillas
30. La Brasa Roja
31. El Fogon
32. California Cafe

Novaplaza

Andes Camping
Montañas Magicas
25
24
22 Parque Ginebra
Money Exchange
Casa de Guias
26 Montañero
21
Parque del Periodista 23
Riders Huaraz/ Piccolo
Montañas Magicas Bike Center
Gear Shops
Av Luzuriaga
BCP

Las Perlas
Rio Quilcay
Progreso
Prof. Caraz
Las Americas
To El Pinar
Gamarra Llupa combi
Augusto B. Leguia
Wilcahuain combi
Linea
Cajamarca
Marco Capac
Renzo & Oltursa
Z Buss
Transportes Ancash
El Veloz
Mariano Melgar
Velez
Comercio
Carhuaz combi
Cavassa
Caraz combi
Naturista Brando
Market Ortiz
Pomatamba
Francisco de Zela
Av Fitzcarrald
Puente Quilcay Pashpa/ Collon combi
3
Pasteleria
Ferreterias
2
San Cristobal
Av Centenario
Huaraz Market
Antonio Raimondi
4
To Carhuaz and Wilcahuain
Hualcan
Guzman Barron
Reyes
Central Market
Clinica San Pablo 50m
Hat makers
Tarapaca
Yungay
Huascaran
Gonzales de Fanning
Alcohol shops
Caraz
Ferreteria Huascaran
Candelaria Villar
Chimbote & Casma combis
5
To Carhuaz and Wilcahuain
13 Diciembre
Sebastian de Aliste
Libertadores
Carhuaz
Movil Tours
Av Confraternidad Oeste
To Puente Interoceanico Raimondi
Stadium
Villazan 1

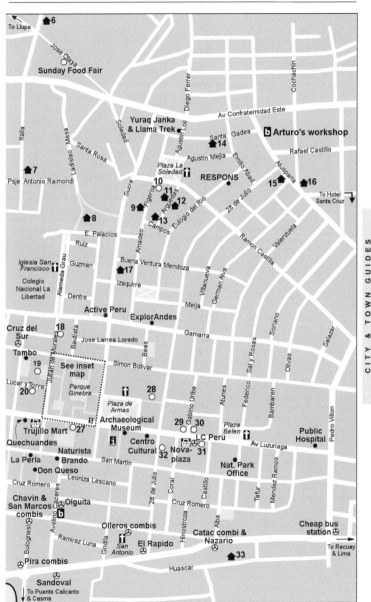

To Llupa
▲6
Jose Oleya
Sunday Food Fair

Jose Oleya
Italia
Ladislao Mesa
Santa Rosa
Soledad
Diego Ferrer
Cochachin

Av Confraternidad Este

Yuraq Janka
& Llama Trek
Santa Gadea
▲14
b Arturo's workshop
Rafael Castillo

Agustin Loli
Agustin Mejia

▲7
Psje Antonio Raimondi
Plaza La
Soledad ℹ
RESPONS
Emilio Abad
Atusparia
15 ▲16
To Hotel
Santa Cruz

Sucre
Figueroa
Argudas
10
▲11
9 ▲12
Eulógio del Río
28 de Julio

▲8
E. Palacios
Ruiz
Amadeo
Campos
▲13
Ramon Castilla
Valenzuela

Iglesia San
Francisco ℹ
Guzman
Alameda Grau
Buena Ventura Mendoza
▲17
Villanueva
German Ava

Colegio
Nacional La
Libertad
Dentre
Izaquirre
Meija
Soriano
Salazar

Active Peru
ExplorAndes
Gamarra
Olivas

Cruz del
Sur ⊘
18
Jose Larrea Loredo
Beas
Sal y Rosas
Federico
Bambaren

Tambo
Julian de Morales
Bautista
19
Simon Bolivar

Lucar y Torre
20
Parque
Ginebra
See inset
map
28
Gabino Uribe
Atunes
Plaza
Belen ℹ
Pedro Villon

Plaza de
Armas
Archaeological
Museum
29 30
LC Peru
Av Luzuriaga
Public
Hospital

Trujillo Mart
27
Quechuandes
ℹ
Centro
Cultural
Nova-
plaza
32
31
Nat. Park
Office
Mendez Ramos

La Perla
Naturista
Brando
San Martin
28 de Julio
Coral
Castillo
Tafur

Don Queso
Leoniza Lescano
Cruz Romero

Chavin &
San Marcos
combis ⊘
Olguita
Avelino Caceres
b
Cruz Romero
Hinostroza
Alba

Bolognesi ⊘
Ramirez Luna
Olleros combis
ℹ
San
Antonio
El Rapido
Catac combi &
Nazario ⊘
Cheap bus
station ⊘

Pira combis ⊘
Gridia
Huascar
▲33
To Recuay
& Lima

Sandoval ⊘
To Puente Calicanto
& Casma

Having said this, ignore touts who sometimes hang out at bus stations, and don't ever buy a tour from anyone on the street.

Stray dogs about town are an annoyance – watch where you step. Cyclists should pay particular attention to the multitude of hazards, including being cut up by taxi drivers and potholes which could swallow a llama.

Getting around

It's easy enough to walk between most places in town, but there's no shortage of taxis (S/.3-4) or mototaxis (S/.1.50-2) for short journeys. Combis are ubiquitous – they're slightly slower and cheaper than colectivos, which are the ones whose drivers insist on tooting their horns at potential customers every two seconds on Luzuriaga. Combi lines E and 10 are particularly useful as they run between Jangas (on the main road north of Huaraz) and Bedoya (south of Huaraz).

WHERE TO STAY

There are literally hundreds of places to bed down for the night, from S/.10 cheapies to luxurious rooms which will set you back rather more. As Huaraz grows haphazardly both upwards and outwards, more and more places have roof terraces with fabulous mountain views. Until a neighbour suddenly plonks three more storeys on his building and blocks the vistas, anyway.

Many accommodation options are in the more tranquil area near Iglesia La Soledad, a 10 minute uphill walk from the centre. All places mentioned here have wifi, though in cheaper places it doesn't necessarily reach every room. All places in the Budget and Mid-range categories have some kind of kitchen facilities for guest use. Rooms in all Mid-range and Expensive options come with attached bathroom and include breakfast, unless otherwise stated.

Budget

Santiago's House (Jr Santa Gadea 830, ☎ 587427, 🖳 santiagoshouse.com) offers good showers and one of the best terrace views. It's popular with cyclists, but some-

times gets overrun by noisy young groups. Guests are charged S/.15pp including light breakfast; all rooms (dbl/twin/2-4 bed dorms) come with AB.

Run more by Vicky than English husband Jo, *Jo's Place* (Jr Villaizan 276, ☎ 425505, 🖳 josplacehuaraz@hotmail.com), north of the centre, is ever-popular with trekkers, mountaineers and cyclists. Rooms are good value and there's a tranquil garden with small lawn for camping (camping/dorm/sgl/dbl S/.10/15/20-30/35-45). English breakfast is available.

The modern rooms at *Akilpo Hostel* (Av Raimondi 510, ☎ 456169) are some of the best value in town. It's right by the market and popular with groups of backpackers, so can be noisy. Per person prices are S/.15/20 in a dorm/private room.

Hostel El Tambo (Av Confraternidad Oeste 122, ☎ 425114, 🖳 marielafm@yahoo.com) is a steal at S/.10 for a bed in a dorm or private room. It's poorly signed and tucked down an alley (between Repuestos Trinidad and Little Boo) opposite the stadium.

Hostal Alpes Huaraz (Jr Ladislau Mesa 112, ☎ 428896, 🖳 hostalalpeshuaraz.com) has friendly staff and rooms set around a pretty courtyard. Dorm/sgl/dbl S/.20/30/60, including breakfast.

Andes Camp Hostel (Jr Huascar 615, ☎ 423842, 🖳 andescamplodge.com) is a sociable place, with a bar and comfortable common rooms. Dorm/dbl S/.15/42-52.

Mid-range

Cosy, colourful and full of character, *Albergue Churup* (Jr Figueroa 1257, ☎ 424200, 🖳 churup.com) is rightfully a perennial favourite. There's a beautiful communal room up top with an open fire. Dorm with SB/sgl/dbl S/.30/85/120.

The large and classy rooms at the new *Casa Ravines* (Jr Arguedas 1217, ☎ 396420, 🖳 casaravines.com; sgl/dbl S/.85/120) are a bargain. Walls are decorated with paintings by owner Juan Quiros (who along with wife Nelly also owns Albergue Churup); the only downside is there's currently no roof terrace or outdoor area with natural light.

Olaza's B & B (Jr Arguedas 1242, ☎ 422529, 🖥 olazas.com; sgl/dbl S/.80/100) offers neat, modern rooms and a lovely communal room with wood fire on the top floor. The roof terrace has fabulous views. The Andean Explorer (🖥 andean explorer.com) agency operates out of here, and owner Tito's brother Julio runs mountain bike tours (see p214).

El Jacal Guest House (Jr Sucre 1044, ☎ 424612, 🖥 jacalhuaras.com; sgl/dbl S/.60/60) has recently been refurbished and is another with excellent breakfast room and roof terrace.

Labyrinthine *La Casa de Zarela* (Jr Arguedas 1263, ☎ 421694, 🖥 lacasa dezarela.hostel.com; sgl/dbl S/.70/90) sports many communal areas and is popular with mountaineers. Breakfast is available but not included.

In a quiet part of town, the rooms at *Morales Guesthouse* (Pasaje Ucanan 232, ☎ 425105, 🖥 moralesguesthouse.com; sgl/dbl S/.100-140) are unspectacular given the price, but there's a nice communal room on the top floor, leading to a terrace with excellent views. English speaking owner Hisao runs the Peruvian Andes agency (see p60).

In the centre of town, *Alpa-K B & B* (Parque Ginebra 308, ☎ 428629, 🖥 hotel-huaraz.com; sgl/dbl S/.45/70-100) is run by knowledgeable and friendly French-Swiss Bertrand. There's a disco nearby so it can be noisy. Only the more expensive doubles have AB; breakfast is available, not included.

Expensive

The tasteful and large rooms at *Casa Hotel* (Jr Maguiña 142, ☎ 221028, 🖥 casahotel house.com.pe; sgl/dbl S/.110/140) are great value, and there are magnificent views from the roof terrace.

One of Huaraz's longest running hotels, *Andino Club Hotel* (Jr Cochachin 357, ☎ 421662, 🖥 hotelandino.com; sgl/dbl/suites S/.240-405/290-405/490-1675) lacks character, but makes up for it with excellent service and facilities. There's a wide range of rooms and suites, some come with terrace, mountain views, open fire, Jacuzzi and sauna.

Hotel San Sebastián (Jr Italia 1124, ☎ 426960, 🖥 sansebastianhuaraz.com; sgl/dbl US$60-66/76-84) is a solid choice with nice lawns and terraces. Rooms are pleasant but moderate in size, and the neighbours are building upwards, eating into the mountain views.

Make sure you get a room with a view of the peaks if you opt for *Hotel Santa Cruz* (Jr Uribe 255, ☎ 396096, 🖥 santa cruzperu.com; sgl/dbl S/.120/170) – they're no more expensive. There's a nice breakfast room and garden.

WHERE TO EAT

Huaraz has an enormous number of budget restaurants which serve up large portions for S/.5-10. Listed here are restaurants which are more of a treat: Mid-Range options offer mains for around S/.8-25; at Splurge places expect prices from S/.20 upwards.

Mid-range

La Brasa Roja (Av Luzuriaga 915, 12:00-00:00, Sun: 17:30-00:00) serves up great value burgers, steaks and chicken. Portions are huge and it's popular with locals as well as tourists looking to gorge after time in the hills. *El Fogón* (Av Luzuriaga 928, 12:00-15:00 & 18:00-00:00, closed lunchtimes on Sun) is one for the carnivores. *Brasas y Parrillas* (Av Luzuriaga 897, lunch and dinner) is another meat option; menus are excellent.

Housed in X-treme Bar, *Pizzeria Franzua* (Av Luzuriaga 646, 19:00-late) prepares tasty, good value pizza. *El Horno Pizzeria* (Parque del Periodista, lunch daily except Sun, dinner daily) has an identical menu to Franzua; come here if you're after more of a restaurant ambience.

El Rinconcito Minero (Jr Morales 757, lunch and dinner) serves up delicious Peruvian fare, both menus and à la carte dishes – it's another that's a hit with locals. For the Peruvian raw fish speciality ceviche, try *Cevicheria el Mordisco* (Jr Amadeo Figueroa 1284, lunch). *Salvia Restaurant* (Pasaje Farfan 793, lunch and dinner) is cheap and one of Huaraz's few offerings for vegetarians.

Splurge

Run by effervescent Graciela, *Mi Comedia Pizzeria* (Av Centenario 351, 17:00-23:00 Mon-Sat) is the classiest place, and whips up the best pizza in town. Travellers who are missing British curry rave about *Chilli Heaven* (Parque Ginebra, 09:30-22:30, Mon-Sat, 17:00-22:00 Sun).

The food at *Trivio Resto-Bar* (Parque del Periodista, 12:00-23:00 Tue-Sun) can be a bit hit and miss, but there's a wide range, it caters to vegetarians, and the atmosphere's congenial. Delicious Sierra Andina craft beer is available on tap, at S/.10 for 330ml. For tasty crêpes, fondue or raclete head to *Creperie Patrick* (Av Luzuriaga 422, 16:00-22:30), which also produces home-made coca liquor and granola.

Cafés

California Café (Jr 28 de Julio 562, 07:30-18:30, to 14:30 Sun) is the place for a relaxed breakfast (S/.16-24) and killer brownies. The staff are happy for you to linger over a coffee and its popularity with local voluntary workers and longer term travellers means there are always useful snippets of information to be gleaned.

Many trekkers, mountaineers and the trendy backpacker crowd head to *Café Andino* (Lucar y Torre 530, 09:00-22:00). As well as breakfasts (S/.12-17) and mains (S/.12-25) including veggie options, there's great coffee, a well-stocked lending library and a terrace with views.

La Boqueria (Parque Ginebra 686, 10:30-22:30 Mon-Sat) and *BooKafé* (Jr Morales 828, 07:30-22:00) are both modern and minimalist, serving good coffee and tasty snacks.

BARS AND NIGHTLIFE

Owner Lucho's artisan beer is available at *13 Buhos* (Parque Ginebra), the coolest bar in town. A short taxi ride north of the centre (ask for '*frente a Coca Cola en Cascapampa*'), the *Sierra Andina Tap Room* (Av Centenario 1690, Cascapampa, Tue-Sun 15:00-22:00) showcases the fruits of Huaraz's second microbrewery's labours. The four flavoursome ales are also on tap at *Trivio* (see above). *X-treme Bar* (Luzuriaga 646, 19:00-late) is a hang-out spot favoured by many; *Tambo* (Jr de la Mar 776, 20:00-late) has been a popular drinking and dancing spot for decades.

❏ WHERE TO GET FUEL FOR STOVES

Stove type	Fuel	Spanish	Price	Available in Huaraz at:	Available elsewhere?
Multi-fuel (MSR/Primus)	White Gas	*Bencina blanca*	S/.6 per litre	Ferreterías, Av Raimondi	Yes *
Multi-fuel (MSR/Primus)	Petrol	*Gasolina*	S/.4 per litre	Petrol Station, Av Raimondi	Yes, widely
Gas (ISO screw thread EN417)	Propane/ Butane Gas	*Gas*	S/.20 for 230g canister	Camping shops, Parque Ginebra	No
Alcohol (Trangia/Esbit)	Grain Alcohol	*Alcohol puro*	S/.4 per litre	Jr Huascarán	Yes **
Alcohol (Trangia/Esbit)	Burning alcohol	*Ron/alcohol de quemar*	S/.6 per litre	Ferretería Huascarán, Av Raimondi	No

* Can sometimes be found in Caraz, Pomabamba & Chiquián
** Though hard to pinpoint

CAMPING GEAR

Montañas Mágicas and **Andes Camping** (🖥 andescamping.com), both on the east side of Parque Ginebra, are **outdoor gear shops** which sell good quality equipment and gas canisters. Other smaller shops are found on the alley between Parque del Periodista and Av Luzuriaga. For cheaper outdoor clothing there are a few shops east of the market on Jr San Martín.

Many agencies in Huaraz **rent outdoor equipment**. It's possible to find sleeping bags, sleeping mats, tents, multi-fuel or gas stoves, rucksacks and down jackets, but some of it is of dubious quality. Check everything for damage before hiring, erecting tents to make sure you know how to and that all parts, including pegs, are there. Take sleeping bags out of their stuff sacks to check the quality and cleanliness. Head to Active Peru, Quechuandes or Montañero (see Agencies) for more reliable gear.

To **patch up outdoor gear**, or buy locally made kit, see Huicho at Yuraq Janka (Pasaje Agustin Loli 465, 🖥 yura qjanka.com), an ethically-run place where owner Uri is involved in a number of community projects. To **fix boots** or leather items, make a beeline for La Perla (Jr San Martín 574), where the work is top class, but they're not averse to inflating prices for tourists.

For **renting bikes**, **cycling spares and gear** see p176. For stove fuel, see box opposite.

AGENCIES

If you elect to trek with a locally based agency, choosing which one will be the most important decision of your trip. In Huaraz the sheer number of companies offering their services can make things daunting and confusing, particularly as there are plenty of cowboy agencies in town.

The list below contains some recommended operators in Huaraz – make contact in advance of your trip to allow arrangements to be made.
● Amongst the budget agencies, **Quechuandes** (Av Luzuriaga 522, 🖥 quechuandes.com) stand out for their integrity and environmental awareness. Run by knowledgeable Peruvian/Belgian couple David and Marie, they organize tours throughout the Blanca and Huayhuash and consistently receive excellent reports from clients. For a small commission, arrieros can be arranged for independent trekkers; they also rent trekking gear.
● **La Cima Logistics** (🖥 cafeandino@hot mail.com, 🖥 cafeandino.com) is a reliable outfit which tailors services to client requirements. Owner Chris Benway runs Café Andino and can sometimes be tracked down there.
● **RESPONSible Travel Peru** (Jr Eulogio del Río 1364, 🖥 responsibletravelperu .com) work with local communities to provide sustainable tourism and allow visitors to see the 'real' Peru. They offer a unique range of environmentally and socially responsible trips including homestays and

CITY & TOWN GUIDES

> ❑ **Asociación de Guías de Montaña del Peru (AGMP)**
> The **Casa de Guías** (Parque Ginebra, 🖳 agmp.pe) is the UIAGM-affiliated Asociación de Guías de Montaña del Peru's headquarters in Huaraz. It was set up to run technical and language courses for mountain and walking guides, and provided impartial advice to mountaineers and trekkers. Nowadays it also operates like an agency, organizing trips, and though staff are knowledgeable and can still provide good information, they are not necessarily the impartial source of yesteryear. Many, but not all, AGMP guides are excellent, so try to get a personal recommendation.

visits to remote ruins, as well as interesting treks.

● Based in Marcará, 25km north of Huaraz, **Don Bosco Andes 6000 Guides** (🖳 don bosco6000.net) have UIAGM qualified guides and offer imaginative trekking, mountain biking and mountaineering routes. (See box p71.)

● **Peruvian Andes Adventures** (Pasaje Ucanan 232, 🖳 peruvianandes.com) is a friendly, family-run agency with an excellent reputation for customer service. They operate out of Morales Guesthouse.

● **Active Peru** (Av Gamarra 699, 🖳 activeperu.com) is another reliable agency with experienced guides. Their office is a good place to rent equipment.

● For two years running **ExplorAndes** (Av Gamarra 835, 🖳 explorandes.com) have won World's Leading Green Tour Operator at the World Travel Awards. They offer excellent service on their comfortable treks to Santa Cruz, Huayhuash and Olleros – Chavín.

● North of town, **Skyline Adventures** (Pasaje Industrial 137, Cascapampa, 🖳 skyline-adventures.com) have a crew of international mountain guides led by US expat Ted Alexander. They offer all the popular treks as well as running a range of mountaineering courses.

● The APOTUM group of agencies provide top notch treks with a very high level of client service. All guides are AGMP qualified, and they hold annual courses for cooks and arrieros. Members of this group include **Montañero** (Parque Ginebra, 🖳 trekkingperu.com) and **Turismo Andino** (Jr Pedro Cochachin 357, 🖳 turismoandino .com.pe) at Andino Club Hotel.

For mountain biking agencies, see p214.

TRANSPORT
Many bus companies make the 7-9 hour journey to **Lima**. These include: **Z Buss** (9 daily, S/.30-50), **Movil Tours** (9 daily, S/.40-80, bikes S/.40), **Cruz del Sur** (11:00/22:00, S/.66-86, bikes S/.20), **Oltursa** (3 daily, S/.40-75), **Linea** (22:15, S/.40-60, bikes S/.20), **Turismo Cavassa** (4 daily, S/.30-60), and **Transportes Ancash** (3 daily, S/.30-35).

All except Movil Tours stop at Plaza Norte in Lima; bike prices are negotiable if not stated. Always ask about taking a bike before you buy your ticket, though it's not usually a problem. Transportes Ancash buses are less comfortable and reliable than others listed, but have big holds for bikes.

LCPerú have offices at Av Luzuriaga 904 for those who prefer **to fly to Lima**.

Movil Tours are among those who have direct buses to **Chimbote** and **Trujillo**.

To the Callejón de Conchucos: Sandoval and Olguita service **Chavín** (3h, S/.12) and **Huari** (4h, S/.15) with many buses each day. For **Pomabamba** (8h, S/.30) via **Chacas** (3h30, S/.16), Renzo and El Veloz both have morning and evening services.

El Rápido and Nazario lay on 05:00 and 14:00 services to **Chiquián** (2h, S/.10).

For **Carhuaz** (40 mins, S/.3.50), **Yungay** (1h, S/.5), **Caraz** (1h20, S/.6) and other towns north of Huaraz in the Río Santa valley, catch one of the combis that leave every few minutes from Puente Quilcay between 04:00 and 20:00.

❏ HOW TO SPEND YOUR TIME IN HUARAZ

Take a soak
There are thermal baths north of Huaraz at both Monterrey (7km, S/.1 on combi No.1, S/.3.50 entry, daily 06:00-17:00) and Chancos (27km, take a Caraz combi to Marcará (S/.3) then a colectivo to the Baños (S/.1.50, entry S/.2-5, daily 06:00-20:00). The latter are better, with natural sauna caves; both see flocks of locals descend at weekends.

Graze the day away...
Delicious street food abounds in Huaraz, and as different snacks are available at different times it's possible to spend the daylight hours contentedly grazing. Early on, try some hot quinoa and papas rellenas, near Puente Quilcay. At lunchtime guzzle an empanada from one of the ladies at the junction of Sucre and Bolivar. In mid-afternoon try some picarones near Iglesia La Soledad. About an hour before sunset, the churros sellers near the central market and pop-corn ladies on Sucre appear.

...go to a feast...
Pachamanca is a pre-Inca dish of meat, potatoes, beans, tamales and corn; it's the ultimate local feasting food. A fire prepared in a hole in the ground is used to heat stones. Raw food is then wrapped in banana leaves and placed between layers of hot stones, before earth is mounded on top to create an oven. After two hours the food emerges, deliciously tender. Try some at the Sunday food fair on José Olaya in Huaraz; or else head out to a *Recreo Campestre* (countryside outdoor restaurant) on a weekend – there are tons on the main road between Huaraz and Yungay.

...or shop for weird fruit and vegetables
Abuelitas selling vegetables like nothing more than finding a gringo who doesn't recognize any of the items on her stall. Pick out some random produce, ask how you prepare it (*¿come se prepara?*), have a nice chat, then go home and tuck in. Unless it's *oca* and the instructions begin with 'put it out in the sun for 3 days'...

Go to the football
Sport Ancash has a flash 18,000-capacity stadium, but a chequered recent history: struggles with relegation, unpaid debts leading to forfeited matches, and even accusations of poisoning opposition players during a match in 2010. There are usually games every other Sunday at 15:00 during high season; tickets cost from S/.15.

Try an elixir
If the dry high altitude air is affecting your throat, or even if it's not, consider hunting down a herbal remedy centre such as Naturista Brando, (see map p54) to sit and sup magic potions alongside a broad range of *Huaracinos*. The slightly-alcoholic Macerados might just hit the spot; Extracto de Rana isn't for the squeamish.

Get involved
There are many volunteering opportunities in the area, for those looking to get involved with community or environmental projects. California Café, RESPONS and Andean Alliance (see The Lazy Dog Inn) are some good places to start the search for more information.

Combis southwards to **Catac** (45 mins, S/.3.50) and **Recuay** (30 mins, S/.3) leave from Av Confraternidad Oeste throughout the day.

Between Huaraz and the **airport at Anta** either catch a taxi (30 mins, S/.40) or jump on a Huaraz-Caraz combi (S/.2.50).

See individual treks for information on reaching trailheads.

❏ Lodges in the Callejón de Huaylas

There are a number of lodges and inns set in the hills high above the Río Santa, which offer relaxing stays in beautiful and often luxurious surroundings.

The Lazy Dog Inn (☎ 943 789330, 🖳 thelazydoginn.com; sgl/dbl S/.120-295/190-365 includes breakfast and dinner) is a sustainable mountain lodge with an idyllic position above Huaraz, near the entrance to Quebrada Cojup (see map p180). Café Yurac Yacu (see p178) is located nearby.

The Hof (☎ 959 473219, 🖳 thehofhostel.com; camping/dorm S/.15/25 per person including breakfast) is a chilled-out place near Pitec (see map p180) that runs courses in natural building and permaculture. Compared to other lodges, facilities are basic, but you can't argue with their claim of being 'on the doorstep of amazingness'. Lunch (S/.15) and dinner (S/.20) are available.

In an unbeatable location within spitting distance of the Huandoy icefall and Llanganuco lakes, *Llanganuco Mountain Lodge* (🖳 llanganucomountainlodge.com; dbl US$192-232, full board) is run by affable Englishman Charlie Good. He's a great source of knowledge about local hiking and biking trails and can organize mountain biking tours.

Cuesta Serena Boutique Hotel (☎ 981 400038, 🖳 cuestaserena.pe; dbl US$190-310, including breakfast) is set in attractive gardens on the lower slopes of the Cordillera Negra, just a few kilometres from the airport at Anta.

The Way Inn (🖳 thewayinn.com) boasts a wonderful position, just downhill from The Hof. Nowadays it concentrates on ayahuasca retreats, rather than providing luxury accommodation.

Caraz
Altitude: 2270m

Charming Caraz is the most northerly town in the Callejón de Huaylas and makes an excellent base for a number of treks and bike rides. Despite the moto-taxis that buzz about the inclined streets, it's a far more relaxed place than Huaraz and the pleasant climate makes it an ideal spot to spend a few days. Don't miss the central market, which is one of the most interesting in the area.

❏ SSHH!

SSHH signs aren't advertising a quiet place, away from car horns or barking dogs; it's simply the *servicios higiénicos*, or toilets.

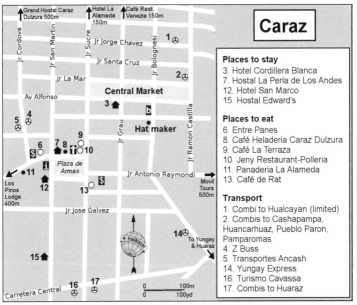

Caraz

Grand Hostal Caraz ↑Hotel La ↑Café Rest.
Dulzura 500m ↑Alameda ↑Venezia 150m
150m

Jr Cordova
Jr San Martin
Jr Sucre
Jr Jorge Chavez
Jr Bolognesi
1

Jr Santa Cruz

Jr La Mar
2

Av Alfonso
Central Market
3
b

Jr Ramon Castilla
Jr Grau
Hat maker
9

5 4
6 7 8 10
i Plaza de
11 Armas
Los 12 13 Jr Antonio Raymondi
Pinos Movil
Lodge Tours
400m 500m

Jr Jose Galvez

14 To Yungay
& Huaraz
trailblazer

15

16 17
Carretera Central

0 100m
0 100yd

Places to stay
3. Hotel Cordillera Blanca
7. Hostal La Perla de Los Andes
12. Hotel San Marco
15. Hostal Edward's

Places to eat
6. Entre Panes
8. Café Heladeria Caraz Dulzura
9. Café La Terraza
10. Jeny Restaurant-Polleria
11. Panaderia La Alameda
13. Café de Rat

Transport
1. Combi to Hualcayan (limited)
2. Combis to Cashapampa,
   Huancarhuaz, Pueblo Paron,
   Pamparomas
4. Z Buss
5. Transportes Ancash
14. Yungay Express
16. Turismo Cavassa
17. Combis to Huaraz

WHERE TO STAY

There are decent options in every price range. All have wi-fi.

Cavernous *Hotel San Marco* (San Martín 1133, ☎ 942 879247, sgl/dbl S/.20-35/25-45) has rooms (with both SB and AB) set around three courtyards; it's a favourite with cycle tourers and trekkers. *Hostal Edward's* and *Hotel Cordillera Blanca* are in a similar price bracket.

The modern rooms at *Hostal la Perla de los Andes* (Daniel Villar 179, ☎ 392007, ⌨ hostal_perladelosandes@hotmail.com, sgl/dbl S/.30/50) are a good deal, particularly if you get a room with balcony and Plaza views.

Neat, clean and with a garden, *Hotel La Alameda* (Av Noe Bazan Peralta 262, ☎ 391177, ⌨ hotellaalameda.com) offers rooms with AB for sgl/dbl S/.40/60, or cheaper rooms with SB for sgl/dbl S/.30/40. Breakfast is available for an additional S/.12.

Run by a Peruvian/British couple, *Grand Hostal Caraz Dulzura* (Jr Saenz

Peña 212, ☎ 392090, ⌨ hostalcarazdulzura.com, sgl/dbl with AB S/.45/70) is located a 10 minute walk north of the Plaza. It's a bit more upmarket, with pleasant communal areas, a bar and rooms set around a courtyard. Prices include breakfast.

Los Pinos Lodge (Parque San Martín 103, ☎ 391130, ⌨ lospinoslodge.pe, sgl/dbl/twin with AB S/.140/160/170) offers sumptuous rooms in a sprawling old building with well-tended gardens. They cater to budget travellers too, with dorm beds (S/.15-20) in a building on another side of the square.

WHERE TO EAT

Café La Terraza (Jr Sucre 1107) prepares good quality food. They offer breakfasts, à la carte mains and also a lunchtime menu (S/.7).

Entre Panes Café House (Jr Daniel Villar) serves real coffee, small but appetizing sandwiches (S/.7-15) and mains (S/.15-25). It's tastefully decorated, has a nice atmosphere and is just off the Plaza.

If you're craving some pasta, try *Café Restaurant Venezia* (Av Noe Bazan Peralta 231) which has dishes for S/.18-28.

Café de Rat (Jr Sucre 1266) serves breakfast (S/.6-15) and evening meals, including pizzas (S/.16-29). The owners run an agency and are a good source of information.

Jeny Restaurant-Pollería on the Plaza is always full of locals. Breakfasts are S/.5, menu lunch and dinners S/.6.

For ice cream head to *Café Heladería Caraz Dulzura*, and for pastries try *Panadería La Alameda*.

INFORMATION AND AGENCIES

The friendly ladies in the **tourist office** (Mon-Fri, 07:45-13:00, 14:30-1700) aren't exactly authorities on the surrounding area, but they do have a few information leaflets.

Pony's Expeditions, below Café de Rat, (☎ 391642, 🖳 ponyexpeditions.com) organize day and multi-day trips and treks. They also rent out equipment and basic mountain bikes (S/.50/day).

Apu Aventura (☎ 391130, 🖳 apuaventura.pe) operates out of Los Pinos Lodge and offers a number of treks and

guided bike rides. They hire out trekking gear, bicycles and quad bikes.

TRANSPORT

Z Buss (S/.40), Movil Tours (S/.45-85) and Turismo Cavassa (S/.30-40) all have multiple daily departures to **Lima** via Huaraz. Movil Tours also go to Trujillo, via Chimbote. From 04:00 to 20:00, combis for **Huaraz** (1h20, S/.6) and all places in between leave every few minutes from the terminal on the Carretera Central.

Accessing treks and cycle routes

Shared transport can be found to Casha-pampa (for the Santa Cruz trek), Huan-carhuaz and Hualcayán (for the Alpamayo Basecamp trek) and Pueblo Parón (for the Artesonraju Basecamp trek). The cycling trips to Laguna Parón and to Winchus can also be attempted from town. For those more interested in flying down big hills on two wheels, than slogging up them, it's possible to put bikes on a Pamparomás combi and get out at Winchus, or on a taxi to Laguna Parón and then bomb the 2000m back down to town. See individual routes for details.

Carhuaz
Altitude: 2650m

Found 30km north of Huaraz by paved road, Carhuaz really comes alive on Wednesday and Sunday mornings for its thriving market. Though it lacks the facilities of Huaraz and the charm of Caraz, it wins hands-down when it comes to ice-cream – get your fill at Helados Porvenir.

The long and spectacular road to Punta Olímpica leaves from the north-east corner of town.

WHERE TO STAY

Hospedaje Rubri (corner of Jrs Comercio and Brasil, ☎ 990 019899, sgl/dbl with AB S/.20/30) has large, modern rooms.

Las Torrecitas (Jr Amazonas 412, ☎ 394213, 🖳 lastorrecitascarhuaz.webnode .es, sgl/dbl with AB S/.35-50/60) is the best mid-range choice, with a roof terrace and

light, clean rooms. For something more old-fashioned, try *Hostal La Merced* (Jr Ucayali 724, ☎ 394280, sgl/dbl S/.45/45).

Run by amiable local map maker and guidebook writer Felipe Díaz, *El Abuelo* (Jr 9 de Diciembre 257, ☎ 394456, 🖳 elabuelohostal.com, sgl/dbl with AB

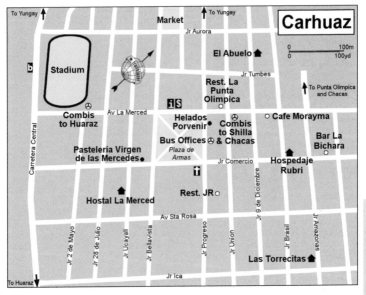

S/.124/162) is the swankiest hotel in town. Prices include American breakfast.

Montaña Jazz Lodge is a tranquil option, a five minute drive from Carhuaz (☎ 630023, 💻 montanajazzperu.com). Bungalows which accommodate 2-5 guests cost S/.300-400.

WHERE TO EAT AND DRINK

The host of uninspiring cheapies in Carhuaz is nothing to get excited about. Standing out slightly from the crowd are *Restaurante JR* (Av Progreso) which offers decent menu fare (S/.6), and *La Punta Olímpica* (Av La Merced) which can rustle you up a quarter of chicken (S/.8) in the evening. *Café Morayma* (Av La Merced 960) serves a range of food, including breakfasts and real coffee.

Helados Porvenir on the Plaza is renowned for its ice cream. Flavours include *cerveza* (beer) and *cushuro*, a type of bacteria which grows in high altitude Andean lakes and is sometimes called 'caviar andino' for its appearance. It tastes better than it sounds.

The most characterful place in the whole area to go drinking, *Restaurant Bar La Bichara* is housed in a beautiful 200 year old courtyarded colonial *casona*, which has been lovingly restored by outgoing owner Murad.

TRANSPORT

Combis for **Huaraz** (45 mins, S/.3.50) leave every few minutes from the stop on Av La Merced. To head north, go to the main road and flag down one of the combis to Caraz which run until around 20:00. For buses to **Lima**, Cavassa, Movil Tours and Z Buss all have offices on the east side of the plaza.

For **Chacas**, via Punta Olímpica, wait on Av La Merced, two blocks east of the Plaza. Buses (S/.15) originating in Huaraz pass here en route to Pomabamba/San Luis and will pick you up if they have room. Your best bet is early morning, around 07:30. Occasionally colectivos (S/.25) to Chacas leave from the same location.

Chavín
(Altitude: 3150m)

Friendly little Chavín in the Callejón de Conchucos was once the centre of the mystical Chavín de Huántar culture. Nowadays it is Ancash's premier archaeological site; a relaxed place with some good accommodation options, a couple of decent restaurants and little going on after dark. For modern day trekkers it's a convenient base or midway break for trips from Olleros, or in Quebradas Carhuascancha and Raria. There's an ATM, but no internet except at the more expensive hotels.

The **Ruins** (S/.10) and **Chavín National Museum** (free) are located at opposite ends of town, both walkable or a short taxi ride from the centre. They're open 09:00-17:00, Tue-Sun.

WHERE TO STAY

Hospedaje Gantu (Jr Huayna Capac 135, ☎ 454030, sgl/dbl S/.15-30/20-40) is a sound choice. The best rooms have AB and Plaza views.

Hostal La Casona (Jr Wiracocha 130, ☎ 454048, 🖥 lacasonachavin.com.pe, sgl/dbl with AB S/.35/60) is in an old building, with bags of character, set about a lovely courtyard and gardens. There may be wi-fi.

Next door to Casona, and equally characterful, is *Hotel Inca* (Jr Wiracocha 170, 🖥 enrique9541@hotmail.com, sgl/dbl with AB S/.35/70).

Chavín Turístico Hostal (Jr Mayta Capac 120, ☎ 454051, 🖥 chavinturisti co1.wix.com/chavin, sgl/dbl with AB S/.40/80) is a modern new option boasting well-appointed rooms. The accommodating owner will let you use her (very slow) internet.

WHERE TO EAT

Restaurante Chavín Turístico (Jr 17 de Enero Sur 439, mains S/.15-20) has been going since 1981 and is a cosy restaurant offering upmarket local dishes.

In a pleasant garden near the ruins, *Buongiorno* (Jr 17 de Enero Sur) serves up tasty Peruvian dishes (S/.15-30).

Restaurant Turístico Pukutay (Jr Túpac Yupanqui 230) dishes up lunch menus (S/.8) and à la carte (S/.15-22). **The Altas Montañas** (☎ 422569, 🖥 altasmon tanas.com/index10.htm) trekking agency, which runs a hotel near Olleros, is housed within.

Café Renato (Jr Huayna Capac), on the Plaza, offers deliciously fresh breakfasts (S/.5-12, from 07:00). It's an enticing place to hang out and chat to the friendly owner, who can organize horse riding in the local area (S/.40/hr).

Las Delicias (Av Julio Tello) is a popular local joint with a reliably good lunch/dinner menu (S/.5). On the opposite side of the street, *Restaurant Alpamayo* is another decent menu choice (S/.5).

TRANSPORT

Combis (2h30, S/.20) and colectivos (2h15, S/.25) to **Huaraz** pass by regularly – wait at the corner of Huayna Capac and Tello.

Many buses for Huaraz and **Lima** also pass this corner. Either jump on there or walk the few blocks to the bus company offices in the ridiculously large Gran Terminal Terrestre to buy a ticket in advance. Rosario, El Solitario, Olguita Tours and Flor Movil all have at least one daily bus to Lima (10-12h, S/.40-50). Sandoval has multiple daily departures to Huaraz (3h, S/.12) and **Huari** (1h, S/.5). El

❏ Chavín ruins and museum

Chavín de Huántar was a pilgrimage centre from 1000-200 BCE. At the heart of the Chavín cult they exerted influence throughout the Andes and coastal areas of present day Peru. The massive, awe-inspiring temple complex consisted of a labyrinth of underground galleries and fantastic friezes with anthropomorphic and zoomorphic iconography of jaguars, caimans and serpents. Gargoyle-like tenon heads hanging from the exterior walls amazed pilgrims arriving at the temple, and represented the transformation from human to feline. Only one tenon head remains in place today.

The Lanzon sculpture, which still stands at the heart of the labyrinth, represents the central deity of the Chavín cult; only the Shamans are believed to have been allowed into the central galleries to see it. In the process of stumbling around in a haze of hallucinogenic drugs and encountering representations of deities, the priests were believed to transform into jaguars and connect with the divine. Most of the decorative stonework has been removed from the site and can now be found at the Chavín National Museum. Allow at least half a day to visit both the ruins and museum.

Places to stay
4. Chavin Turistico Hostal
7. Hotel Inca
8. Hostal La Casona
9. Hospedaje Gantu
Places to eat
1. Buongiorno
2. Rest. Turistico Pukutay
3. Rest. Chavin Turistico
5. Rest. Alpamayo
6. Las Delicias
10. Cafe Renato

CITY & TOWN GUIDES

Solitario has a bus to **Pomabamba** most days, via Huari.

See individual treks for details on getting to trailheads.

OTHER INFORMATION

Sweet old Donato Melgarejo from ASAAM (☎ 944 607909) can, with a few days' notice, help organize local treks including Carhuascancha and the route to Huánuco Pampa on the Qhapaq Ñan (6 days, see p28). He's best found at the wool shop (Av Julio Tello 275) where his wife sells home knitted socks and hats. Altas Montañas (see Where to eat) can also arrange local trips.

To see (or buy) some weaving or stone carving, head to the CETPRO teaching workshop (Av Julio C Tello).

Chiquián
Altitude: 3400m

Perched on a plateau with Cordillera Huayhuash views, 'Espejito del Cielo' ('Mirror to the Sky') is a town of narrow streets and little traffic. Add to this welcoming locals, traditional architecture and some hat shops and it's easy to see why many a trekker has begun dreaming of a quiet retirement in the gateway to the Huayhuash. There are internet cafés and both hotels below have wi-fi, but there's no ATM.

WHERE TO STAY AND EAT

Chiquián has a surprisingly good place to stay, in the form of *Hotel Los Nogales* (Jr Comercio 1301, ☎ 447121, 🖳 hotelnogaleschiquian.com). The thick walls of this old house were built by current owner Manuel's grandfather and survived the 1970 earthquake intact.

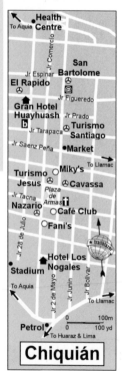

There is a variety of rooms with SB/AB for S/.15/35 per person. Breakfast is available.

If Nogales is full try *Gran Hotel Huayhuash* (Jr 28 de Julio 400, ☎ 447049, sgl/dbl with AB S/.20-30/50) which occupies an ugly multi-storey building a few blocks north of the Plaza. Rooms are large, and there's also a roof terrace.

There are a few other very basic places in town for S/.10 per person.

Café Club on the Plaza offers meat and fish dishes (S/.18-30) as well as real coffee. Cheap menu places include *Fani's* and *Miky's*.

AGENCIES

A couple of family-run operations from Chiquián know the mountains well, charge reasonable prices and regularly receive good reports from trekkers. **Los Amigos de Huayhuash** (☎ 447096, 🖳 losamigosdehuayhuash.free.fr) are the Valdez brothers Abner, Alcides and Adolfo, assisted by English-speaking sister Anamin who deals with enquiries. The Obregon family run **Huayhuash Aventura** (☎ 447185, 🖳 huayhuash_aventura@hotmail.com) – father Sabino works as an arriero, and English-speaking daughter Lina is a knowledgeable guide.

TRANSPORT

El Rápido, Nazario and Turismo Jesús all have daily buses to and from **Huaraz** (2h, S/.10, 05:00/14:00). Nazario runs a minibus to **Pocpa** (2h, S/.12) via **Llamac** (1h30, S/.10), leaving daily at 08:00. San Bartolomé also has a few minibuses a week to Pocpa, leaving at 08:00.

Cavassa goes twice daily to **Lima** (8h, S/.30, 09:30/21:30); Turismo Santiago has three micros a day to the coast at **Barranca** (4h, S/.15).

Pomabamba
Altitude: 2960m

Pomabamba is a typically rustic Conchucos town which styles itself the 'Folklorica Capital of Ancash'. Many residents have migrated to Lima in recent decades, but most return to pack the town for the colourful fiestas of San Juan el Bautista in late June and San Francisco de Asís in early October. Until 1967, when the 'City of Cedars' was finally connected by road to the outside world, it was a long two days on horseback to Yungay. Nowadays access is much easier, but the rough road and town's remoteness mean it still receives few foreign visitors.

With thermal baths a short walk from town, it makes a good stopover place for trekkers tackling the Alpamayo Basecamp trek, or cyclists looping the northern part of the Cordillera Blanca. There's an ATM on Plaza San Francisco and slow internet cafés dotted about. Wi-fi is yet to reach these parts.

WHERE TO STAY AND EAT
In a charming courtyarded house, parts of which are over a century old, *Hospedaje Las Begonias* (Jr Huamachuco 206, ☎ 451057, 🖳 lasbegonias_20@yahoo.es, dbl with SB/AB S/.25/40) survived the destruction wrought in this area by an earthquake in 1946. A few doors down, the corresponding modern offering *Las Begonias II* (sgl/dbl/twin with AB S/.30/50/60) has neat, functional rooms; both places have hot water.

Don't worry about the initial fussing of doting owner Doris (which is especially frenzied if you arrive with muddy boots or a dirty bike) at *Estrada Vidal* (Jr Huaraz 209, ☎ 504615): this place is excellent value. Large rooms have thick walls and there's a courtyard. Guests are charged S/.20 per bed, making it a particularly good deal for couples who don't mind sharing. Give some notice if you want a warm shower.

Hostal Leo (Plaza de Armas, ☎ 451307, sgl/dbl with AB S/.20-25/35-40) is central, with acceptable rooms.

Hotel El Mirador (Corner of Jrs Moquegua and Centenario, ☎ 451067, sgl/dbl/twin with AB S/.43/61/73) is the plushest hotel in town and also boasts the best views. It's a short walk uphill from the centre.

For those on very tight budgets, there is a handful of insalubrious cheapies on or near the Plaza de Armas.

There are no stand-out eateries in town, with the cheap restaurants mostly offering much of a muchness. *Mesa Rumi* (Jr Chávez, menu S/.5 and à la carte) is better than average and opens for breakfast and lunch.

TRANSPORT
All rides to and from Pomabamba are on clapped-out old buses, and almost all offices are on Jr Huaraz. Renzo (08:45/19:00) and El Veloz (08:45/18:45) go daily to **Huaraz** (8h, S/.30), as do Sandoval most days in dry season. All now travel via Túnel Olímpica rather than Llanganuco.

For direct buses to **Lima** (16h or more) there's also a choice of operators; note it's quicker to go via Túnel Olímpica than Huari. Fama Tours, Chavín Express, Turismo Andino and El Solitario all have services for S/.50. None are very 'lux', so it's probably better to change in Huaraz.

Richivan and San Francisco, both near Plazuela Yanapampa offer a few buses a week to **Chimbote** (S/.35-40).

See p76 for getting to Alpamayo Basecamp trailheads.

❏ Cuy cuy cuy
Yes, you did just see that sack in the market wriggling; it's probably full of whistling guinea pigs, onomatopoeically called *cuy* in Peru. They're a local culinary delicacy, usually baked or fried and served up with head and paws still attached. Look out for *picante de cuy* on restaurant menus.
(Photo © Cass Gilbert)

Other towns

YUNGAY (2490m)
Yungay's ebullience belies its tragic recent history (see p104). Though most tourists just pass through on the way to Quebrada Llanganuco, the town is well located for many of the biggest sights in the Blanca.

You're unlikely to find a warmer welcome in the Callejón de Huaylas than at *Hostal Gledel* (Av. Aries Graziani, ☎ 393048). Basic rooms with new mattresses are S/.15pp. *Hotel Rima Rima* (Jr Grau 275, ☎ 393257, ✉ jrodriortiz@hotmail.com, sgl/dbl S/.55/80) is the best place in town.

Serving up fresh breakfasts, sandwiches, salads and menus, *Kawaq Yaku Café* (Calle 8, ✉ kawaqyakucafe.com) is run by Americans Julia and Scott, and provides employment opportunities for young men who have been raised at the nearby orphanage in Ongo. The coffee's good and there's wi-fi. On the main road in the northern part of town, *Alpamayo Restaurante Turístico* is a reliable choice.

Daily **combis** for Yanama leave from the terminal on the main road, a two minute walk from the Plaza. There are also combis every few minutes from here to Caraz and Huaraz.

YANAMA (3390m)

With one of the most picture-perfect settings in the Cordillera, laid-back little Yanama couldn't be any more *tranquilo*. With more animal- than motor-traffic on the roads it's an adorable place, perfect for whiling away a few days mid- or post-trek. Abutting the Plaza is an astounding new church; President Ollanta Humala's wife attended the grand opening in August 2013. It's possible to use the internet in the Municipalidad building, but there's no ATM. See p90 for details of daily combis to Yungay.

Hostal El Pino is the best of the budget accommodation options (dbl S/.25) and its namesake restaurant on the plaza is the pick of the eateries. For something more upmarket try the excellent *Andes Lodge Peru* (Jr Chavín, ☎ 765579, 🖳 andeslodgeperu.com, sgl/dbl S/.60-70/10-150, including breakfast), which has comfy beds, roof terrace and temperamental wi-fi. The owners can arrange numerous trips to local sights.

CHACAS (3380m)

Picturesque Chacas is another gem and a favourite with visitors to Conchucos. Tiled two storey adobe houses with ornately carved wooden balconies surround a grassy plaza which is dominated by the Santuario (Sanctuary) Mama Ashu.

The small but well-presented **Archaeological Museum** (Wed-Sun, 09:00-12:00, 14:30-19:30) under the church has interesting objects from the Recuay, Wari and Inca periods.

There's an **internet café** by the bank on the plaza, but no ATM.

In an old casona, *Hostal Pilar* (Jr Ancash 110, ☎ 943 486316, sgl/dbl S/.30/50-100) is the best place in town.

The pick of the budget options are *Hospedaje Carina* (Jr Buenos Aires, ☎ 782836, 🖳 hospedajecarina@yahoo.es, sgl/dbl S/.25/30) which has super-friendly owners, but is let down by its showers; and *Hostal Asunción* (Plaza Mayor, ☎ 990 798654, 🖳 asuncion.chacas@gmail.com, dbl S/.40-50).

❏ Operación Mato Grosso

Over 30 years ago the Italian NGO Operación Mato Grosso (run by the Salesians of Don Bosco) arrived in Ancash with the aim of combatting poverty by training young campesinos in trades. A wood carving school was established in Chacas and there are now two famed workshops (*Talleres Don Bosco*) in town, making religious artefacts and funky modern furniture which is shipped worldwide. The artefact workshop is just off the square and easiest to access – ask if you'd like to be shown round (Mon-Fri).

Throughout the Cordillera, Chacas' Mama Ashu hospital is a source of great pride. It offers treatment to the neediest campesinos and employs young women trained by the Don Bosco Institute of Nursing. The Don Bosco Andes 6000 project instructs those wishing to become mountain guides, cooks and porters at the Andes School of Guides – many are subsequently employed at the agency based in Marcará (see p60).

CITY & TOWN GUIDES

The restaurant scene is somewhat lacking. The **menu place** opposite Hospedaje Carina and *Chifa Sabor Oriental* (on a stairway en route to the hospital) are both acceptable. If you're around on a Sunday, *Pizzeria San Francisco* by the church is open from 19:00.

All Huaraz – Pomabamba and Huaraz – San Luis **buses** pass through Chacas.

HUARI (3110m)

Huari is a provincial capital that sits in a side valley, surrounded by green, eucalyptus-studded hills. Known for its May cat-eating, it's a mellow place (except during fiestas), with plenty of steep, concrete streets.

There are many accommodation options in the mid to basic range, including: *Hotel Tucu* (Jr Libertad 867, ☎ 457727, 🖳 hoteltucu.com, rooms S/.10-30), *Hostal El Dorado* (Jr Bolivar 341, ☎ 453028, rooms S/.20-30), *Hostal Huagancu II* (Jr Sucre 335, ☎ 630424, sgl/dbl with AB S/.30/50) and *Hotel Tang* (Jr Guzmán Barrón 325, ☎ 941 955110, sgl/dbl with AB S/.30/45).

Crillón Chico (Jr San Martín 565) and *Luchitos* (Jr Bolivar 530) are the pick of the menu options; *Chifa Mana* is okay.

Buses (for Lima, Huaraz, Pomabamba) leave from the bus park a few minutes' walk south of the centre, but buy tickets beforehand from offices on Parque Vigil. Colectivos for San Marcos (S/.6) leave from a corner, two blocks west of the Parque. There are a couple of very basic **bike shops** in town – Multiservicios Eliachito is the cheapest.

SAN MARCOS (2980m)

Monies received from the nearby Antamina mine make San Marcos one of the richest villages in Peru, but you wouldn't know just by looking at it. *Hotel Casona Las Magnolias* (Plaza de Armas, dbl with AB S/.60) is nice and houses a restaurant within. *Hotel Erick* (sgl/dbl with AB S/.25/30), by the junction at the south side of town is good value. *Junagan* (Plaza de Armas) is a stylish menu restaurant with à la carte options.

There's internet on the Plaza, but no ATM.

Colectivos to Chavín (S/.2) leave regularly from opposite Hotel Erick; nearby Sandoval has multiple daily buses to Huari (S/.5) and Huaraz (S/.12). Combis (S/.20) and colectivos (S/.25) to Huaraz go from the Plaza, via Chavín.

❏ **Internet and tourist information in small towns**
Many small towns and villages in the Cordillera don't have public internet facilities. If you desperately need to get online, try heading to the Municipalidad building – if there's a connection, staff are often happy to allow you to use it and can usually also offer some information about local sights and fiestas.

HIKING ROUTES & MAPS

Using this guide

ROUTE DESCRIPTIONS

Directions in this chapter are shown as an instruction to go left (L) or right (R) and as a compass point (N/S/E/W). For instance, if the instruction stated 'go L/N', it would indicate that north is to your left. In the case of describing walking along river valleys, the terms true left (TL) and true right (TR) have been used to describe which side of the river when facing downstream.

Popular multi-day routes have been split into days which end at official campsites. On quieter routes we have noted places where camping is possible, but not split the description into set days.

Direction

Almost all trekking routes in this book could be walked in either direction. They have been described either in the way they are usually walked, or, in the case of routes such as Alpamayo Basecamp which are frequently walked in either direction, the way which the authors feel is preferable.

Route maps

Trekking maps are drawn at one of two scales. The well-known multi-day hikes (Alpamayo Basecamp, Santa Cruz, Huayhuash Circuit) as well as the day hike to Laguna Wilcacocha are drawn at 1:50k (20mm = 1km). All other treks are drawn at 1:100k (10mm = 1km).

The times included on maps and in descriptions refer to walking times only, and do not include any breaks. Overall you'll find you need to add on around 20-30% to the walking times to calculate the actual time taken.

Gradient arrows on maps point uphill. If the path is a steep climb from A to B, it's illustrated as: A --->>--- B. Double arrows represent steeper gradients than single arrows.

GPS waypoints are marked on the maps – all waypoints can be downloaded for free from 🖥 blancahuayhuash.com.

Place names

Many Quechua names can be spelt several ways as the original language had no alphabet. In trekking descriptions and maps, the version used is the one most commonly found locally.

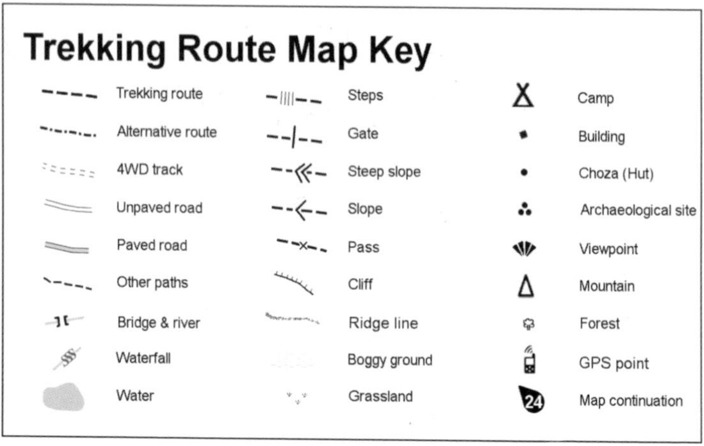

Trekking Route Map Key

– – – –	Trekking route	– ‖ – –	Steps	✕	Camp
–·–·–·–	Alternative route	– –	– –	Gate	●	Building
≈≈≈≈≈	4WD track	– – ≪ –	Steep slope	•	Choza (Hut)
══	Unpaved road	– – ⟨ –	Slope	⁂	Archaeological site
══	Paved road	– – ✕ –	Pass	🕊	Viewpoint
╲– – –	Other paths	⌒⌒⌒	Cliff	△	Mountain
–⌐	Bridge & river	⌒⌒⌒⌒	Ridge line	☘	Forest
ℳ	Waterfall	⋯⋯	Boggy ground	📱	GPS point
▬	Water	ᵛ ᵛ ᵛ	Grassland	㉔	Map continuation

Altitudes and vertical distances

Heights on trekking (and cycling) routes are given to the nearest 10m. All altitudes have been measured by GPS and should be accurate to about 20m. Peak heights used are from John Biggar's list at 🖥 andes.org.uk, which is thought to be the most accurate list of Andean mountain heights. Vertical climbs are given to the nearest 50m.

Northern Cordillera Blanca

ALPAMAYO BASECAMP

The Alpamayo Basecamp trek (also known as Cedros – Alpamayo, or simply Alpamayo) showcases much of the Cordillera Blanca's finest mountain scenery. Most of the hike is a wild, wilderness route through gorgeous landscapes, where the only sounds are the cracking of glacial ice and the murmur of ichu grass in the wind.

An international survey once declared Alpamayo the 'Most Beautiful Mountain in the World', but this trek is by no means a one-mountain show. Pucajirca's sheer bulk and the immensity of Santa Cruz's glaciers are in many ways more impressive than Alpamayo's perfect, yet petite, summit pyramid.

Many of the best views are to be found by delving into quebradas south of

> **ALPAMAYO BASECAMP**
> ● **Start** Pomabamba
> ● **End** Hualcayán
> ● **Distance** 68km/42 miles +
> ● **Trekking time** 5-9 days
> ● **Vertical climb** 4000m/13,100ft
> ● **Max altitude** 4860m/15,950ft
> ● **Navigation** 2
> ● **Terrain** 2

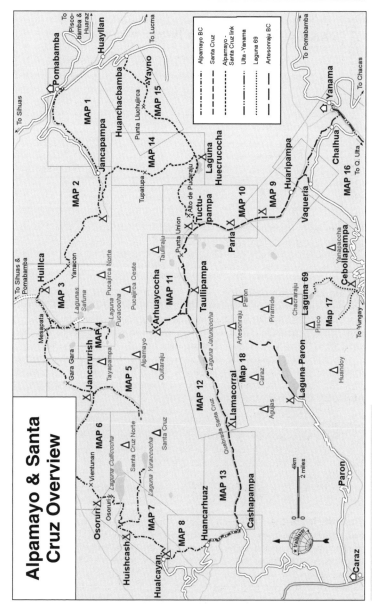

Alpamayo & Santa Cruz Overview

Alpamayo BC	
Santa Cruz	
Alpamayo - Santa Cruz link	
Ulta -Yanama	
Laguna 69	
Artesonraju BC	

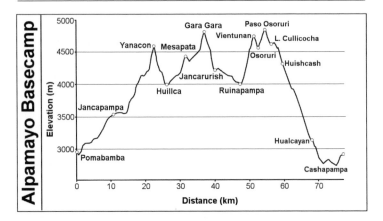

the main trail – entering sanctuaries surrounded by icy peaks. It's well worth spending a couple of days exploring these.

Despite its attractions, the trek is far less popular than Santa Cruz – outside of July and August you can go days without seeing another hiker.

Timing and which direction

The basic route from Pomabamba to Hualcayán can be completed in five days (not including the day for travelling between Huaraz and Pomabamba), however the many permutations of side trips and start/finish points mean it's possible to lengthen the walk to as much as a fortnight.

Opinion is divided as to the best direction in which to hike. We describe the route from east to west to avoid beginning with a 2000m climb to the highest pass. Trekking the route in reverse makes it easier to cross many of the passes earlier in the day, when the sky is more likely to be clear.

Each of the three recommended there-and-back side trips south of the main route adds a day.

Taking transport between Pomabamba and Jancapampa shortens the trek by half a day. Finishing/starting in Cashapampa or Huancarhuaz rather than Hualcayán adds half a day, but makes it easier and cheaper to find transport back to Caraz.

See p99 for the popular option of combining the Alpamayo and Santa Cruz treks.

To and from the trailhead
There are daily buses from Huaraz to Pomabamba (see p60). Usually two combis a day leave from Plazuela Yanapampa in Pomabamba for Jancapampa (1h, S/.5), one very early in the morning (around 06:00) and another in the early afternoon. They don't hang around long in the village before returning. Try to confirm timetables beforehand as the driver changes them on a whim. A taxi costs around S/.70.

Hualcayán is only served by public transport to Caraz on market days (Sun/Wed) when a lone (and usually full) combi (1h30, S/.8) descends to town in the night, and returns around midday (see map p63). It's easier to go by taxi (1h15, S/.90).

Some colectivos from Caraz to Cashapampa (see p90) continue to Huancarhuaz (1h15, S/.8) if there's enough interest. A taxi between Huancarhuaz and Caraz costs around S/.45.

Preparations Trekkers need to be self-sufficient, so buy all necessary supplies beforehand. There is a very basic snack and soft drink shop in Jancapampa (day 1) and reasonably well stocked shops in Hualcayán (final day), but absolutely nothing in between.

Between Pomabamba and Hualcayán there are many vertical metres to ascend and five high passes to negotiate – trekking poles come in handy as a couple of these are steep. Though there are few signposts, navigation is not especially tricky.

It's possible, but not particularly easy, to find arrieros in Hualcayán or Jancapampa; it's better to arrange them from Huaraz. Much of the route is within PNH, but there's nowhere on the trail to buy a ticket. The Hualcayán community charge trekkers an additional S/.20 fee; ensure you get a receipt.

Day 1: Pomabamba – Jancapampa camp   [Maps 1 & 2, pp78-9]

● **Duration** 4h30-5h
● **Summary** Begin with an easy walk up to a camp on Jancapampa meadow which is towered over by Pucajirca's mammoth glaciers. Most of this first day can be bypassed by catching transport to the village of Jancapampa, and walking up to the camp from there.

Leave Pomabamba's Plaza de Armas at the NW corner on Jr Peru, before descending on steps to the main road. Turn R and soon take a path down to the Río Pomabamba, crossing on a footbridge then climbing to the Chuyas road (20 minutes). Go R, following the road or footpath shortcuts. After passing an electricity substation and a 'Pomabamba – Chuyas' road sign, leave the road (30 minutes), descending R/N for a few metres to a water channel.

Follow the channel into green, wooded Quebrada Jancapampa. Despite *Hidrandina* disclaimers about not walking next to the channel, it's a good path and the main one used by locals. The quebrada becomes narrow, with near-vertical walls, and after 45 minutes the channel meets the main river, crossing on a bridge to the N bank.

Soon recross and continue upriver on the eucalyptus-shaded main path, through small villages where children (and some adults) will ask you for *caramelos*. One hour and 45 minutes from the bridges, the path emerges onto the meadow of Jancapampa – continue for 15 minutes to reach the road bridge in Jancapampa village. Cross the bridge, and take the shortcut that leaves the road at the first bend. When this rejoins the road soon after, go straight over onto a footpath that heads up valley, contouring high above the river on the N side. After 45 minutes the path descends to the pampa.

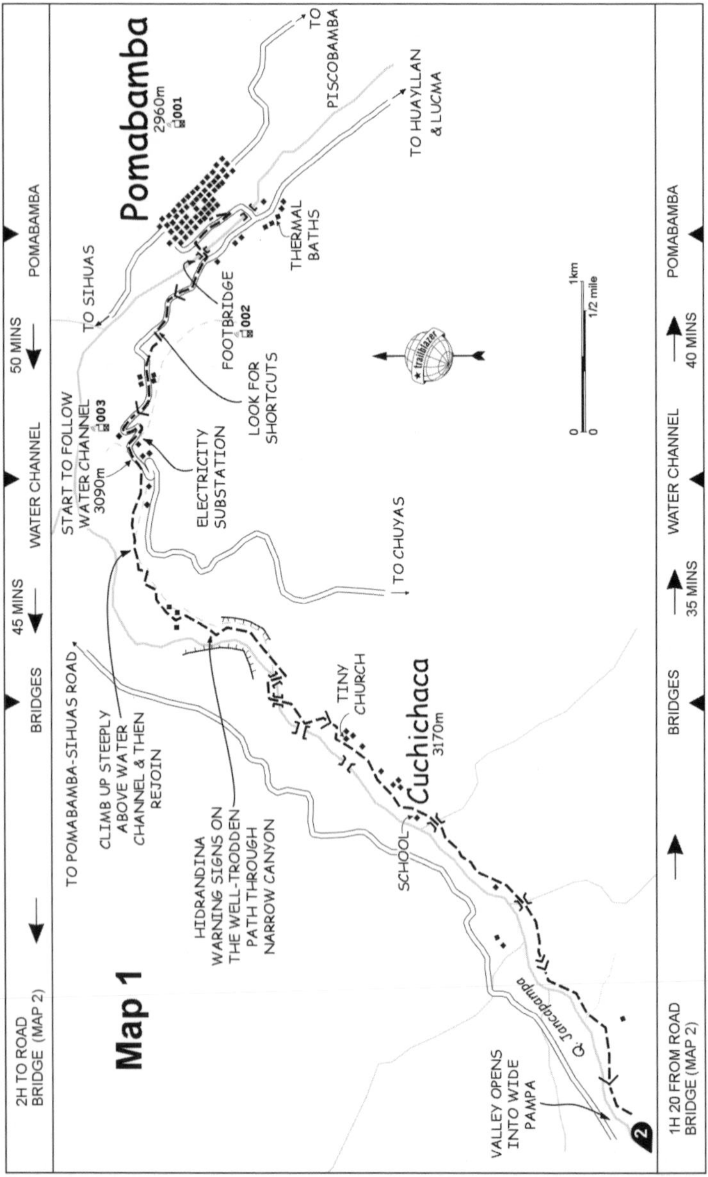

Map 1

Pomabamba 2960m ⛪001

TO SIHUAS

TO PISCOBAMBA

TO HUAYLLAN & LUCMA

THERMAL BATHS

FOOTBRIDGE ⛪002

LOOK FOR SHORTCUTS

START TO FOLLOW WATER CHANNEL 3090m ⛪003

ELECTRICITY SUBSTATION

TO CHUYAS

TO POMABAMBA-SIHUAS ROAD

CLIMB UP STEEPLY ABOVE WATER CHANNEL & THEN REJOIN

HIDRANDINA WARNING SIGNS ON THE WELL-TRODDEN PATH THROUGH NARROW CANYON

TINY CHURCH

Cuchichaca 3170m

SCHOOL

Q Tancapampa

VALLEY OPENS INTO WIDE PAMPA

2

0   1km
0   1/2 mile

2H TO ROAD BRIDGE (MAP 2) → | ← BRIDGES | ← 45 MINS | WATER CHANNEL | ← 50 MINS | POMABAMBA ▶

1H 20 FROM ROAD BRIDGE (MAP 2) → | ← BRIDGES | ← 35 MINS | WATER CHANNEL | ← 40 MINS | POMABAMBA ◀

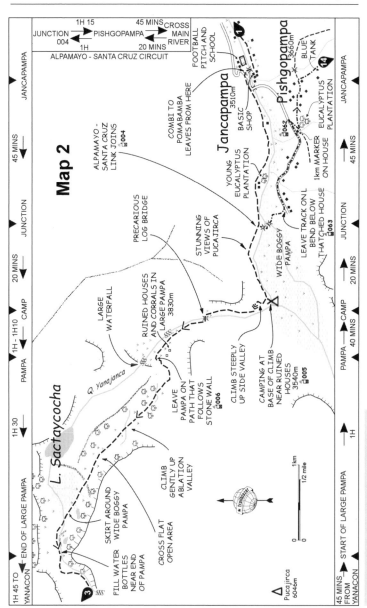

Map 2

ALPAMAYO - SANTA CRUZ CIRCUIT

JUNCTION 004 →← PISHGOPAMPA →← CROSS MAIN RIVER

1H 15 · 45 MINS · CROSS MAIN RIVER · FOOTBALL PITCH AND SCHOOL

1H · 20 MINS

JANCAPAMPA · 45 MINS · JUNCTION · 20 MINS · CAMP · 1H – 1H10 · PAMPA · 1H 30 · END OF LARGE PAMPA · 1H 45 TO YANACON

ALPAMAYO - SANTA CRUZ LINK JOINS ▲004

COMBI TO POMABAMBA LEAVES FROM HERE

Pishgopampa 3660m
BLUE TANK ▲14
EUCALYPTUS PLANTATION
Jancapampa 3510m
BASIC SHOP
▲062
YOUNG EUCALYPTUS PLANTATION
1km MARKER ON HOUSE
LEAVE TRACK ONL BEND BELOW THATCHED HOUSE ▲063
WIDE BOGGY PAMPA

PRECARIOUS LOG BRIDGE
STUNNING VIEWS OF PUCAJIRCA
LARGE WATERFALL
RUINED HOUSES AND CORRALS IN LARGE PAMPA 3830m
Q Yanajanca
LEAVE PAMPA ON PATH THAT FOLLOWS STONE WALL ▲006
CLIMB STEEPLY UP SIDE VALLEY
CAMPING AT BASE OF CLIMB NEAR RUINED HOUSES 3540m ▲005

L. Sactaycocha

SKIRT AROUND WIDE BOGGY PAMPA
CLIMB GENTLY UP ABLATION VALLEY
CROSS FLAT OPEN AREA
FILL WATER BOTTLES NEAR END OF PAMPA
▲3

△ Pucajirca 6046m

1km
1/2 mile
trailblazer

JANCAPAMPA · 45 MINS · JUNCTION · 20 MINS · CAMP · 40 MINS · PAMPA · 1H · START OF LARGE PAMPA · 45 MINS FROM YANACON

Ignore a small bridge to the L/S – this is the way to Tupatupa (see Santa Cruz Alpamayo link p99) – continuing instead up valley. The path fizzles out, but reforms, skirting above the boggy pampa. Follow it along the straight-sided N shore of the pampa for 20 minutes until the pampa edge curves round to the L/S. There's good camping here, level with the last houses on the opposite, southern, side.

Day 2: Jancapampa camp – Huillca   [Map 2, p79 & Map 3]

● **Duration** 5h30-6h
● **Summary** Tackle imposing Yanacon, the first of the route's high passes, with its close-up views of Pucajirca's ice and folded rock strata. Descend to camp in the vicinity of the pastures at Huillca.

From camp, a small path leads up wooded slopes to the N, into Quebrada Yanajanca. After 45 minutes the path crosses the river, then continues up valley, heading towards a serrated, toothy ridge. Twenty minutes of gentle climbing brings you to a large pampa; stay on the left hand side, heading for a path which leaves the pampa by a stone wall.

Climb for 40 minutes to another pampa, continuing on the L/S side of the valley. Jade green Laguna Sactaycocha lies in a dip to the N, but is not visible from the trail until nearer the pass. Cross to the far end of a large pampa (50 minutes), then follow the path of least resistance up the grassy slopes towards the pass. The views of Pucajirca improve and the climb steepens on nearing Yanacon (1h45); the final section is a real lung-burster.

The descent on zigzags into Quebrada Yanta Quenua is equally steep, the path sticking to the slopes on the R/N of the valley, before emerging onto the pampa after 30 minutes. Descend further, now on the TL/S side, past another pampa with water and possible camping (10 minutes) to a couple of buildings and corrals (30 minutes). Carry on straight, aiming for the few buildings that comprise Huillca (20 minutes). Ask the local residents for permission if you wish to camp in this area. There are many domestic animals around, often including herds of alpaca which are a rarity in this region.

Day 3: Huillca – Jancarurish camp   [Map 3 & Map 5, p83]

● **Duration** 6h
● **Summary** Crossing two passes, this is the most strenuous day of the trek. A short climb to Mesapata gives access to a remote valley, which is exited via the challenging Gara Gara pass. The panoramas that await at the top should turn lack-of-oxygen gasps into gasps of amazement; the views remain stunning all the way down to Jancarurish.

Pass the buildings and cross the concrete bridge over the main river, before climbing to the 4WD track beyond. Head up valley on the 4WD track, aiming at Nevados Tayapampa and Jancarurish; after a while, Alpamayo makes its first appearance of the trek. In 50 minutes, a faint path, which is difficult to spot, leads off R/W, climbing towards Mesapata. The side trip to Lagunas Pucacocha and Llullacocha continues straight – see p82.

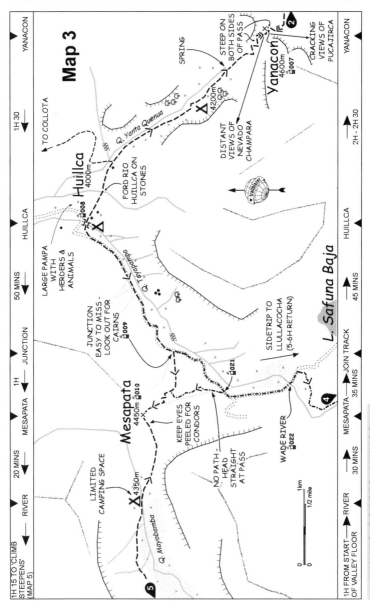

Map 3

1H 30 → TO COLLOTA

↑ YANACON

Q. Yanta Quenua

SPRING

STEEP ON BOTH SIDES OF PASS

△ 4200m

Huillca 4000m

FORD RIO HUILLCA ON STONES

🏠 008

DISTANT VIEWS OF NEVADO CHAMPARA

Yanacon 4600m

🏠 007

CRACKING VIEWS OF PUCAJIRCA

LARGE PAMPA WITH HERDERS & ANIMALS

△

Q. Taulipampa

JUNCTION EASY TO MISS - LOOK OUT FOR CAIRNS

🏠 009

Mesapata 4450m 🏠 010

KEEP EYES PEELED FOR CONDORS

🏠 021

SIDETRIP TO LLULLACOCHA (5-6H RETURN)

L. Safuna Baja

NO PATH - HEAD STRAIGHT AT PASS

WADE RIVER 🏠 022

LIMITED CAMPING SPACE

△ 4350m

Q. Mayobamba

1km
1/2 mile

0

Scale bars / route times (top):
1H 15 TO 'CLIMB STEEPENS' (MAP 5) → RIVER ← 20 MINS → RIVER ← MESAPATA ← 1H → JUNCTION ← 50 MINS → HUILLCA ← 1H 30 → YANACON

Route times (bottom):
1H FROM START OF VALLEY FLOOR → RIVER ← 30 MINS → MESAPATA ← 35 MINS → JOIN TRACK ← 45 MINS → L. Safuna Baja ← HUILLCA ← 2H - 2H 30 → YANACON

2

5

4

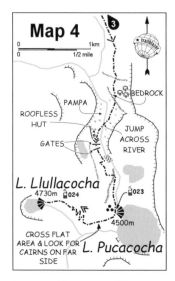

Map 4

On the climb to Mesapata (1 hour), the easiest pass on the trek, the western aspect of Pucajirca dominates the horizon behind you. Over the pass lies green Quebrada Mayobamba, and in the distance sit Nevados Pilanco and Milluacocha.

From the pass descend gradually to the main river (20 minutes) then make your way gently up the valley on the other side. After 1h15 the climb steepens and the path splinters into many branches, all of which soon meet up. It's a further, steep, 1 hour to Gara Gara, but all becomes worth it at the top when the Santa Cruz massif, Abasraju and Quitaraju appear in all their glory. Peeking out below is a slither of Laguna Jancarurish.

The gradients on the way down are equally relentless, but the views only improve. Alpamayo and Tayapampa come into view on the knee-jarring descent to a small green laguna (20 minutes). Fifteen minutes later an inky-blue laguna appears, offset dramatically against turquoise Laguna Jancarurish behind. Pass to the R/W of this laguna, descending through ichu grass by a small stream. Cross the main stream in the side valley (40 minutes) en route to the concrete bridge (10 minutes) over Río Alpamayo. (Opposite direction: from the concrete bridge, aim straight for cairn-topped boulders. The path, which is visible from the valley floor, climbs to the L/W of the left-hand side valley.)

The wonderful Jancarurish camp lies just downriver from the bridge and sports excellent views of Alpamayo's famous triangular NW face.

Side trip to Lagunas Pucacocha and Llullacocha
[Map 3, p81 & Map 4]

● **Duration** 5-6h return
● **Summary** Delving into the quebrada south of Huillca, this is the first (and probably least spectacular) of the wonderful side trips.

From the turn-off to Mesapata, walk up valley on the 4WD track for 40 minutes to a fording point. Wade the river, then leave the 4WD track by cutting S to the obvious, but sometimes overgrown, path traversing the hillside. Follow this to a large pampa, which you skirt on the L/E. After 40 minutes, descend to avoid a rock and scree slide on the E slopes, before climbing to the next pampa.

Leave from near a roofless hut at the SW corner (20 minutes) from where it's 35 minutes further to a superb spot by more ruined walls which looks out over Pucacocha. Pucajirca's heavily glaciated flanks lurk behind, while to the

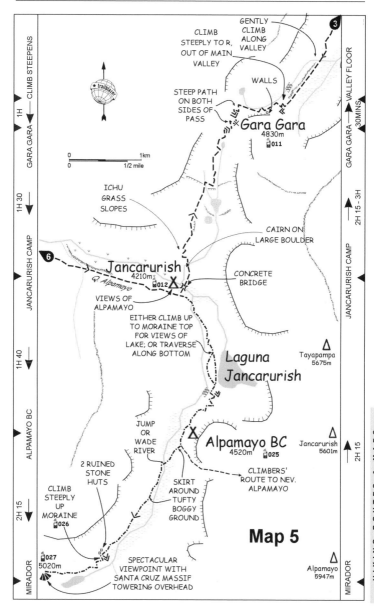

GENTLY
CLIMB
ALONG
VALLEY

CLIMB
STEEPLY TO R,
OUT OF MAIN
VALLEY

WALLS

STEEP PATH
ON BOTH
SIDES OF
PASS

Gara Gara
4830m
011

CLIMB STEEPENS

GARA GARA ▸ 1H

1H 30

JANCARURISH CAMP

1H 40

ALPAMAYO BC

2H 15

MIRADOR

VALLEY FLOOR

GARA GARA ▸ 30MINS

2H 15 – 3H

JANCARURISH CAMP

2H 15

MIRADOR

trailblazer

0   1km
0   1/2 mile

ICHU
GRASS
SLOPES

CAIRN ON
LARGE BOULDER

Jancarurish
4210m
012

CONCRETE
BRIDGE

VIEWS OF
ALPAMAYO

EITHER CLIMB UP
TO MORAINE TOP
FOR VIEWS OF
LAKE; OR TRAVERSE
ALONG BOTTOM

Laguna
Jancarurish

△ Tayapampa
5675m

JUMP
OR
WADE
RIVER

Alpamayo BC
4520m
025

△ Jancarurish
5601m

2 RUINED STONE
HUTS

SKIRT
AROUND
TUFTY
BOGGY
GROUND

CLIMBERS'
ROUTE TO NEV.
ALPAMAYO

CLIMB
STEEPLY
UP
MORAINE
026

027
5020m

SPECTACULAR
VIEWPOINT WITH
SANTA CRUZ MASSIF
TOWERING OVERHEAD

Map 5

△ Alpamayo
5947m

HIKING ROUTES & MAPS

W are Nevados Alpamayo, Jancarurish and Tayapampa.

If this is not sufficient reward and you still have the energy, climb on to Llullacocha. From the walls, continue SW, aiming at Alpamayo. Cross some small ridges on the moraine, going just to the L/S of some rounded bedrock (10 minutes) at the start of a pampa in a bowl. Continue into the bowl, heading W, and after 2 minutes turn R/NW following cairns to the rocky moraine. This initial section has an indistinct path, but it becomes clear and easy to follow once you hit the moraine. It's a 45-minute climb to reach the shores of little Llullacocha, a turquoise lake topped up by waterfalls sliding down Nevado Tayapampa.

Returning, it's 2 hours back to the junction where a shortcut begins climbing up to meet the main trail to Mesapata, longer if you decide to detour up to the Lagunas Safuna.

Side trip past Alpamayo's northern Basecamp to the Santa Cruz Sanctuary [Map 5, p83]

● **Duration** 6-7h return
● **Summary** The strenuous day hike into the Santa Cruz Sanctuary is a must, entering an enchanting valley which cries out for a day of exploration. The path ends at 5000m with snowy peaks in all directions, overlooking glacial turquoise lakes.

From Jancarurish camp, follow the path up valley towards Alpamayo. Cross a large stream on stones, by the ruins of a bridge (20 minutes), then begin climbing steeply up the lateral moraine which dams the W side of Laguna Jancarurish. Turn L at a junction (R is a slightly more direct route, but foregoes some excellent views) and 20 minutes from the stream hit the top of the moraine and a sight of the turquoise lake with waterfalls and Alpamayo behind. Don't walk on the very edge of the unstable ridge-top – it's a long and rapid fall to the lake. Fifteen minutes later the paths meet and climb steeply on switchbacks to Alpamayo Basecamp (45 minutes).

Continue up the valley, crossing the main river after 15 minutes, and begin climbing into a mountain amphitheatre dominated by Quitaraju, Abasraju and Santa Cruz.

Forty minutes from the river crossing, the path veers R/SW, passing two ruined stone huts. Beyond, climb extremely steep switchbacks up a moraine bank, before easing W, in the direction of Santa Cruz Chico. The path finally ends on a large slab of bedrock (1h20) at the princely height of 5020m – a perfect place to lunch and enjoy the avalanches which regularly ravage Santa Cruz's gargantuan NE face.

Returning to Jancarurish camp by the same route takes around 2h15.

Day 4: Jancarurish camp – Osoruri camp [Map 5, p83 & Map 6]

● **Duration** 5-6h
● **Summary** Leave Alpamayo behind as the route heads west, before climbing over Vientunan to the high camp at Osoruri.

Climb up to the main path which traverses the slopes behind camp. After 1 hour, cross two large side streams on slippery rocks before continuing the gentle walk down valley to Ruinapampa camp (1 hour). Cross a log bridge over a side

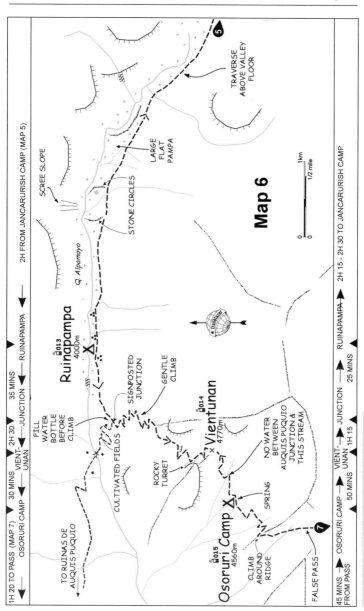

Map 6

TRAVERSE ABOVE VALLEY FLOOR

2H FROM JANCARURISH CAMP (MAP 5)

SCREE SLOPE

LARGE FLAT PAMPA

STONE CIRCLES

Q. Alpamayo

FILL WATER BOTTLE BEFORE CLIMB

SIGNPOSTED JUNCTION

GENTLE CLIMB

Ruinapampa
4000m

Vientunan
4770m

CULTIVATED FIELDS

ROCKY TURRET

NO WATER BETWEEN AUQUIS PUQUIO JUNCTION & THIS STREAM

SPRING

Osoruri Camp
4560m

TO RUINAS DE AUQUIS PUQUIO

CLIMB AROUND RIDGE

FALSE PASS

0   1km
0   1/2 mile

1H 20 TO PASS (MAP 7) ◀ OSORURI CAMP ◀ 30 MINS VIENT-UNAN ◀ 2H 30 JUNCTION ◀ 35 MINS RUINAPAMPA ◀ 2H FROM JANCARURISH CAMP (MAP 5)

45 MINS FROM PASS ▶ OSORURI CAMP ▶ 50 MINS VIENT-UNAN ▶ 1H 15 JUNCTION ▶ 25 MINS RUINAPAMPA ▶ 2H 15 - 2H 30 TO JANCARURISH CAMP

HIKING ROUTES & MAPS

stream (35 minutes), then stay L/up on the main path at two subsequent junctions. The long, zigzag climb to Vientunan crosses rocky slopes which support little vegetation, and there's no water higher up. To the N, the three snow-topped summits of Milluacocha dominate the scene. It takes 2h30 to reach Vientunan, a pass with views of the highest tops in the Cordillera Negra as well as of Huaylas, the small town from which the Río Santa valley takes its name.

It's a 30 minute descent to the high Osoruri camp, where there's water and room for a handful of tents.

Day 5: Osoruri camp – Hualcayán   [Map 6, p85 & Map 7]

● **Duration** 5h30-6h
● **Summary** End with a crossing of Osoruri, the highest pass of the trek. Views of the Santa Cruz massif are magnificent at the start of the long, long descent to civilization.

From the low point beyond the camp, the path climbs to round a conspicuous rocky ridge (40 minutes), before continuing for a further 40 minutes to Paso Osoruri.

It's an unusual, hemmed-in pass with few views, but before dismissing it totally, descend a few minutes to allow the magnificent Santa Cruz massif to reveal itself to the E. This snow and ice beacon illuminates an otherwise bleak landscape; a world of dark rock and eroding ridges, which over the eons crumble into scree slides and stony slopes.

The path weaves its descent through boulders, staying on the slopes to the N of Laguna Cullicocha which shines bright against the neutral-coloured rock backdrop. The laguna has a small hydro dam, as well as smooth, humped bedrock that nearly forms a natural dam at the W end of the lake. Descend to and cross these dams 45 minutes from the pass.

After the last hydro buildings, climb up above a water channel, before shadowing the channel westwards. To the R/N is inaccessible little Laguna Azulcocha, nestled in a deep hollow far below the path. The descending traverse eventually transforms into wide, sweeping zigzags which drop down a bare hillside to the camp at Huishcash (1h30). The turn-off to Laguna Yuraccocha (see below) is 10 minutes above the camp, on a right-hand switchback.

The path descends to Calamina camp (40 minutes), where a signposted trail leads off to Laguna Yanacocha. The main path begins a long traverse to avoid a landslide-prone side valley, then descends gradual switchbacks to Hualcayán, whose green and orange fields can be seen from afar.

Nearing town after 1h30, go R at a fork above some reservoirs, and immediately after turn R on a 4WD track. (Opposite direction: climb up/L on a small footpath, heading to the R of a large waterfall.) The path descends past blue concrete cisterns to the road in Hualcayán, emerging by a wooden barrier across the road (10 minutes). (Opposite direction: Turn R/up onto a footpath immediately after the barrier, before crossing the water channel.)

Independent trekkers finishing here should continue 5 minutes to the plaza to try and find a taxi to Caraz. Hualcayán has well stocked shops, but no restaurant or accommodation. Camping is possible – ask.

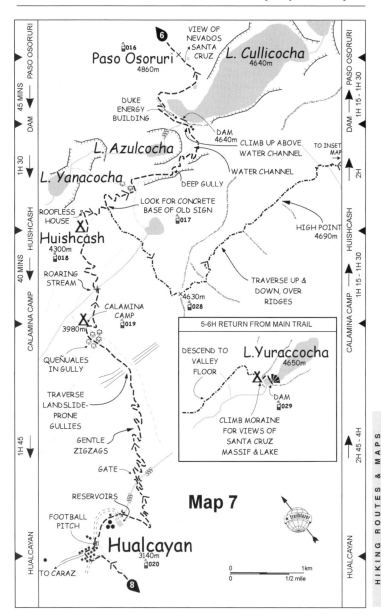

PASO OSORURI

45 MINS — PASO OSORURI

1H 30 — DAM

40 MINS — HUISHCASH

1H 45 — CALAMINA CAMP

HUALCAYAN

VIEW OF
NEVADOS
SANTA
CRUZ

6

Paso Osoruri
4860m
016

L. Cullicocha
4640m

DUKE
ENERGY
BUILDING

DAM
4640m

CLIMB UP ABOVE
WATER CHANNEL

L. Azulcocha

WATER CHANNEL

TO INSET
MAP

L. Yanacocha

DEEP GULLY

LOOK FOR CONCRETE
BASE OF OLD SIGN
017

ROOFLESS
HOUSE

Huishcash
4300m
018

HIGH POINT
4690m

ROARING
STREAM

CALAMINA
CAMP
3980m
019

4630m
028

TRAVERSE UP &
DOWN, OVER
RIDGES

QUEÑUALES
IN GULLY

TRAVERSE
LANDSLIDE-
PRONE
GULLIES

GENTLE
ZIGZAGS

GATE

RESERVOIRS

FOOTBALL
PITCH

Hualcayan
3140m
020

TO CARAZ

8

5-6H RETURN FROM MAIN TRAIL

DESCEND TO
VALLEY
FLOOR

L. Yuraccocha
4650m

DAM
029

CLIMB MORAINE
FOR VIEWS OF
SANTA CRUZ
MASSIF & LAKE

Map 7

trailblazer

0   1km
0   1/2 mile

PASO OSORURI

1H 15 - 1H 30 — DAM

2H — HUISHCASH

1H 15 - 1H 30 — CALAMINA CAMP

2H 45 - 4H — HUALCAYAN

Side trip to Laguna Yuraccocha   [Map 7, p87]

• **Duration** 5-6h return
• **Summary** This long diversion from the main trail leads to memorable Yuraccocha, a dazzling lake which boasts the unbroken wall of the Santa Cruz massif as a backdrop. Many ins and outs to avoid rocky outcrops mean that though the lake is only 200m higher than the turn-off from the main trail, the return trip necessitates 800m of climbing.

From the junction, on a zigzag above Huishcash camp, a path leads off S from the main trail. Climb for 50 minutes to a small pass, then veer L/E into Quebrada Ragranco (Yuraccocha). After 1h10 on a rollercoaster of a path, descend an ancient set of zigzags to a low point. Continue up valley for a further one hour, climbing the moraine to the dam at the lake's W end. There's room for a fantastic camp by the dam, or lower down on the moraine. Returning, it's 2h30 back to the main trail.

Alternative finish – Cashapampa   [Map 8]
Turn L/S one block before reaching the Plaza in Hualcayán and a minute later turn L again on a 4WD track which morphs into a footpath as it descends to another motorable road. Follow this road, or shortcuts, S towards Cashapampa. It's a colourful and bucolic scene, through patchwork fields tended by campesinos, but it's a hot walk on a sunny day.

An hour from Hualcayán go L when the 4WD track forks, and less than 10 minutes later leave the track onto a footpath which climbs up/L before a large boulder marked with '47.00' in red paint. After 40 minutes reach the road in Huancarhuaz by a blue church. If you don't find transport here, turn L, cross the bridge (30 minutes) over the Río Santa Cruz by the derelict Baños Huancarhuaz, then climb steeply on shortcuts to the Santa Cruz trailhead (1 hour) in Cashapampa (see p90). Regular colectivos to Caraz leave from here.

SANTA CRUZ

Santa Cruz is the classic Cordillera Blanca trek and by far the most popular multi-day hike in the range. This popularity stems first and foremost from the spectacular mountain views on show – the Blanca's big names, Alpamayo and Artesonraju, as well as lesser known, but no less impressive peaks such as Quitaraju and Taulliraju provide a snow and ice extravaganza not to be missed.

Add to this a clear path, one of the simpler high passes in the range, towering rock bastions and countless waterfalls; it's easy to see why so many visitors to the area choose to tramp this route.

SANTA CRUZ
• **Start** Vaquería
• **End** Cashapampa
• **Distance** 55km/34 miles
• **Trekking time** 4 days
• **Vertical climb** 1800m/5900ft
• **Max altitude** 4780m/15,700ft
• **Navigation** 1
• **Terrain** 1

Timing and getting to and from the trailhead
The trek can be done in either direction, though it's more common to begin in

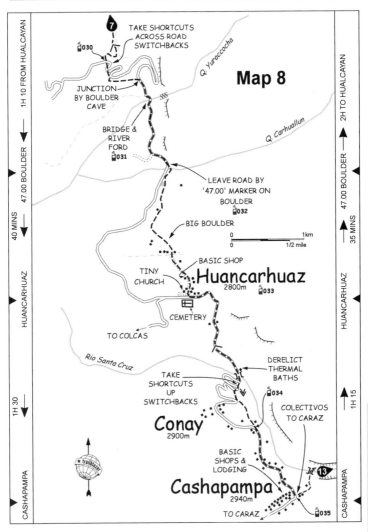

Vaquería. This has the advantage of simpler transport logistics, less climbing, and makes it easier to buy a PNH ticket if you are trekking independently.

Sticking to the route described on pp92-9, it's a comfortable four days from Vaquería to Cashapampa or vice versa. Missing out the side trip to Laguna

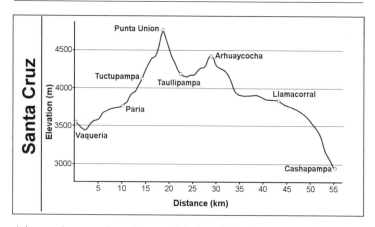

Arhuaycocha means foregoing one of the best viewpoints on the trek, but makes it possible to complete the walk in three days.

For a more comprehensive trek through much of the Blanca's finest scenery, consider linking the Santa Cruz and Alpamayo Basecamp treks (see p99). Another nice variant is to tack on Ulta – Yanama to Quebrada Santa Cruz, for a five- or six-day route.

To/from Vaquería/Yanama Vaquería is just a collection of houses by the road with a couple of basic shops and a menu restaurant. Extremely basic accommodation can be found for S/.10pp. See p71 for Yanama info.

The only way to reach Vaquería (3h, S/.15) or Yanama (3h30, S/.15) by public transport is on a combi from Yungay (see p70). These leave early (06:00-07:00), though there's sometimes also a service around 13:00. Either overnight in Yungay, or catch a very early combi there from Huaraz (1h, S/.5). A Yungay-Yanama taxi costs around S/.180.

Returning to Yungay, combis leave Yanama in the late morning and also sometimes in late afternoon, passing through Vaquería after 45 minutes. They often don't have spare room by the time they reach Vaquería.

To/from Cashapampa Cashapampa is a village with some basic shops and drink stalls. Rustic accommodation can be found at homestays (S/.10pp) – ask around. There's no internet.

Regular colectivos leave Cashapampa for Caraz (1 hour) during the day until around 16:00. It costs S/.7, but the tourist price is S/.10. Happy haggling! Hiring the whole taxi will set you back around S/.40. In reverse, colectivos for Cashapampa leave the Santa Cruz stop in Caraz, from about 06:00 to 17:00.

Preparations All agencies in Huaraz and Caraz offer guided Santa Cruz treks, and this competition keeps prices extremely low – see City and town guides for recommended agencies. Finding arrieros is simpler for this route than almost any other; still, they're easier to find in Cashapampa than Vaquería.

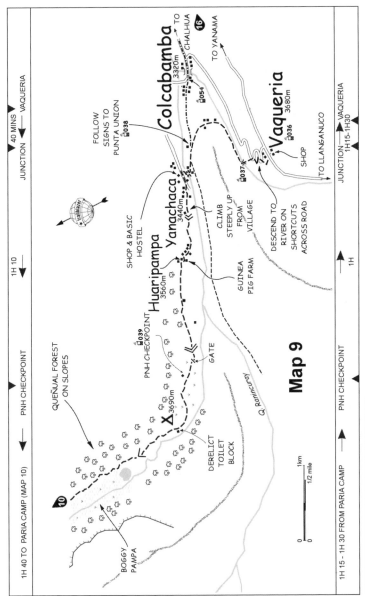

Map 9

Colcabamba 3320m

TO CHALHUA

TO YANAMA

16

△054

△038

FOLLOW SIGNS TO PUNTA UNION

Yanachaca 3440m

SHOP & BASIC HOSTEL

CLIMB STEEPLY UP FROM VILLAGE

Vaqueria 3680m

△036

SHOP

TO LLANGANUCO

△037

DESCEND TO RIVER ON SHORTCUTS ACROSS ROAD

Huaripampa 3560m

GUINEA PIG FARM

QUEÑUAL FOREST ON SLOPES

△039 PNH CHECKPOINT

GATE

Q. Ranincuroy

X 3690m

DERELICT TOILET BLOCK

BOGGY PAMPA

10

0 ────── 1km
0 ────── 1/2 mile

40 MINS — VAQUERIA

JUNCTION ◄

1H 10

PNH CHECKPOINT

1H 40 TO PARIA CAMP (MAP 10)

JUNCTION — VAQUERIA 1H15-1H30

1H

PNH CHECKPOINT

1H 15 - 1H 30 FROM PARIA CAMP

❑ **Old-school treks**

Many agencies still offer Llanganuco – Santa Cruz, Chacas – Yanama and treks through Quebrada Honda. From Llanganuco to Vaquería, on the Llanganuco – Santa Cruz trek, the scenery is superb, but the road over Portachuelo de Llanganuco goes this way. Though the walking path doesn't follow it exactly, we've included this part as a cycling route, not a hiking route. Likewise Chacas – Yanama is now connected directly by a quiet road. Walking in Quebrada Honda is best avoided these days as it is marred by the many mines (both legal and illegal) that operate in the valley.

As with all multi-day treks in PNH, trekkers require a 21 day ticket. There are checkpoints in Huaripampa (near Vaquería) and Cashapampa. Everyone can buy tickets at the Huaripampa post, but the guardaparques at Cashapampa sometimes refuse to sell tickets to independent trekkers. Note that if you already have a ticket you'll be allowed through no problem; go figure. This aside, trekking independently is straightforward.

Being the most popular trek in the range has some downsides, one of them being rubbish left behind by irresponsible tourists and their crews. Please read the Minimum Impact chapter and only camp at official campsites, even if you see unscrupulous agencies doing otherwise. There are toilet blocks at all the official campsites, but many are in disrepair. The PNH authorities don't expect to build replacements until at least 2016, so in the meantime bring a trowel.

Day 1: Vaquería – Paria camp   [Map 9, p91 & Map 10]

● **Duration** 3-4h
● **Summary** Leaving Huaraz on a tour, or Yungay on early morning public transport, it's possible to fit this short walk in on the same day. It's a gentle introduction, passing through villages before entering PNH and the green, wood-filled Quebrada Huaripampa.

Leave the road in Vaquería on a path near a blue Yanama information sign. Drop down to a 4WD track, immediately leaving it on a shortcut. On meeting the track again, follow it to a signed junction, where you turn L, on a footpath down to the river (15 minutes).

Cross the bridge, then wander gently downstream for 10 minutes, before turning L on a 4WD track which becomes a footpath and heads into Quebrada Huaripampa. After 15 minutes, turn L at a signed junction (R is for Colcapampa – see Alternative start p94). Pass a signpost to Quebrada Ranincuray (off limits to tourists, despite the sign), cross the main river and climb to a road in Yanachaca. Soon leave the road, going R onto a footpath that climbs through Huaripampa village to the PNH checkpost (1h10) where it's possible to get information and buy park tickets.

The path climbs up the green valley, past queñuales and in 15 minutes reaches a pampa with a derelict toilet block at its northern end. Continue climbing gently, arriving at a small green lake at the start of a large pampa 20 minutes later. This boggy meadow takes 35 minutes to skirt round after which the path climbs gently again through queñuales to Paria camp (30 minutes).

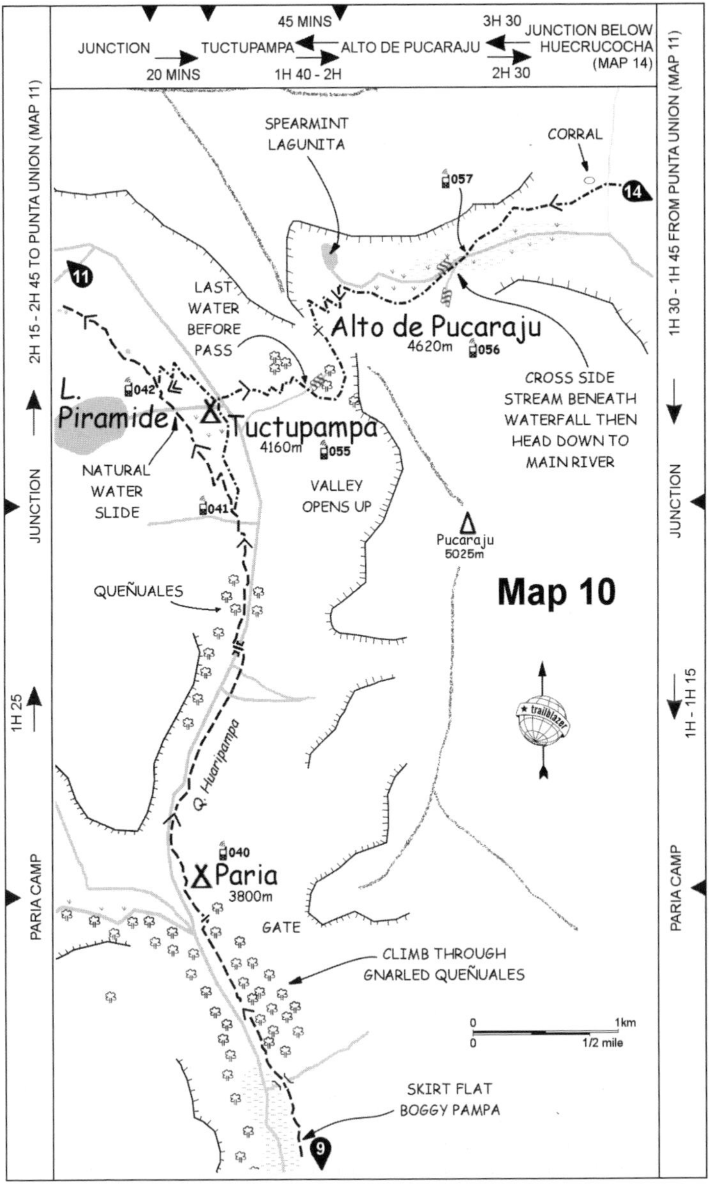

JUNCTION ⟶ TUCTUPAMPA ⟵ ALTO DE PUCARAJU ⟵ JUNCTION BELOW HUECRUCOCHA (MAP 14)

45 MINS   3H 30

20 MINS   1H 40 - 2H   2H 30

SPEARMINT LAGUNITA

CORRAL

057

2H 15 - 2H 45 TO PUNTA UNION (MAP 11)

1H 30 - 1H 45 FROM PUNTA UNION (MAP 11)

11

LAST WATER BEFORE PASS

Alto de Pucaraju
4620m   056

CROSS SIDE STREAM BENEATH WATERFALL THEN HEAD DOWN TO MAIN RIVER

L. Piramide   042

Tuctupampa
4160m   055

NATURAL WATER SLIDE

041

VALLEY OPENS UP

JUNCTION

JUNCTION

QUEÑUALES

Pucaraju
5025m

Map 10

trailblazer

1H 25

1H - 1H 15

Q. Huaripampa

PARIA CAMP

PARIA CAMP

Paria
3800m   040

GATE

CLIMB THROUGH GNARLED QUEÑUALES

0   1km
0   1/2 mile

SKIRT FLAT BOGGY PAMPA

9

HIKING ROUTES & MAPS

Alternative start in Yanama   [Map 16, p105]

Enchanting Yanama is a convenient start/end for the Santa Cruz trek, or stopover on a longer Ulta – Santa Cruz route.

From the village, walk up the road towards Llanganuco, then turn R after 25 minutes, onto a wide path that descends to a bridge over the Río Ichic Ulta. Climb to Chalhua (45 minutes) and join a road which you follow for 45 minutes to Colcabamba. You could try hitching, but there's almost no traffic and it's a pleasant enough walk. Leave the road in Colcabamba, climbing up concrete steps by a balconied house just after the bridge. It takes 20 minutes to reach the main trail.

Day 2: Paria camp – Punta Unión – Taullipampa
[Map 10, p93 & Map 11]

● **Duration** 5-6h
● **Summary** This is the most taxing day of the trek, with a 900m climb to Punta Unión. From this notch in a rocky ridge there are fabulous mountain panoramas, from Taulliraju to Quitaraju, Artesonraju to Contrahierbas. End the day relaxing by the gurgling river at idyllic Taullipampa.

Continue up valley from Paria Camp; Chacraraju's Matterhorn-esque E summit is visible to the L/W. After 50 minutes, cross a bridge over the main river and wander for 35 minutes to a junction on a bend. L (climbing) goes to Punta Unión; straight goes to Tuctupampa camp and links with the Alpamayo Basecamp trek.

Going L, it's a 40-minute climb to a natural water slide which emanates from Laguna Piramide. A minute after is another junction where a small trail leads down to Tuctupampa. Continue on the main trail which, though a veritable motorway at this point, can be muddy in the early season.

Punta Unión comes into view ahead as the path slowly gains height before levelling off and passing some of the smaller Lagunas Morococha (35 minutes). The path begins climbing again, around rocky cliffs and over inclined slabs of bedrock, passing above the largest of the Morococha lakes (40 minutes). This section has fine views of Taulliraju, which has been towering to the N all day, as well as more distant vistas of Contrahierbas, Chopicalqui and Chacraraju to the S.

Punta Unión (30 minutes) is reached by a flight of built-up stone steps. Passing through the rocky cleft reveals the stunning peaks of Rinrijirca and Quitaraju to the W; far below loiter colourful Taullicocha and Jatuncocha. Wander either way along the ridge for better panoramas.

The descent to Taullipampa (1h30) is steady, with some long stone-paved sections and superb alpine views. The pampa is large, with a number of different camping areas. Choose well and you'll be able to gaze at Alpamayo and Taulliraju from the comfort of your tent; all plots come with Artesonraju and Quitaraju views as standard.

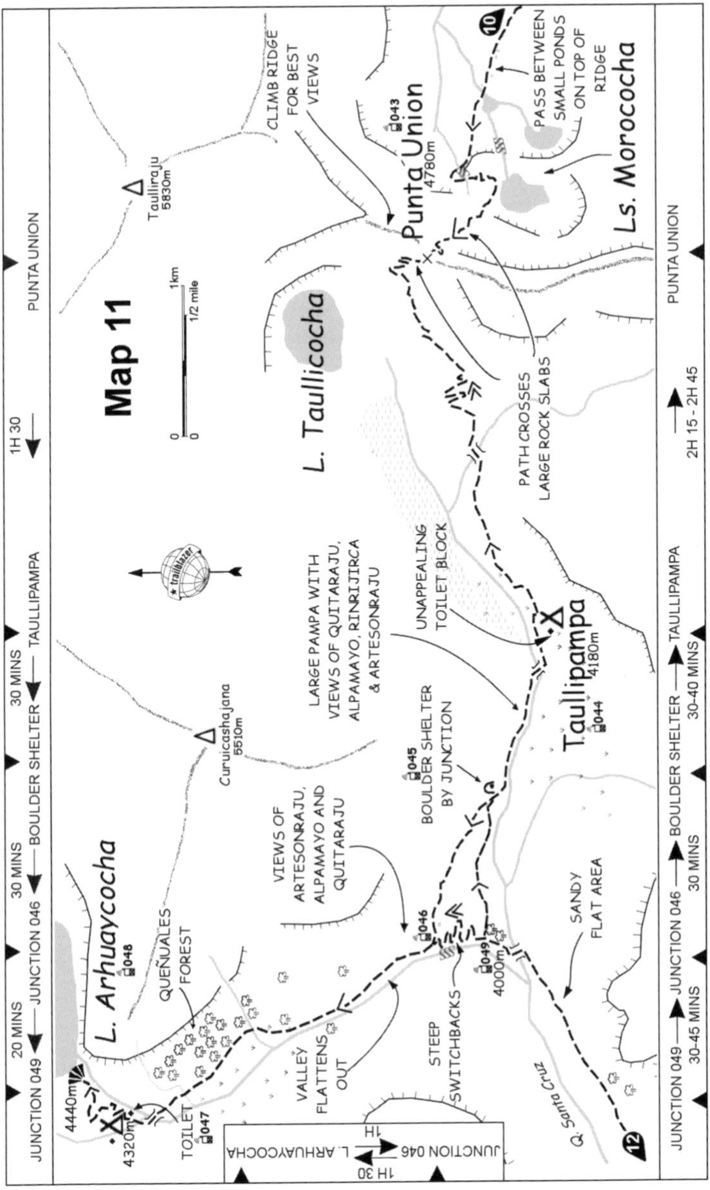

Map 11

Taulliraju 5830m

CLIMB RIDGE FOR BEST VIEWS

Punta Union 4780m □043

10

PASS BETWEEN SMALL PONDS ON TOP OF RIDGE

Ls. Morococha

L. Taullicocha

PATH CROSSES LARGE ROCK SLABS

Curuicashajana 5610m

LARGE PAMPA WITH VIEWS OF QUITARAJU, ALPAMAYO, RINRIJIRCA & ARTESONRAJU

1km
1/2 mile
0
0

UNAPPEALING TOILET BLOCK

VIEWS OF ARTESONRAJU, ALPAMAYO AND QUITARAJU

L. Arhuaycocha

QUENUALES FOREST

4440m

TOILET □047

4320m

□045 BOULDER SHELTER BY JUNCTION

Taullipampa 4180m □044

□046

□049
4000m

STEEP SWITCHBACKS

VALLEY FLATTENS OUT

SANDY FLAT AREA

Q. Santa Cruz

12

JUNCTION 046 ← L. ARHUAYCOCHA 1H
1H 30

PUNTA UNION ▶
1H 30 →

BOULDER SHELTER ▶
30 MINS →

TAULLIPAMPA ▶
30 MINS →

JUNCTION 049 ← 20 MINS → JUNCTION 046 ← 30 MINS → BOULDER SHELTER ← 30 MINS → TAULLIPAMPA

PUNTA UNION ▶
2H 15 - 2H 45 →

TAULLIPAMPA ▶
30-40 MINS →

BOULDER SHELTER ▶
30 MINS →

JUNCTION 046 ▶
30-45 MINS →

JUNCTION 049

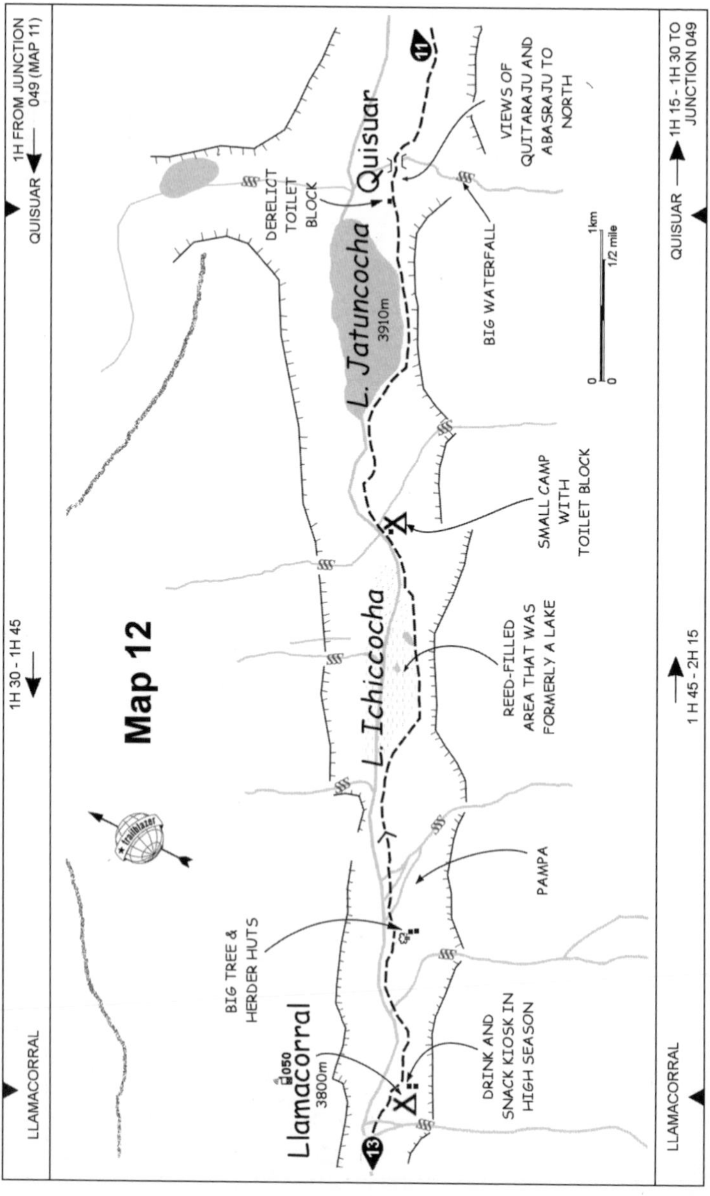

Map 12

Llamacorral
3800m

Quisuar

L. Jatuncocha
3910m

L. Ichiccocha

QUISUAR ← 1H FROM JUNCTION 049 (MAP 11)

QUISUAR ← 1H 15 - 1H 30 TO JUNCTION 049

LLAMACORRAL ← 1H 30 - 1H 45

LLAMACORRAL ← 1 H 45 - 2H 15

VIEWS OF QUITARAJU AND ABASRAJU TO NORTH

DERELICT TOILET BLOCK

BIG WATERFALL

SMALL CAMP WITH TOILET BLOCK

REED-FILLED AREA THAT WAS FORMERLY A LAKE

PAMPA

BIG TREE & HERDER HUTS

DRINK AND SNACK KIOSK IN HIGH SEASON

1km
1/2 mile

0
0

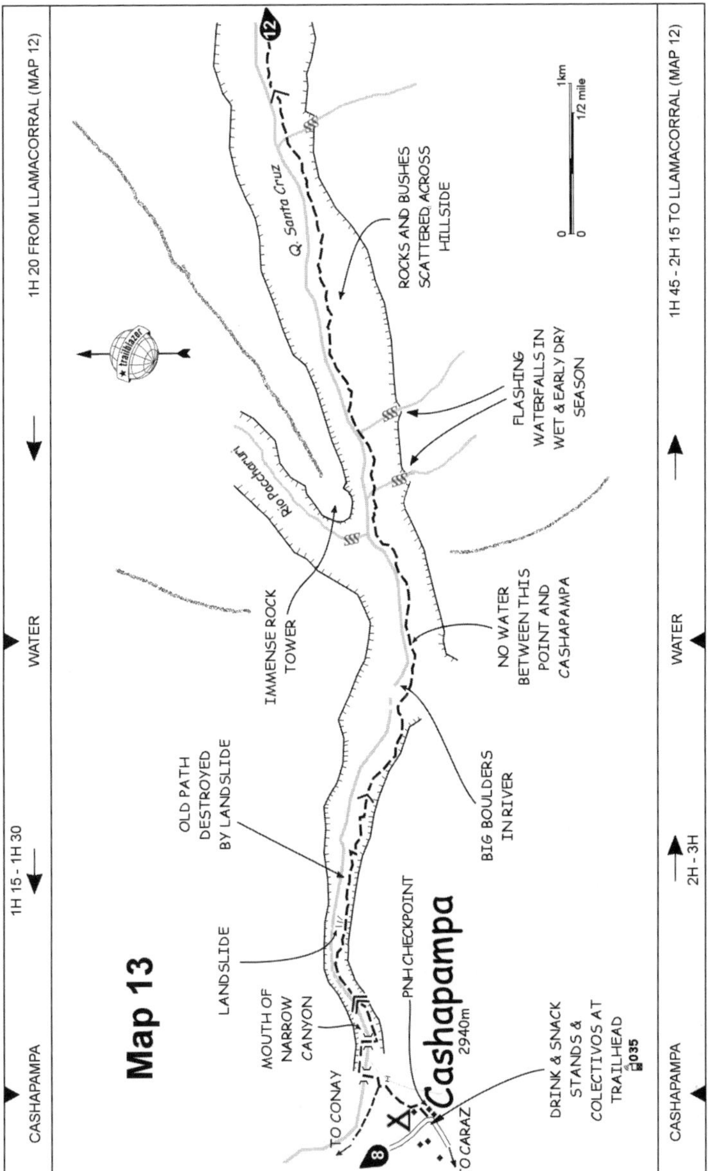
Map 13
CASHAPAMPA
1H 15 - 1H 30
WATER
1H 20 FROM LLAMACORRAL (MAP 12)
CASHAPAMPA
2H - 3H
WATER
1H 45 - 2H 15 TO LLAMACORRAL (MAP 12)
Cashapampa
2940m
PNH CHECKPOINT
TO CONAY
TO CARAZ
8
12
DRINK & SNACK STANDS & COLECTIVOS AT TRAILHEAD
035
MOUTH OF NARROW CANYON
LANDSLIDE
OLD PATH DESTROYED BY LANDSLIDE
BIG BOULDERS IN RIVER
NO WATER BETWEEN THIS POINT AND CASHAPAMPA
IMMENSE ROCK TOWER
Río Pacchanuri
FLASHING WATERFALLS IN WET & EARLY DRY SEASON
ROCKS AND BUSHES SCATTERED ACROSS HILLSIDE
Q. Santa Cruz
trailblazer
0
1km
0
1/2 mile

Day 3: Taullipampa – Laguna Arhuaycocha – Llamacorral
[Map 11, p95 & Map 12, p96]

● **Duration** 6-7h
● **Summary** The side valley housing shimmering Arhuaycocha offers arguably the best views of the whole trek. After gazing at Alpamayo, Pucajirca and Artesonraju, descend to Llamacorral, passing turquoise Jatuncocha and numerous waterfalls en route.

Head W from Taullipampa camp and cross the main river on a bridge (5 minutes). To the NW Alpamayo comes into view for the first time all trek – from this angle it looks nothing like the perfect pyramid seen on the Alpamayo Basecamp trek. To the S it's not hard to spot the source of a landslide which fell from Artesonraju in February 2012. The trail and valley have altered somewhat as a result; most noticeably through the disappearance of Laguna Ichiccocha. Surveying the devastation further down valley near Cashapampa, it's a miracle no-one was killed.

Reach a junction by a boulder cave 25 minutes from the bridge. For Arhuaycocha take the smaller path which leads R, traversing the northern slopes of the valley. (To bypass Laguna Arhuaycocha, follow the mule route L, and in 20 minutes reach the junction where the route from Arhuaycocha rejoins.) A 30 minute traverse brings you to a larger path, climbing up from the valley floor – go R/N into the Arhuaycocha valley.

By now there are again wonderful mountain views, as you head into a valley surrounded by great peaks. The path stays on the R/E of a pampa and eases up to the quiet Arhuaycocha camp (1 hour) – continue ascending to the top of the moraine encasing Laguna Arhuaycocha (30 minutes). Either carry on to the lake shore, or, for better views of Pucajirca and Rinrijirca, climb the moraine ridge.

Returning, it's 1 hour retracing steps to the junction where the traverse joins, heading all the while at Artesonraju. From this angle the peak bears a striking resemblance to Paramount Pictures' live logo and is far more beautiful than when viewed from Punta Unión. Go R at the junction and descend through woods to the mule path (20 minutes). It's usually a hot and energy-sapping walk along the sandy valley floor to Quisuar (1 hour), which is not an appealing camp spot since the landslide, despite its proximity to Laguna Jatuncocha.

❏ **A deadly beauty**

Despite not being one of the higher summits in the Blanca, Alpamayo is high on many a mountaineer's wish list. In 1966 an international survey declared it the 'Most Beautiful Mountain in the World' and this beauty draws climbers from afar. But a dangerous peak it can be too. Walking the trail in May 2013 we encountered a rescue team with horse carrying the body of a Huaraz guide killed in an avalanche on the peak a few days before. A chilling reminder of the danger these alluring mountains pose.

Continue along the S shores of the lake to a dam at its western end (30 minutes). Ignore a signpost which suggests it's possible to head R and reach Quitacocha; it's not – being so overgrown as to be impassable.

Continue 15 minutes to the next possible camp before the trail passes the ex-Ichiccocha – now just a muddy bed filled with reeds. Press on down valley for 50 minutes to Llamacorral, which has a stand selling cold drinks in high season.

Day 4: Llamacorral – Cashapampa　　[Map 12, p96 & Map 13, p97]

● **Duration** 2h30-3h
● **Summary** The trek ends gently with a short walk down the verdant Santa Cruz valley, passing under looming rock towers. It shouldn't be difficult finding a colectivo to Caraz, provided you arrive sufficiently early.

Leaving Llamacorral the gradients are initially gentle before the descent steepens. After 1 hour there's an amazing rock 'table' to the L – a huge boulder supported in the most unlikely manner by a set of smaller rocks. Cross a small stream (20 minutes) – the last water source until near Cashapampa – before leaving the banks of the main river. Descend, over old rock slides, to cross a bridge spanning the roaring river (1h10). The path soon recrosses and climbs briefly to a junction and information board. Go L for the road and guardaparque post in Cashapampa (15 minutes).

SANTA CRUZ – ALPAMAYO CIRCUIT (LINKING SECTION)

It's common to combine the Santa Cruz and Alpamayo treks into a sublime seven- to fourteen-day circuit from Cashapampa or Vaquería to Hualcayán or Cashapampa. Walking the loop in an anticlockwise direction leaves the highest altitudes until the end, but it's perfectly possible to do in reverse.

Use the Santa Cruz route description (p92) for details of the trail from Vaquería to Tuctupampa, and reverse it for details of Cashapampa to Tuctupampa. See the Alpamayo description (p80) for Jancapampa to Cashapampa. Here we describe the middle, linking section from Tuctupampa to Jancapampa, as well as the Alternative Route to Huanchacbamba via the impressive ruins at Yayno. Both of these take two days.

SANTA CRUZ – ALPAMAYO CIRCUIT (LINKING SECTION)
● **Start** Tuctupampa
● **End** Jancapampa
● **Distance** 23km/14 miles
● **Trekking time** 2 days
● **Vertical climb** 1100m/3600ft
● **Max altitude** 4620m/15,150ft
● **Navigation** 2
● **Terrain** 1

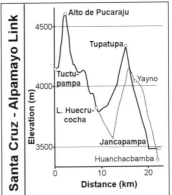

Timing and getting to and from the trailhead

For Cashapampa and Vaquería, see p90. For Hualcayán, Huancarhuaz and Jancapampa, see p76. Vaquería to Jancapampa/Huanchacbamba takes three days. From Cashapampa it takes five.

There's a daily combi between Huanchacbamba and Pomabamba (30 minutes, S/.4), usually leaving Pomabamba around 06:00 and returning in the early afternoon. A taxi between the two is around S/.40. There is more transport between Huayllán (walkable from Huanchacbamba) and Pomabamba.

Preparations See Santa Cruz (p90) for details about arrieros and PNH tickets. Bring all food with you – there are extremely basic shops at Jancapampa and Quisuar (Alternative route) but nowhere you could properly resupply. If you're unable to carry enough supplies for the full trek, it's possible to break a Santa Cruz – Alpamayo circuit at Jancapampa village (a 15 minute detour from the trekking route) by catching a combi (1h, S/.5) to Pomabamba (see p69); stock up, then return to Jancapampa.

Coming from Cashapampa   [Map 10, p93]

About 1h30 after Punta Unión, go L a minute before the water slide from Laguna Piramide and descend for 15 minutes to Tuctupampa camp.

Coming from Vaquería   [Map 10, p93]

Go straight at the junction 30 minutes after crossing Río Huaripampa and continue for 20 minutes to Tuctupampa camp.

Tuctupampa camp – Jancapampa
[Map 10, p93, Map 14 & Map 2, p79]

Continue up valley from Tuctupampa camp and in 5 minutes cross the river at an 'Alto de Pucaraju/Yaino' sign. The mountain views improve with altitude on the steep climb to Alto de Pucaraju (1h40-2h) and by the time you reach the top a whole cluster of peaks is on show. Scamper up the ridge to the N for best views of Taulliraju's fearsome SW face.

On the zigzag descent a spearmint lagunita immediately comes into view under Taulliraju's SE ridge. The path doesn't go to the lake, instead descending into the Huecrucocha valley ahead. The switchbacks give way to a traverse down the valley and the route becomes hard to follow, splitting into many cow paths (40 minutes). Stay R/S of the pampa until you reach a side stream from a waterfall. Cross, shadowing this downhill to stepping stones over the main river (15 minutes). On the far bank, the path immediately becomes large and easy to follow again.

Stick to the TL/N side, contouring high above the main river and boggy pampa to a possible **campsite** (40 minutes). The contouring continues awhile before the path descends to Laguna Huecrucocha and follows the N shore round to the lake's outflow (50 minutes). There's a trout farm on the lake, initiated by the Mayor of Lucma, and you could ask to camp.

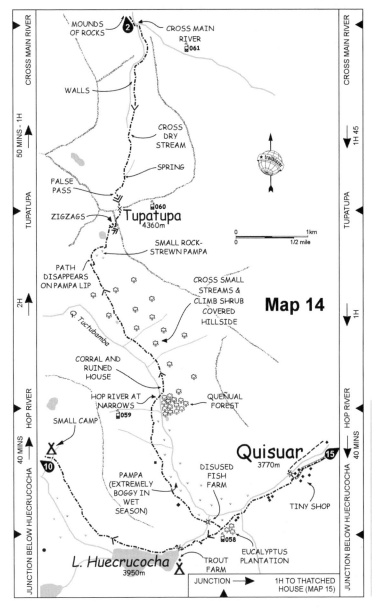

MOUNDS OF ROCKS

CROSS MAIN RIVER

061

WALLS

CROSS DRY STREAM

SPRING

FALSE PASS

ZIGZAGS

060

Tupatupa
4360m

SMALL ROCK-STREWN PAMPA

PATH DISAPPEARS ON PAMPA LIP

CROSS SMALL STREAMS & CLIMB SHRUB COVERED HILLSIDE

Map 14

0   1km
0   1/2 mile

Tuctubamba

CORRAL AND RUINED HOUSE

HOP RIVER AT NARROWS
059

QUEÑUAL FOREST

SMALL CAMP

10

Quisuar
3770m

15

PAMPA (EXTREMELY BOGGY IN WET SEASON)

DISUSED FISH FARM

TINY SHOP

L. Huecrucocha
3950m

TROUT FARM

058

EUCALYPTUS PLANTATION

JUNCTION →   1H TO THATCHED HOUSE (MAP 15)

CROSS MAIN RIVER

50 MINS - 1H

TUPATUPA

2H

HOP RIVER

40 MINS

JUNCTION BELOW HUECRUCOCHA

CROSS MAIN RIVER

1H 45

TUPATUPA

1H

HOP RIVER

40 MINS

JUNCTION BELOW HUECRUCOCHA

HIKING ROUTES & MAPS

Descend a further 10 minutes on the wide main trail until it reaches the start of a eucalyptus plantation. The large path continues down valley – this is the route to Yayno (see below) – but for Jancapampa turn L (no real path) to a bridge (5 minutes). Stick to a path which passes houses on the TR/W side of the river for 40 minutes until level with a stand of queñuales on the E bank. Just upriver from the queñuales, the river narrows and it's possible to leap to the far bank. Climb up to the path traversing northwards and follow this towards Tupatupa.

After 1h15, reach a rock-strewn pampa in a bowl to the R/E of the path, and climb round the pampa to a lake (15 minutes). The path becomes steep, zigzagging up the ridge to the NE which is crossed en route to Tupatupa (25 minutes), a pass with wide mountain views.

The descent crosses and recrosses the valley's main, and often dry, stream. The surrounding slopes are covered in ichu, punctuated with stripes of black rock strata. Stick to the E side until a side valley joins from the R/E (55 minutes) and the path splits. It's quickest to cross the river to the W side here, traverse, then descend steeply past a blue water tank to the few houses of Pishgopampa (20 minutes). Make your way to the buildings and line of eucalyptus at the L/NW end and follow a path down to the 4WD road in Jancapampa, joining at the '0+900' road marker (30 minutes).

For supplies, head R to Jancapampa village (15 minutes). To continue trekking, go L up the road for 25 minutes, before leaving it by heading R, over bridges, to the main trail from Pomabamba on the N side of the pampa (10 minutes).

Alternative route: near Quisuar – Yayno – Huanchacbamba
[Map 14, p101 & Map 15]

• **Duration** 5-6h

• **Summary** This alternative finish allows trekkers to visit the deserted pre-Inca ruins at Yayno, before continuing to Pomabamba and a chance to resupply.

Rather than turning L for Tupatupa, remain on the main trail down the populated Lucma valley to Quisuar (30 minutes). The path becomes a 4WD track and after 25 minutes a bridge appears below; take the path down to it that leaves just before some thatched buildings. Cross the bridge and turn R, to a bridge over a side river (10 minutes). Soon after, go L at a fork and begin the climb to Punta Lluchujirca, curving round a ridge topped with a cross, into the next side valley, on a well-used trail.

After 1h30 of climbing, an alternative path from Quisuar (marked as the main path on *Alpenvereinskarte*) joins from the L. For Yayno, continue climbing NE to the pass (55 minutes).

On Punta Lluchujirca, Yayno comes into view ahead, crowning a conical hill. The wide, ancient path traverses to the ruins (35 minutes), which dominate the area and are the largest and most impressive in the Cordillera Blanca. They are thought to be a Recuay period fortress which was inhabited from 400-800 CE. Spend an hour or two rambling around, admiring the huge walls which are constructed from the full gamut of stone sizes.

HIKING ROUTES & MAPS

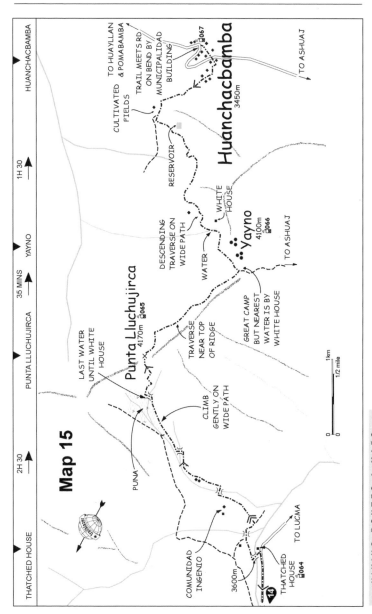

Map 15

THATCHED HOUSE ▲ 2H 30 → PUNTA LLUCHUJIRCA ▲ 35 MINS → YAYNO ▲ 1H 30 → HUANCHACBAMBA ▲

COMUNIDAD INGENIO

PUNA

3600m

THATCHED HOUSE
☐064

14

TO LUCMA

CLIMB GENTLY ON WIDE PATH

LAST WATER UNTIL WHITE HOUSE

Punta Lluchujirca
4170m ☐065

TRAVERSE NEAR TOP OF RIDGE

GREAT CAMP BUT NEAREST WATER IS BY WHITE HOUSE

WATER

DESCENDING TRAVERSE ON WIDE PATH

Yayno
4100m
☐066

TO ASHUAJ

WHITE HOUSE

RESERVOIR

CULTIVATED FIELDS

TO HUAYLLAN & POMABAMBA

TRAIL MEETS RD ON BEND BY MUNICIPALIDAD BUILDING

☐067

Huanchacbamba
3450m

TO ASHUAJ

1km
1/2 mile

HIKING ROUTES & MAPS

The main trail on the N side of the ridge descends past a white house (15 minutes, first **water** since before the pass) to the village of Huanchacbamba (1h15).

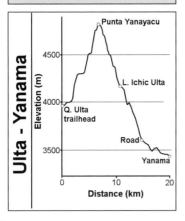

ULTA – YANAMA
- **Start** Quebrada Ulta
- **End** Yanama
- **Distance** 20km/12 miles
- **Trekking time** 2 days
- **Vertical climb** 900m/3000ft
- **Max altitude** 4840m/15,900ft
- **Navigation** 2
- **Terrain** 2

ULTA – YANAMA

For two years following the 1970 earthquake, when their traditional trading town of Yungay and access route via Llanganuco were wiped out by an aluvión, this became Yanama's main trading route to the Callejón de Huaylas. There's still a good path as a result, and the views of Chopicalqui and Huascarán Sur on the climb to the exciting Punta Yanayacu are exceptional.

The descent is dramatic, as the path traverses a steep rock face before dropping to a pair of sparkling lakes in verdant Quebrada Ichic Ulta. Most trekkers choose to tack this walk onto a Santa Cruz or Alpamayo trek, extending those routes by one or two days.

Timing and getting to and from the trailhead

Transport logistics favour beginning in Quebrada Ulta. From Huaraz, El Veloz, Renzo and Sandoval all have early morning buses (see map pp54-5) for San Luis and Pomabamba which pass the trailhead (2h, S/.16, book the day before). Ask to be dropped at the bridge before the switchbacks ('*el puente antes de las curvas*') to Punta Olímpica begin. If ending in Quebrada Ulta, buses for Huaraz pass through in the early morning and mid-afternoon.

❏ **Aluviones**
There is a long and tragic *aluvión* history in the Cordillera Blanca. These flash floods of mud and gravel are usually sparked by earthquakes rupturing the moraine encasing a lake. The Spanish first made mention of such an event in 1705 and since then various catastrophic incidents have occurred. The most significant were: in 1941 when Palcacocha burst, killing 5000 in Huaraz; 1962 when an aluvión left 4000 dead in Ranrahirca; and 1970 when Yungay was destroyed, leaving 23,000 dead.

Many towns in the Blanca now have street signs advising which way to head in order to escape an aluvión. Follow the directions, in the event of a 'quake.

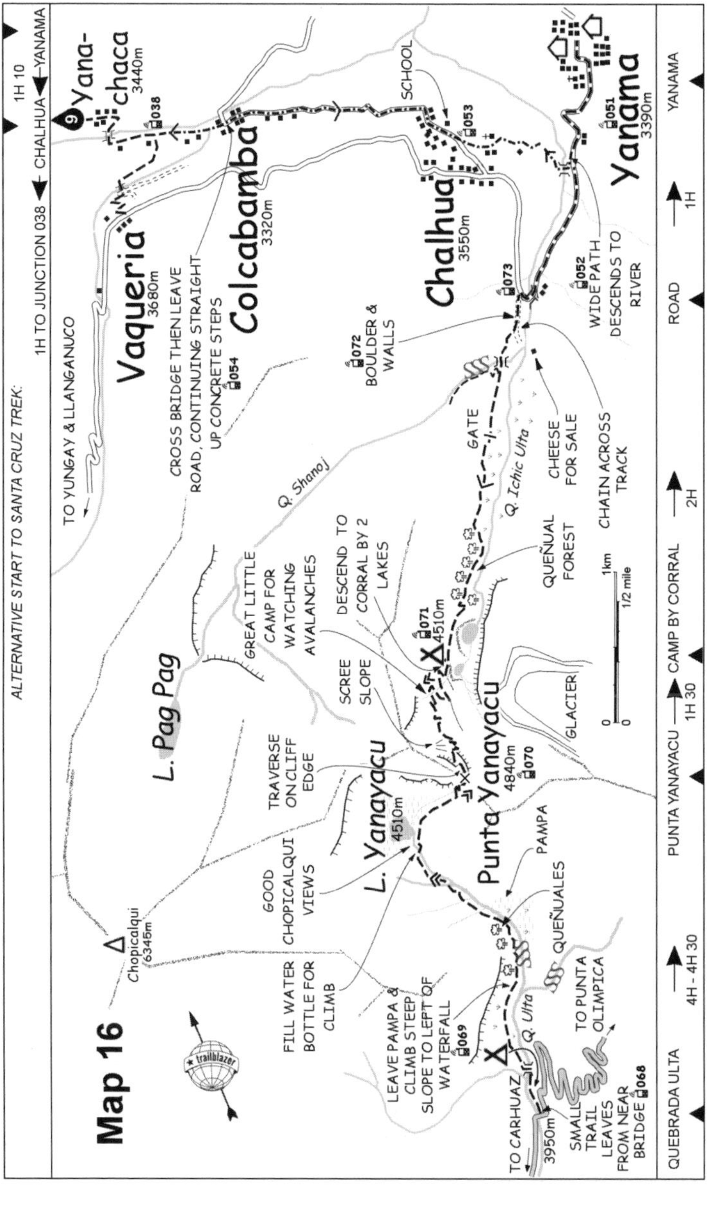

ALTERNATIVE START TO SANTA CRUZ TREK:

1H TO JUNCTION 038 ◀ CHALHUA ◀ YANAMA

1H 10

Map 16

Chopicalqui
6345m

L. Pag Pag

9 Yana-
chaca
3440m
⌂038

Vaqueria
3680m

Colcabamba
3320m
⌂054

CROSS BRIDGE THEN LEAVE
ROAD, CONTINUING STRAIGHT
UP CONCRETE STEPS

TO YUNGAY & LLANGANUCO

SCHOOL
⌂053

Chalhua
3550m
⌂072 BOULDER &
WALLS
⌂073

Yanama
3390m
⌂051

⌂052
WIDE PATH
DESCENDS TO
RIVER

Q. Shanoj

GREAT LITTLE
CAMP FOR
WATCHING
AVALANCHES

DESCEND TO
CORRAL BY 2
LAKES

SCREE
SLOPE

GATE

Q. Ichic Ulta

CHEESE
FOR SALE

QUEÑUAL
FOREST

CHAIN ACROSS
TRACK

TRAVERSE
ON CLIFF
EDGE

L. Yanayacu
4510m

✗⌂071
4510m

GLACIER

1km
1/2 mile

0
0

GOOD
CHOPICALQUI
VIEWS

Punta Yanayacu
4840m
⌂070

PAMPA

FILL WATER
BOTTLE FOR
CLIMB

QUEÑUALES

TO PUNTA
OLIMPICA

LEAVE PAMPA &
CLIMB STEEP
SLOPE TO LEFT OF
WATERFALL

✗⌂069

Q. Ulta

TO CARHUAZ
3950m

SMALL
TRAIL
LEAVES
FROM NEAR
BRIDGE ⌂068

trailblazer

QUEBRADA ULTA   4H – 4H 30   ◀   PUNTA YANAYACU   1H 30   ▶   CAMP BY CORRAL   2H   ◀   ROAD   1H   ▶   YANAMA

The trail hits the Llanganuco road an hour's walk from Yanama. As there's no guarantee there'll be room in the combis to Yungay when they pass this spot in the late morning, it's best to head to Yanama for a ride. To link up directly with the Santa Cruz or Alpamayo trek, walk, or hitch, the other way along the road, to Chalhua.

It takes two days from Quebrada Ulta to Yanama, though faster walkers can reach the road in time to give themselves a chance with transport on the second day.

Preparations There are no facilities whatsoever on this route, so bring all supplies. There are no mules in Quebrada Ulta, and organizing to go with arrieros from Vaquería is tricky. Some Huaraz agencies can arrange the trek as an extension to a Santa Cruz trek. The hike is within PNH, but there's no checkpoint en route to buy a ticket.

Quebrada Ulta – Yanama [Map 16, p105]

From the S side of the road bridge in Quebrada Ulta, follow the small trail up valley on the TL/S of the river. There are good, hidden **campsites** away from the road, views of the white wall of Contrahierbas to the E and the beautiful cone of Nevado Ulta to the S. Cross a small bridge over the main river (15 minutes) and continue upriver for 25 minutes to some large boulders. Turn L and leave the valley floor here, before reaching a N-S ridge that cuts across the valley, forming a waterfall.

The path morphs from indistinct to clear as it climbs steeply up a side valley, through queñuales. Emerge onto a pampa (45 minutes) in Quebrada Cancahua, to the L/W of another waterfall; these lower reaches of pampa are boggy and tufty, but further up are good **camp spots**.

Follow the trail across the pampa, then up through ichu grass, crossing the river flowing down from Chopicalqui on stones (35 minutes). The path now becomes steep, climbing tight zigzags before swinging N on a rising traverse to Laguna Yanayacu (50 minutes). Soon after the dark, inky-blue lake comes into view there's a small path leading off L, descending to the lake's shore. You could **camp** down there, but it's a struggle to find a flat, non-boggy site.

At this small junction, continue straight/R on the main path that climbs eastwards. In 40 minutes cross a reddish, mineral-loaded stream (don't drink), on the steep, breathless climb to Punta Yanayacu (45 minutes). The pass is a notch in a ridge which boasts magnificent views of Chopicalqui and Huascarán Sur; on the Yanama side ahead lies emerald and lime-green Quebrada Ichic Ulta.

Initially it's a thrilling descent, but one that will not be appreciated by vertigo sufferers. The route traverses on a good path, but with a rock face one side and a large drop-off on the other. Soon this gives way to zigzags down a scree slope, which in turn becomes a grassy slope laden with colourful flowers in early season. Forty-five minutes into the descent is a great **campsite**, with **water**, on a balcony with bird's-eye views over the valley to Contrahierbas' glaciers.

Descend on switchbacks to the upper lake (Ichic Ulta) and a corral (40 minutes). There's good **camping** here too and free aural entertainment in the form of ice blocks calving off the glacier above and smashing thunderously on the high rock cliffs. Continue down, past Laguna Jatun Ulta (viewed by detour only), on a good path which winds through queñuales. Pass through a gate in 1h10 from the corral, and in a further 20 minutes ignore a small path which climbs off L into Quebrada Shanoj – this is a restricted zone not open to trekkers. In 15 minutes join a 4WD track, between a chain across the track and some walls built against a boulder. It's 10 minutes from here to the Llanganuco road and a further 1 hour to Yanama.

LAGUNA 69

The walk to prosaically-named Laguna 69 (*Sesenta y Nueve*) is, quite rightly, the most popular day hike in the range. Cradled in a bowl at 4600m and towered over by colossal Chacraraju, many of the Blanca's highest and most striking peaks are visible on the climb to the lake's azure waters. Acclimatize on other, lower, trails in the area before attempting to reach this altitude.

Timing and getting to and from the trailhead

All agencies in Huaraz offer Laguna 69 day trips for S/.30-50. It's 3 hours each way by vehicle from town to the trailhead, which results in a 10-12 hour total trip. To avoid a tour and beat the groups, try catching an early morning Yanama combi from Yungay (06:00-07:00; check the day before,

LAGUNA 69
- **Start & End** Cebollapampa
- **Distance** 13km/8 miles
- **Trekking time** 4h-5h30
- **Vertical climb** 700m/2300ft
- **Max altitude** 4600m/15,100ft
- **Navigation** 1
- **Terrain** 1

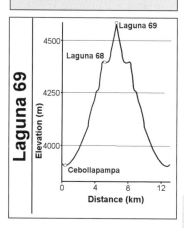

❑ **Laguna 69 two-day loop**
For even better views, including of Huandoy, acclimatized trekkers can turn this into an excellent two day loop, without the necessity of camping. On the first day, climb to and overnight at *Refugio Peru* (2h30 – 3h30, 4660m), a hut used by mountaineers attempting Nevado Pisco. In the morning, find a way across (or round) the moraine to the east and join an obvious path which climbs to 4860m en route to Laguna 69 (2h30-3h30); descend via the main trail. Note that though much of the dynamic moraine has a path across, other sections are wracked by rock fall and slides – it's not always possible to cross safely. Take a guide, or ask for information at the Refugio, and if you're not comfortable about crossing the moraine, follow a more circuitous cross country route skirting round on grassy slopes to the south of the moraine, before meeting the path on the east side.

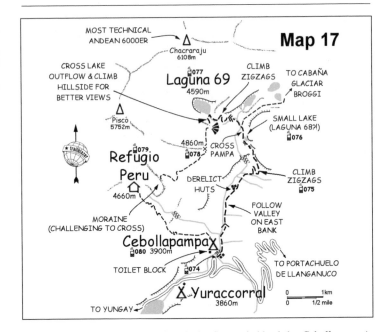

S/.15) and jump out at the trailhead (the first switchback by Cebollapampa). Another way to beat the crowds is to camp at Cebollapampa and set off at the crack of dawn. Both of these options rely on hitching, or finding a spare seat in a combi, to return you to Yungay.

Alternatively, from Cebollapampa you can walk, via the road or footpath shortcuts, over Portachuelo de Llanganuco to Vaquería in a day, to link up with the Santa Cruz trek.

Preparations The lake is within PNH – tickets can be bought at the office at the entrance to the Llanganuco valley. Snacks are available here, but nowhere on the walk itself, so bring supplies.

Cebollapampa – Laguna 69 – Cebollapampa   [Map 17]

From the switchback on the road, descend briefly by a stream to the valley floor. Cross a small bridge and in a few minutes reach a signed junction. L, crossing the main river, goes to the Cebollapampa campsite and Refugio Peru (see box p107), but for Laguna 69 continue straight on the main path. After 50 minutes of gentle walking with views of the Huascaráns, Chacraraju and Yanapaccha, cross a couple of streams, then begin a steeper 1 hour climb to a small lake at the start of a pampa.

Cross the pampa, ignoring a sign to 'Cabaña Glaciar Broggi' (2km, R) after 10 minutes. Continue straight, climbing a further 45 minutes to Laguna 69.

Returning to the road takes 1h30-2h.

ARTESONRAJU BASECAMP

Exploring Laguna Parón's mountain arena is a highlight of the Cordillera Blanca. Though possible as a day excursion from Caraz, it's more rewarding to allow two (or three) days for the trip, overnighting at the idyllic camp at the east end of the lake. In the morning, when the peaks are most likely to be cloud-free, climb to Artesonraju's moraine basecamp (ABC) for stunning vistas of its perfect pyramid and a host of other 6000m summits.

Timing and getting to and from the trailhead

A motorable road rises from Caraz (p62) to the western end of Laguna Parón (33km). Taxis (1h30 each way) charge S/.120 return including a 2 hour wait, though you'll have to negotiate a price for a longer wait to complete the trek to ABC and back. Without your own transport this is the only realistic way to complete the hike in a day.

Although more time-consuming, the cheaper alternative is to catch a combi (1h, S/.7) from the Cashapampa stop in Caraz to Pueblo Parón – generally two leave per day at around 07:00 and 11:00. As always, it's best to confirm timetables the day before, and on your way up check the return times from Pueblo Parón. A taxi from Caraz to Pueblo Parón costs S/.35.

Preparations The hike is on a clear path and easy to undertake independently, though it may be possible to find arrieros in Pueblo Parón. There's a control gate on the road at 3300m where the Parón community charge visitors S/.5 to enter the quebrada. Despite the trek being within PNH, you are not asked to purchase a PNH ticket. Buy all supplies in Caraz.

Pueblo Parón – Artesonraju Basecamp – Pueblo Parón [Map 18, p110]

From Pueblo Parón (3250m) it's a 4 hour walk to the lake, following the unpaved road and/or footpath shortcuts through queñuales. High granite walls loom overhead on both sides of this, the most impressive of the many steep-sided valleys leading off the Callejón de Huaylas. The giant 800m *Esfinge* (Sphinx) face to the N attracts big-wall rock climbers.

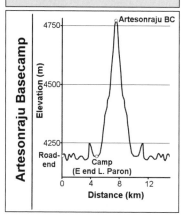

ARTESONRAJU BASECAMP
- **Start & End** Pueblo Parón (or Laguna Parón)
- **Distance** 32km/20 miles (15km/9 miles)
- **Trekking time** 2 days (1 day)
- **Vertical climb** 1600m/5200ft (700m/2300ft)
- **Max altitude** 4770m/15,650ft
- **Navigation** 1
- **Terrain** 2

HIKING ROUTES & MAPS

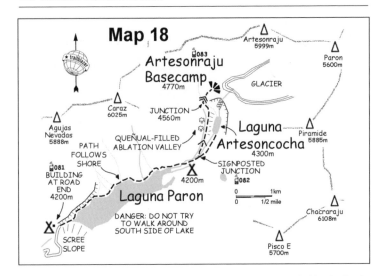

Map 18

Artesonraju 5999m

Paron 5600m

083

Artesonraju Basecamp 4770m

GLACIER

Caraz 6025m

JUNCTION 4560m

Laguna Artesoncocha 4300m

Piramide 5885m

Agujas Nevadas 5888m

PATH FOLLOWS SHORE

QUEÑUAL-FILLED ABLATION VALLEY

SIGNPOSTED JUNCTION

081

BUILDING AT ROAD END 4200m

4200m

082

Laguna Paron

Chacraraju 6108m

0   1km
0   1/2 mile

DANGER: DO NOT TRY TO WALK AROUND SOUTH SIDE OF LAKE

Pisco E 5700m

SCREE SLOPE

At road-end is a building owned by Duke Energy, but occupied by the Parón Community, (see box opposite) where it's possible to camp. Here the turquoise waters of the Blanca's largest lake come into view, along with Nevados Piramide and Chacraraju. To the S, the multiple summits of Huandoy dominate the skyline.

The road gives way to a wide path which contours round above the lake's N shore, to a hydro-electric building (10 minutes). Beyond, the trail narrows and the views unfurl, with first Pisco East and then its more frequently climbed western brother appearing to the SE. After 1h20 reach a serene **campsite**, with Artesonraju-views, on a meadow straddling the river.

The footpath heads up valley through camp to a signed junction (5 minutes). Go L for ABC (R for the side trip to Laguna Artesoncocha – 30 minutes return) following cairns northwards on a trail that crosses two rivers before beginning to climb. By the path are plaques to climbers who tragically paid the ultimate price for being drawn to Artesonraju's geometric beauty.

The trail runs near the top of a moraine ridge above an ablation valley full of queñuales and after 40 minutes there are good views of little turquoise Laguna Artesoncocha below. Continue along the ridge, then climb L of a cliff and roaring waterfall. In 30 minutes reach another signed junction – stay R/NE for ABC, crossing a stream.

After 45 minutes of rapid altitude gain and ever-improving panoramas reach ABC, a moraine camp encircled by peaks. If the weather is clear, feast your eyes on the summits of Piramide, Chacraraju, Pisco, Huandoy, Caraz and the great pyramid of Artesonraju, arguably the most beautiful mountain in the range.

Once sated by the icy visual offerings, it's 2h30 back to the road and 2 hours further to Pueblo Parón. Don't return via the southern side of the lake – sections are exposed and dangerous.

❏ **Power to Parón**
For years, a battle has raged between the Parón community and Duke Energy, the US-owners of the hydroelectric centre in the Cañón del Pato. The lake was originally dammed and water level lowered for safety reasons following the earthquake of 1970, but locals are unhappy at the continued high release rate from the lake, which they fear erodes downstream irrigation systems and has a negative effect on local water quality. The Parón community currently have control of the lake and are allowing water levels to rise.

Hikes near Huaraz

LAGUNA LEJIACOCHA

The fit and acclimatized will enjoy this very long but varied day hike. There are ample opportunities for discourse with locals before a zigzagging climb through beautiful old gnarled polylepis forest leads to a fantastic viewpoint of milky-green Laguna Lejiacocha and Nevado Copa's fluted west face.

After negotiating the maze of trails in the fields around Vicos, the path to the lake is good and clear, as this is the route used by mountaineers to climb Nevado Copa. Those with sufficient acclimatization could camp near the lake, splitting the route into two more manageable days.

Timing and getting to and from the trailhead

This is a long day walk, so leave very early. Take a Caraz/Carhuaz combi from Huaraz and alight at Paradero Chancos (30 minutes, S/.3) in Marcará. Colectivos for Vicos (via Chancos) leave regularly from here (10 minutes, S/.1.50). Returning, colectivos from Vicos to Marcará run until dusk.

Preparations The walk has a significant vertical height gain, so you should be well acclimatized before attempting it. Part of the route is within PNH, but there are no checkpoints.

LAGUNA LEJIACOCHA
- **Start & End** Vicos
- **Distance** 23km/14 miles
- **Trekking time** 9 hours
- **Vertical climb** 1700m/5600ft
- **Max altitude** 4640m/15,200ft
- **Navigation** 2
- **Terrain** 1

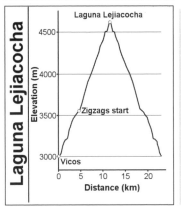

Laguna Lejiacocha (chart, Elevation (m) vs Distance (km))

Bring all the supplies you need as there are no shops after Vicos.

RESPONS (see p59) runs community treks led by local guides in this area, some of which visit the lake. This local knowledge can make for an extremely rich and rewarding experience, for those who are looking for more cultural interaction. If you have time, it's well worth going for a dip at the hot baths (06:00-20:00) in Chancos after your walk.

Vicos – Laguna Lejiacocha – Vicos [Map 19]

From the plaza in Vicos, take the road to the L/N of the church, passing a large building with a curved roof. Climb up the hillside behind, following the road or shortcuts. After 40 minutes of height gain, reach a right-hand bend in the road with a circular blue building/water tank just above. Leave the road here, taking the path to the R/E of the building that descends to a bridge (5 minutes).

Five minutes after, leave the wide, traversing path for a large, rough foot-path which climbs up R/NE, through eucalyptus woods. Twenty minutes later go straight at a junction, on a 4WD track, and continue straight at two further junctions, still climbing through woods. After this third junction, the 4WD track crosses a water channel and continues climbing. Round a ridge and leave the eucalyptus grove, after which the 4WD track becomes a walking path (30 minutes) which follows a small valley.

In 10 minutes reach another eucalyptus plantation and slice straight through. From the far end of the plantation (10 minutes) a path, which soon becomes wide, leads off up the hill in zigzags, ascending through queñual forest. After 1h30 cross a stream – the most reliable **water source** on this part of the climb – then leave the polylepis forest for the remaining 2-3 hour climb to the lake. Returning, it's 3h-3h30 back to Vicos.

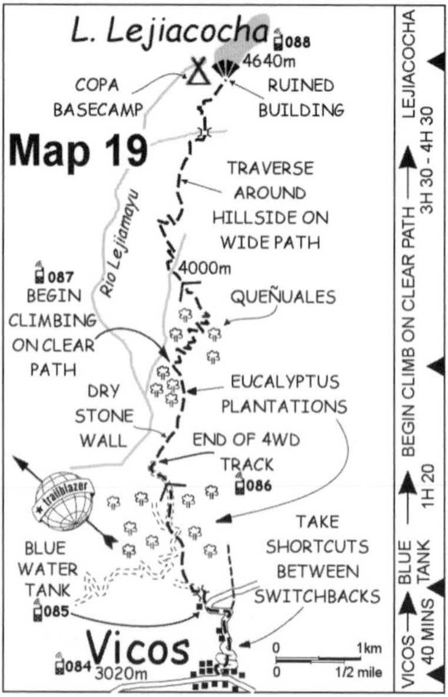

L. Lejiacocha ⌂088
4640m
COPA BASECAMP
RUINED BUILDING

Map 19

TRAVERSE AROUND HILLSIDE ON WIDE PATH

Río Lejiamoyu
⌂087 4000m
BEGIN CLIMBING ON CLEAR PATH
QUEÑUALES

DRY STONE WALL
EUCALYPTUS PLANTATIONS
END OF 4WD TRACK
⌂086

BLUE WATER TANK
⌂085.
TAKE SHORTCUTS BETWEEN SWITCHBACKS

Vicos ⌂084 3020m

0 ——— 1km
0 ——— 1/2 mile

LEJIACOCHA
← 3H 30 - 4H 30 →
BEGIN CLIMB ON CLEAR PATH
← 1H 20 →
BLUE TANK
VICOS ← 40 MINS →

AKILPO – ISHINCA

In many ways this is the perfect three- or four-day trekking circuit near Huaraz. There are interesting Wari period ruins to explore at Honcopampa before the trail passes through polylepis forest in both Quebradas Akilpo and Ishinca. Turquoise alpine lakes await at the heads of both valleys, and the mountain scenery on crossing 5060m Paso Urus is magnificent.

Unfortunately there is also a very big drawback. The descent from Paso Urus to Quebrada Ishinca is a nightmare – the most difficult trekking terrain in this book. Just below the pass is a short, steep section on loose rock that requires scrambling skills. It's not a good idea to trek alone – a companion to pass packs down to is invaluable. Don't attempt to descend from the pass if it's raining or recent snow has settled on the ground – this renders the steep section slippery and dangerous, and any fall would be extremely serious.

The remaining 500m descent to the valley floor is no less slow and difficult. There's no path and the steep hillsides are covered in ankle-spraining, clumpy ichu grass: this is a route for experienced, sure-footed trekkers only.

Take care and once down make sure to allow time for side trips to Lagunas Ishinca and Milluacocha.

AKILPO – ISHINCA
● **Start** San Miguel de Aco
● **End** Collón/Pashpa
● **Distance** 38km/24 miles +
● **Trekking time** 3 or 4 days
● **Vertical climb** 2200m/7200ft
● **Max altitude** 5060m/16,600ft
● **Navigation** 3
● **Terrain** 3

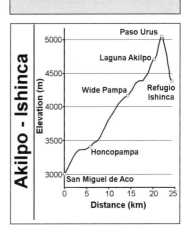

Getting to/from the trailhead

Access from Huaraz is rapid. Take a Caraz or Jangas-Bedoya (10 or E) combi from by Puente Quilcay and alight at the Taricá junction (20 minutes, S/.2.50) just before Puente Jangas. From here, combis leave regularly for San Miguel de Aco (20 minutes, S/.1.50), and occasionally for Honcopampa (S/.5). A taxi straight to Honcopampa from Taricá is S/.25.

It's possible to finish the walk in either Collón or Pashpa. See Ishinca trek (p116) for details.

Mules can't cross the pass, so hiring an arriero is not an option. For navigation purposes, taking a guide is more useful on this trek than any other in this book. Arrange it with an agency in Huaraz, ensuring first that your guide knows the pass well.

Preparations The walk is within PNH – buy a ticket as you leave Quebrada Ishinca if the guardaparque's there. Unlike most treks in the Cordillera Blanca, it's not that feasible to walk the route in reverse. Paso Urus is difficult to locate and extremely steep when climbing up from Refugio Ishinca.

Tourists are charged S/.5 to pass through Honcopampa village, whether or not they visit the ruins.

In season, meals can be bought at Refugio Ishinca (see box p116), but for Quebrada Akilpo bring all supplies with you.

Paso Urus is one of the highest in the range, so ensure sufficient acclimatization before attempting the crossing.

San Miguel de Aco – Laguna Akilpo – Collón/Pashpa   [Map 20]

From the combi stop in San Miguel de Aco, continue up the road for a minute, rounding a left-hand bend and crossing a bridge. Just after, turn R onto a broad path and climb. The route takes the road or shortcuts, past a tiny church, to Pampamaca plaza (50 minutes). Locals here weave typical Andean garments which make great souvenirs.

Cross the plaza and climb to rejoin the road on a plateau. Go R through Shirapucro, remaining on the road to the pay station in Honcopampa (1 hour). Leave the road at the barrier, onto a large path with stairs. After 15 minutes pass the ruins (fenced on the L) – continue straight, aiming at Quebrada Akilpo.

Twenty minutes from the ruins, cross a road by a 'Puente Vehicular' sign, and continue climbing to a fork (15 minutes). Go R towards the last house in the village; L goes to waterfalls. Fork L before the house and start climbing steeply, staying on the TL/S of the river, which is out of sight below. Enter an ancient queñual forest, which, like all queñuales in PNH, is protected, so don't deviate from the clear path which slices through it.

After 50 minutes, cross the first of many bridges spanning the main river. Six more crossings later, leave the cool, enchanting forest as the valley opens out onto a pampa which makes for good **camping** (1h30).

There are a further three bridges to cross; after the final one (50 minutes), stick to a faint trail which skirts a pampa on the TL/S side. In 45 minutes reach some rock corrals – climb above these to a good path that traverses L, up valley towards the cascade emanating from Laguna Akilpo, which is reached (45 minutes) on a good zigzagging path.

This bright laguna is a lovely spot, with views of Nevado Tocllaraju as well as of Paso Urus – the low point on the ridge, due S. Walk anti-clockwise round the W shore on a small path, passing a possible (but very high) **campsite**. After 10 minutes leave the lake and follow cairns towards the pass. The path is sometimes faint and the way steep, but the going is not overly difficult. Climb straight up, before traversing R/SW near the top, to the pass (1h15).

Paso Urus offers great panoramas back to Nevados Copa, Paccharaju, Akilpo and forward to majestic Ranrapalca and Ocshapalca; but the descent down to Refugio Ishinca is horrible, so stay focussed. From the pass, cairns lead you L/SE, on a gentle downwards traverse for 20 minutes. Here you reach very steep ground with many loose rocks and it's difficult to find the way down. Head back R/W and scramble down a short, steep section of rock.

From the bottom of the steep section, a path leads over a small ridge and down towards some lakes (20 minutes, often dry). Head S to the edge of this flat area, then off the end. It's awkward with no path or good route – head straight down to the valley floor and Refugio Ishinca (1h20).

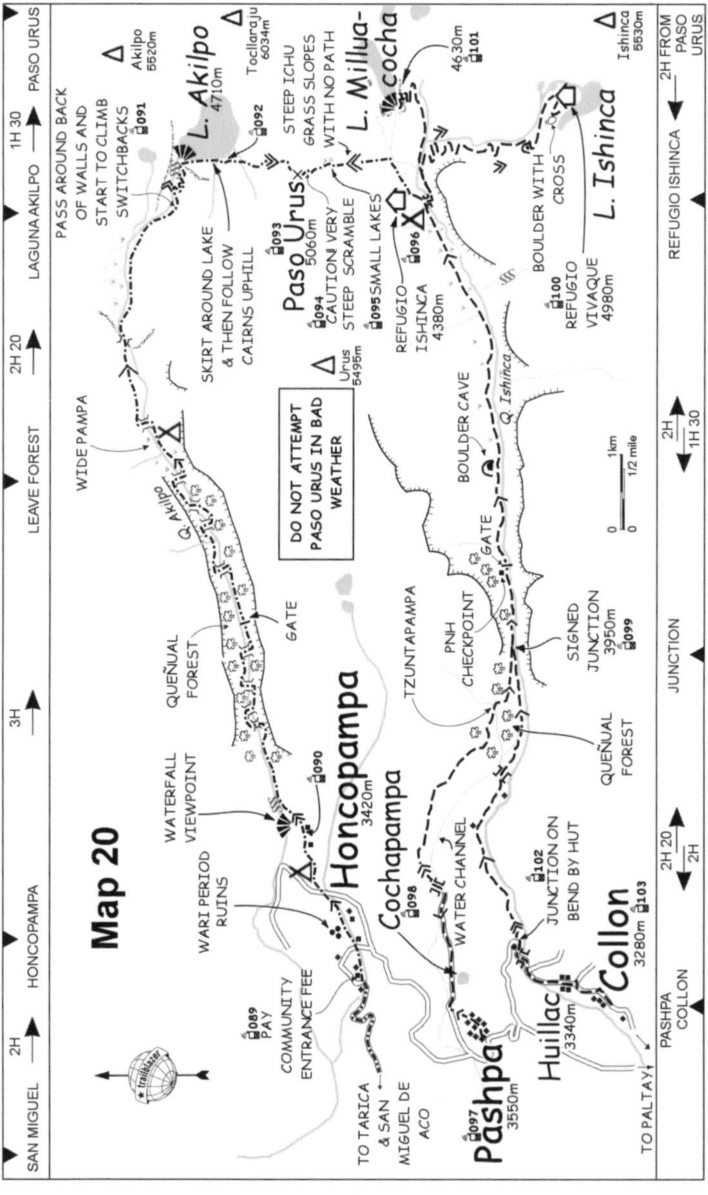
Map 20
SAN MIGUEL
2H
HONCOPAMPA
3H
LEAVE FOREST
2H 20
LAGUNA AKILPO
1H 30
PASO URUS
PASHPA COLLON
2H 20
2H
JUNCTION
2H
1H 30
REFUGIO ISHINCA
2H FROM PASO URUS
089 PAY
COMMUNITY ENTRANCE FEE
TO TARICA & SAN MIGUEL DE ACO
WARI PERIOD RUINS
WATERFALL VIEWPOINT
Honcopampa 3420m
090
QUEÑUAL FOREST
GATE
Q. Akilpo
WIDE PAMPA
SKIRT AROUND LAKE & THEN FOLLOW CAIRNS UPHILL
PASS AROUND BACK OF WALLS AND START TO CLIMB SWITCHBACKS
091
L. Akilpo 4710m
Akilpo 5520m
Tocllaraju 6034m
092
STEEP ICHU GRASS SLOPES WITH NO PATH
Paso Urus 5060m
093
094 CAUTION! VERY STEEP SCRAMBLE
095 SMALL LAKES
Urus 5495m
DO NOT ATTEMPT PASO URUS IN BAD WEATHER
L. Millua-cocha
4630m 101
REFUGIO ISHINCA 4380m
096
BOULDER WITH CROSS
100 REFUGIO VIVAQUE 4980m
L. Ishinca
Ishinca 5530m
Q. Ishinca
BOULDER CAVE
GATE
PNH CHECKPOINT
TZUNTAPAMPA
SIGNED JUNCTION 3950m
099
QUEÑUAL FOREST
Cochapampa
098
WATER CHANNEL
102 JUNCTION ON BEND BY HUT
Collon 3280m 103
Huillac 3340m
097 Pashpa 3550m
TO PALTAY
0 1km
0 1/2 mile

From the hut it takes 1h30 to the Collón/Pashpa junction and 2 hours more to Pashpa or Collón. See Ishinca trek below for details, including side trips to Lagunas Ishinca and Milluacocha.

QUEBRADA AND LAGUNA ISHINCA

Quebrada Ishinca is one of the most visited valleys in the Cordillera Blanca. Popular with climbers attempting Nevados Tocllaraju, Urus and Ishinca, its impressive 360 degree mountain views likewise make it an excellent trekking destination.

QUEBRADA & LAGUNA ISHINCA
- **Start** Pashpa
- **End** Collón
- **Distance** 38km/24 miles
- **Trekking time** 3 days
- **Vertical climb** 1500m/4900ft
- **Max altitude** 4980m/16,350ft
- **Navigation** 1
- **Terrain** 1

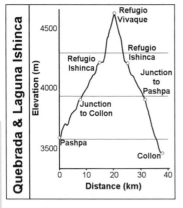

The trailhead villages of Pashpa and Collón are easily accessed from Huaraz, meaning you can be out walking on the trail within an hour of jumping on transport in town. Make sure you are sufficiently acclimatized before heading up this valley, as although it's a gentle climb, the first refugio and official campsite are at nearly 4400m. The existence of two refugios in the valley make it possible to complete this there-and-back trek without camping.

Even if you choose not to stay at Refugio Vivaque (see opposite), the day walk to it for close-up views of milky-green Laguna Ishinca, backdropped by Ranrapalca, is a highlight that shouldn't be missed.

Timing and getting to and from the trailhead

You can begin and end in either Collón or Pashpa. Beginning in Pashpa and ending in Collón makes for a more varied walk with fewer vertical metres to climb. Reaching Refugio Ishinca only takes a day, but

❏ **Refugios**
The Don Bosco Andes 6000 guides (see p60) run five *refugios* in the Cordillera Blanca, providing a touch of Alpine comfort and allowing trekkers to enjoy overnight trips without the need for camping. Huts (half/full board – US$32/37) are open May-September and located in Quebrada Ishinca and at the bases of Pisco, Huascarán and Contrahierbas. All proceeds are funnelled back into helping some of the most deprived campesinos in the Cordillera.

> ❑ **Mountain climbing**
> The Blanca and Huayhuash draw mountaineers from around the world wishing to test themselves on the continent's toughest and most technical 6000ers. There are almost no summits over 5000m which could be considered trekking peaks – even the easier and more popular peaks such as Urus, Ishinca, Vallunaraju and Pisco shouldn't be attempted by those with little experience, unless accompanied by a good guide.

most people choose to include side trips and spend at least three days in the valley.

There are a couple of direct combis daily to each of these villages from Huaraz (1 hour, S/.5, from Puente Quilcay), generally leaving around 07:00 and 13:00. They're hard to pin down; try checking times beforehand. A taxi from Huaraz is around S/.50 to Collón and S/.70 to Cochapampa (above Pashpa and where most groups begin treks).

If you're not rushed for time and can't track down the direct combis, take a northbound combi (10 or E towards Jangas, or one bound for Caraz) and alight at Puente Paltay (20 minutes, S/.2). From here there's very occasional shared transport to Pashpa or Collón (30 minutes, S/.3) – expect a long wait. A taxi from this junction costs around S/.20 to either village.

Preparations Comfortable **Refugio Ishinca** (bunk beds, food and a very basic shop in season, see box opposite) and the basic **Refugio Vivaque** (unmanned but has beds) make it possible to complete this trek without camping gear. If camping, it's best to bring all supplies from Huaraz. At the **campsite**, cattle have acquired a taste for trekking food and can be a pain. Don't leave any tasty morsels unattended outside your tent.

Tickets for PNH can be bought at the guardaparque post at the entrance to Quebrada Ishinca, though it's not always manned.

It's usually easier to find arrieros in Pashpa than Collón.

Pashpa – Laguna Ishinca [Map 20, p115]
From Pashpa's plaza take the path which climbs to the R/E of the church to a 4WD track (15 minutes) on the plateau N of the village. Turn R along the track which has extensive views of the Callejón de Huaylas and peaks from Huandoy to Vallunaraju. Pass Cochapampa after 10 minutes, then veer L onto a wide footpath when the motorable track ends in a further 20 minutes. Pass between stone walls and cross a water channel, sticking to this path all the way to Quebrada Ishinca.

The trail passes a signed junction (15 minutes) to 'Joncopampa', whose ruins can be seen below, before traversing across to Manantial Lachoccuta (45 minutes), a spring by a pampa, where the shady queñual forest begins. Stay L/up at a fork just before reaching the signed Collón/Pashpa junction (35 minutes).

Fifteen minutes of easy walking brings you to a PNH hut which is dwarfed by looming rock towers and pinnacles to the N. Go through the gate beyond and enter the valley's inner reaches. The landscape opens out and the path wanders gently up the valley, making for a lovely riverside walk. Up ahead the Tocllaraju-Palcaraju ice wall comes into view, and occasionally Urus to the N and Ocshapalca to the S reveal themselves. Grassy meadows tempt an early camp, but to minimize the impact on this popular valley please heed PNH rules by only erecting your tent at the official campsite.

From the gate it takes 1h40 to reach **Refugio Ishinca** and attached, free **campsite**, with its two toilet huts. Campers should watch out for small, spiky cacti that will pierce an inflatable sleeping mat or an unsuspecting backside; then allow themselves to be lulled to sleep by the distant roar of avalanches down the active Tocllaraju-Palcaraju face.

Continuing to Laguna Ishinca (3h return)

From the W end of the campsite, cross a small bridge and head upstream for 10 minutes to a signed junction. Go R for Laguna Ishinca; straight goes to Laguna Milluacocha (see below). Zigzag gently upwards for 40 minutes to a flat, boggy area which the path contours round for 10 minutes.

Climb again near a small waterfall and in 10 minutes reach a smaller flat area with views of glaciated Nevado Ishinca (5530m). Twenty minutes of climbing brings you to a junction where a small path heads off L towards this peak and two small lakes at its base. Stay straight and climb for a further 15 minutes to the moraine ridge just above Refugio Vivaque which offers magnificent views of glacial Laguna Ishinca and giant Ranrapalca.

Retracing your steps, it's 1h15 back to Refugio Ishinca.

Side trip from Refugio Ishinca to Laguna Milluacocha (2h return)

Continue straight at the junction 10 minutes into the Laguna Ishinca route, reaching a large, derelict building after a further 30 minutes. Take the path that leads L, up the moraine, from just beyond the building, climbing gentle, sweeping zigzags. It's 20 minutes to the top of the moraine and an excellent viewpoint of turquoise Laguna Milluacocha, as well as serac-etched Tocllaraju.

Exiting from Refugio Ishinca to Collón

Heading back down from Refugio Ishinca, it's an easy 1h30 to the Collón/Pashpa junction. Either retrace your steps to Pashpa, or to stay nearer the Río Paltay head L to Collón (described here).

Continue through queñuales on the main trail to a water channel (25 minutes). Cross, and in a further 15 minutes, having left the forest, cross a bridge over a side river. The path forks 35 minutes later, but both soon meet up again. Less than 10 minutes from the fork the footpath reaches a motorable 4WD track

---

❏ **A Wilcahuaín day walk**
For another nice gentle introductory walk, catch a combi from Huaraz (Av Bolivar, S/.1.50) to Wilcahuaín. Visit both sets of ruins, then wander along the deserted road to Café Yurac Yacu (2 hours). After lunch, descend to Marian (1 hour) and catch combi 15 back to town. See map p181 and cycle route p178 for more details.

on a hairpin bend. Go L to Huillac (20 minutes), a small village with little in the way of public transport. To improve your chances of a lift, carry on down to the larger Collón (15 minutes), by turning R by a 'No Arrojar Basura' sign at the far end of Huillac. Continue a few minutes past Collón to rejoin the 'main' road; wait for transport there. If your luck is out, the walk down to Paltay takes 1h15.

LAGUNA WILCACOCHA

The half-day return hike to Laguna Wilcacocha makes an ideal first acclimatization hike in the Callejón de Huaylas. From the main road just south of Huaraz, a wide and easy-to-follow path leads up into the Cordillera Negra, and a small plateau at 3700m housing the lake. From the peaceful shores there are superb, expansive views of the whole western side of the Cordillera Blanca – pick out the peaks from Huandoy in the north, to Shacsha and beyond.

LAGUNA WILCACOCHA
● **Start & end** Chihuipampa
● **Distance** 7km/4 miles
● **Trekking time** 3 hours
● **Vertical climb** 600m/2000ft
● **Max altitude** 3720m/12,200ft
● **Navigation** 1
● **Terrain** 1

Getting to the trailhead
The trailhead at Puente Santa Cruz in Chihuipampa is just a 15 minute ride on combi 10 or E (S/.1, direction Bedoya) from the centre of Huaraz. The walk isn't in PNH, so no tickets are needed.

Chihuipampa – Laguna Wilcacocha   [Map 21]
From the main road, cross the bridge over the Río Santa and begin climbing up a 4WD track. After a couple of minutes, turn L up a wide, steep footpath.

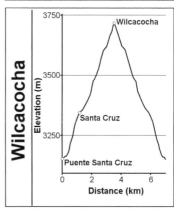

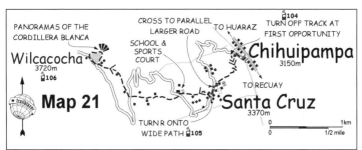

Map 21

HIKING ROUTES & MAPS

In 30 minutes reach a rough 4WD track in the village of Santa Cruz; cross the track to a larger road just behind and turn L/SW. Continue for 5 minutes, past houses, before leaving the motorable track by turning R/NW onto another wide footpath, under power lines.

This passes a sports court (15 minutes), twice crosses the 4WD track which is zigzagging up the hill and leads all the way to Wilcacocha (1 hour from the court).

Descending to the main road takes 1 hour.

Quebradas above Huaraz

There is a myriad of hiking options in the Blanca near Huaraz. As well as the three trips described in detail here, you could explore Quebradas Llaca and Rajucolta, or wander up to Lagunas Mullaca or Ahuac.

Getting to and from the trailhead

Treks in Quebradas Churup, Shallap and Quilcayhuanca can all be started in either Llupa or Pitec. Llupa is easier and cheaper to reach on public transport from Huaraz, but lengthens the walks by 2 hours on the climb and 1 hour on the descent. As Llupa-Pitec is such a pleasant route, a good option is to take transport up to Pitec, then walk down to Llupa at the end of your hike.

Combis for Llupa (30 minutes, S/.3 – ask for '*Cruce Pitec*'), leave when full throughout the day from the *grifo* (petrol station) on Av Gamarra in Huaraz. They are more frequent in the early morning, around 07:00, and because of the popularity of this combi route with trekkers, drivers usually charge a tourist price of S/.5. Some drivers may agree to continue to Pitec for an increased fare (usually S/.10pp, minimum five people).

Taxi costs vary with the quality of vehicle and negotiating skills – expect S/.30 to Llupa and double that to Pitec. The last combi down from Llupa leaves around 18:00.

Preparations
All three hikes are within PNH – you can buy tickets from the guardaparque at Pitec. There's a very basic shop in Llupa, but nowhere to buy supplies higher up on any of the hikes (despite appearing on many maps, Pitec is just a few scattered houses, with no facilities). See box p62 for nearby accommodation options.

Llupa – Pitec (4km each way)

From '*Bodega El Cruce*' in Llupa, take the R fork, up a 4WD track. After 25 minutes go R, off the track, by a blue water cistern, climbing steps on an ancient path. Rejoin and follow the 4WD track, leaving it again by going R/up onto a broad, earthy path, just before the ruined walls of a house (20 minutes). Soon cross the 4WD track again and continue climbing on steps. Ask one of the many campesinos in the area if you need to confirm the way. Considering the proximity to Huaraz, it's a surprisingly rural walk to Pitec, a further 1h15 uphill.

LAGUNA CHURUP

The half-day hike to Laguna Churup is one of the Cordillera Blanca's popular acclimatization trips. It's a largely straightforward route; however, there are a number of short, rocky scrambles, three of which have metal cables to assist hikers. These are not difficult, but care needs to be taken, particularly in wet or icy conditions. The altitude of the lake means that this should not be a first walk in the area, and, if arriving from sea level, certainly shouldn't be attempted within the first two days.

Timing

From Pitec, this is a half day walk; it can be made into a full day by beginning and ending in Llupa (see opposite).

Pitec – Laguna Churup
[Map 22, p122]

In Pitec, take the signposted Churup path, which climbs, then flattens off and heads into Quebrada Churup. The gradients crank up again to a small

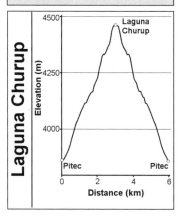

LAGUNA CHURUP
● **Start & end** Pitec
● **Distance** 6km/4 miles
● **Trekking time** 2½ – 4 hours
● **Vertical climb** 650m/2100ft
● **Max altitude** 4470m/14,650ft
● **Navigation** 1
● **Terrain** 3

camp spot by a cascade and are even steeper on the short climb over rocky slabs to the lake. The shores of Laguna Churup (1h30-3h) make a great lunch spot; with slightly improved views if you climb a bit to the R/SE.

Side trip to Laguna Churupita (1h30 return)

For close-up views of Nevado Churup and panoramic views of its namesake lake, continue round Laguna Churup's NW shore, then climb steep moraine to Laguna Churupita.

Returning from the SW end of Laguna Churup, it's 1 hour back to Pitec.

LAGUNA SHALLAP

Virtually no-one hikes in Quebrada Shallap, and we're not quite sure why. True, it's a long way from Pitec to the bean-green laguna, but with little vertical ascent this makes an excellent acclimatization walk. The quebrada is in many ways more modest and under-

LAGUNA SHALLAP
● **Start & end** Pitec
● **Distance** 23km/14 miles
● **Trekking time** 6-7 hours
● **Vertical climb** 550m/1800ft
● **Max altitude** 4280m/14,050ft
● **Navigation** 1
● **Terrain** 1

HIKING ROUTES & MAPS

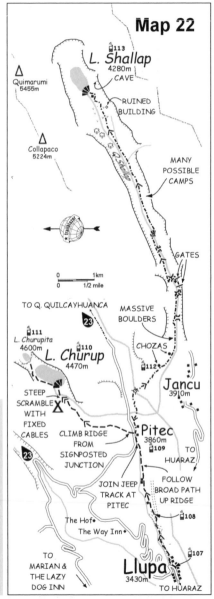

Map 22

stated than its neighbours –
the cliffs are lower and less
vertical; 5843m San Juan is
the highest peak on view. But
in one respect Shallap wins
hands down: big boulders.
Leviathans the size of (blue)
whales laze haphazardly all
along the valley floor. **Camp**
spots are plentiful on the
pampa above 4000m for those
who'd prefer to turn it into an
easy overnight trek.

Timing and getting to and from the trailhead
It's a long day from Pitec (see
p120) so start early. If beginning in Llupa, the trip takes
two days. Entering from
Jancu on the S side of the
Shallap river valley renders
the hike slightly shorter than
from Pitec, but there's very
little public transport. A taxi
to Jancu from Huaraz costs
around S/.80.

Pitec – Laguna Shallap [Map 22]
From Pitec, head R, to the S of
the 4WD track that leads into
Quebrada Quilcayhuanca, and
descend a footpath to the Río
Quilcay (20 minutes). Cross
the bridge, then climb gently
over the hump between valleys, following the main trail
past some chozas into
Quebrada Shallap (appropri-
ately, Quechua for 'boulder').
At a fork (50 minutes) stay
straight, aiming at the heart of
the quebrada (R crosses a
bridge and is the path from
Jancu). Stick to the main trail,

crossing the river three times on bridges, to Laguna Shallap (2h30). Climb the moraine path to the R/S for better lake views and a large cave. It's 3 hours back to Pitec.

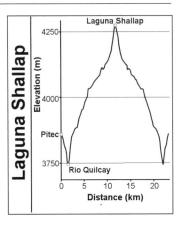

QUILCAYHUANCA – COJUP

Those looking for a quieter, more accessible and more demanding alternative to Santa Cruz, without compromising on dramatic scenery, will find this trek fits the bill. One of the best routes for spotting condors, you can camp near glaciers, under the gaze of giant peaks, only a day out of Huaraz. Navigation skills are required as locating the trail to high camps in each quebrada is not straightforward. Paso Huapi is the highest pass described in this book, so ensure you have sufficient acclimatization before attempting it.

Timing and getting to and from the trailhead
The trek is usually undertaken in three days or a leisurely four from Llupa (see p120), but the very acclimatized and fit should be able to complete it in two, by hiring transport to and from the entrances to each of the quebradas (a taxi from Huaraz to either *portón*

QUILCAYHUANCA – COJUP
- **Start** Llupa
- **End** Marian
- **Distance** 47km/29 miles
- **Trekking time** 3 or 4 days
- **Vertical climb** 1800m/5900ft
- **Max altitude** 5080m/16,650ft
- **Navigation** 3
- **Terrain** 2

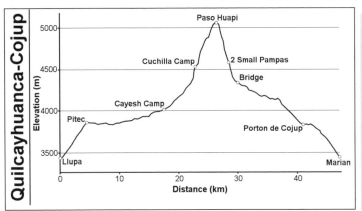

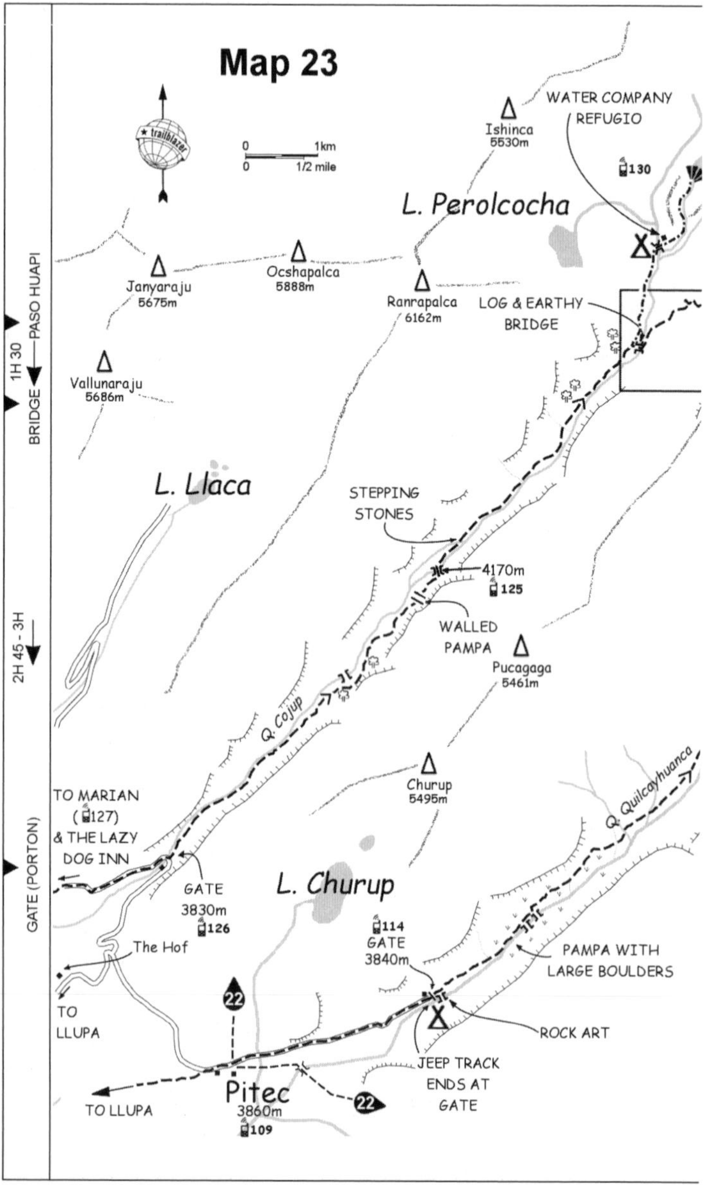

Map 23

trailblazer

0   1km
0   1/2 mile

WATER COMPANY
REFUGIO

Ishinca
5530m

🏠130

L. Perolcocha

Janyaraju
5675m

Ocshapalca
5888m

Ranrapalca
6162m

LOG & EARTHY
BRIDGE

Vallunaraju
5686m

L. Llaca

STEPPING
STONES

4170m
🏠125

WALLED
PAMPA

Pucagaga
5461m

Q. Cojup

Churup
5495m

Q. Quilcayhuanca

TO MARIAN
(🏠127)
& THE LAZY
DOG INN

GATE
3830m
🏠126

L. Churup

🏠114
GATE
3840m

PAMPA WITH
LARGE BOULDERS

The Hof

TO
LLUPA

ROCK ART

22

Pitec
3860m
🏠109

TO LLUPA

JEEP TRACK
ENDS AT
GATE

22

BRIDGE ◄── PASO HUAPI   1H 30

2H 45 - 3H

GATE (PORTON)

HIKING ROUTES & MAPS

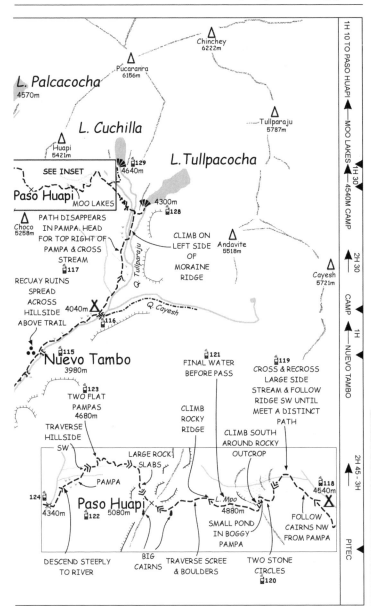

L. Palcacocha
4570m

Chinchey
6222m

Pucaranra
6156m

Tullparaju
5787m

L. Cuchilla

L. Tullpacocha

Huapi
5421m

SEE INSET

129
4640m

Paso Huapi

MOO LAKES

4300m
128

CLIMB ON
LEFT SIDE
OF
MORAINE
RIDGE

Choco
5258m

PATH DISAPPEARS
IN PAMPA. HEAD
FOR TOP RIGHT OF
PAMPA & CROSS
STREAM
117

Andavite
5518m

Cayesh
5721m

RECUAY RUINS
SPREAD
ACROSS
HILLSIDE
ABOVE TRAIL

4040m

116

Q. Cayesh

Nuevo Tambo
3980m

115

121
FINAL WATER
BEFORE PASS

119
CROSS & RECROSS
LARGE SIDE
STREAM & FOLLOW
RIDGE SW UNTIL
MEET A DISTINCT
PATH

123
TWO FLAT
PAMPAS
4680m

TRAVERSE
HILLSIDE
SW

CLIMB
ROCKY
RIDGE

CLIMB SOUTH
AROUND ROCKY
OUTCROP

LARGE ROCK
SLABS

PAMPA

124

Paso Huapi
122 5080m

L. Moo
4880m

118
4540m

4340m

SMALL POND
IN BOGGY
PAMPA

FOLLOW
CAIRNS NW
FROM PAMPA

DESCEND STEEPLY
TO RIVER

BIG
CAIRNS

TRAVERSE SCREE
& BOULDERS

TWO STONE
CIRCLES
120

1H 10 TO PASO HUAPI | MOO LAKES | 1H 30 | 4540M CAMP | 2H 30 | CAMP | 1H | NUEVO TAMBO | 2H 45 – 3H | PITEC

HIKING ROUTES & MAPS

(gate), is around S/.60-80). It's best to trek in the anti-clockwise direction described here, due to the steepness of the Cojup side of Paso Huapi.

Combi 15 leaves regularly from Marian to Huaraz (20 minutes, S/.1.50) until around 18:00.

Preparations You could try arranging mules in Llupa, or with a Huaraz agency, but they can't cross the pass, having to take the long route round instead. Bring all supplies.

Pitec – Paso Huapi – Marian   [Map 23, pp124-5]
See p120 for description from Llupa to Pitec. From Pitec, follow the 4WD track for 50 minutes to the portón guarding the quebrada's entrance – jump the wall if the gate is locked and unattended. The valley is wider than others in the area, with lush pampa on the valley floor. Nevado Andavite (Chopiraju on *Alpenvereinskarte*) commands the valley ahead on the gentle 2 hour walk to Nuevo Tambo. These early-Recuay period ruins, mostly *chullpas,* on slopes above the path, are a good spot to spend some time exploring, before continuing 1 hour to a **campsite** and turn-off to Quebrada Cayesh.

> ### Side trip to Quebrada Cayesh (2-3h return)
> It's well worth crossing the bridge near the campsite and wandering into Quebrada Cayesh. The views get better the higher you go – stick to the TL/W side.

The main trail swings into Quebrada Tullparaju and steepens en route to a large pampa (40 minutes), with views of Nevado Chinchey, amongst others. Keep L of the pampa and climb to a smaller grassy pampa. Here the path becomes indistinct – go to the upper end, leaving from the right-hand (NE) corner. Immediately cross the river from Laguna Cuchilla, to climb a clear path on the L/W slopes of the moraine hill in the middle of the valley. After 45 minutes reach another good camp spot on a riverside platform.

> ### Side trip to Laguna Tullpacocha (30 minutes return)
> From the platform, a path heads R/E, contouring round to the retaining wall on Laguna Tullpacocha and views of Tullparaju.

The main path crosses two rivers then climbs broad zigzags for 1 hour to a great **camp** at the base of the moraine enclosing Laguna Cuchilla.

> ### Side trip to Laguna Cuchilla (45 minutes return)
> From camp, cross the stream to the R/E and climb zigzags to the lake and a viewpoint of the immense Pucaranra.

The next section of trail is difficult to follow. From the stone walls at the camp, head L/W and climb for a minute onto a small ridge, where you should veer R/NW, following boulder-top cairns, aiming at horned Nevado Huapi. Continue in a straight line for 25 minutes, slowly gaining altitude and crossing side streams, until you encounter a green side valley with a larger stream cascading out of it. Go L/SW up this, briefly by the river, then follow cairns on the TR/S side of the stream. Climb fairly steeply up the left-hand side of the flat ridge in the foreground ahead, to the L of a rocky outcrop, heading SW. Next, traverse L/SW, going to the L of a second small ridge (20 minutes).

Here the path becomes clear again and climbs for 10 minutes past two stone circles to a lake and boggy pampa. Turn L/SW and climb steeply to the 'Moo' lakes (30 minutes). This last possible (but very high) **camp** before the pass sports wonderful views – to the W the ridge separating you from Quebrada Cojup is visible (the pass is out of sight, round a corner), while to the NE and E are Pucaranra and Tullparaju.

The path bisects the two largest lakes, then climbs to a scree and boulder field of sheep-sized rocks. It's largely clear, traversing W across rocky ground, with regular cairns to mark the way. Look back, and with a little imagination the lakes spell out 'Moo'. After 1h10 of mostly gentle climbing, reach Paso Huapi. Ranrapalca pokes its head out first, while Nevado Ishinca appears little more than a bump on the ridge ahead. Palcaraju dominates the head of the Cojup valley.

Descend straight down on a steep path. Soon a refugio and Laguna Palcacocha appear – the obvious moraine gap revealing where the lake disgorged its contents in 1941 (see p104). After 20 minutes the path begins heading R/N, crossing small boulder fields and steeply descending a rock outcrop to a stream (first water since 'Moo' lakes). Follow this downhill; as the terrain improves, the path becomes less obvious.

Thirty minutes of continued descent brings you to a pampa, the highest **camping** possibility on this side. Drop to a second small pampa, then go L/SW on a path that traverses, crossing the stream and zigzagging steeply down a ridge which is barer than earlier grassy slopes.

After 25 minutes reach the top part of a pampa; continue down to the far end and descend on a wide path to a rocky/grassy area by the main river. Walk downstream, before crossing a bridge and climbing briefly to the main path on the N side (20 minutes).

Side trip to Laguna Palcacocha (2h return)
Go up valley to the *Ministerio de Agua* refugio (unmanned, not open to tourists) and climb beyond to the bright turquoise waters of Laguna Palcacocha. The final part is an aluvión and waterworks mess – but hovering above are the fabulous summits of Palcaraju and Pucaranra.

From the junction, the main path out of the quebrada leads downriver, passing a couple of **camp spots**. After 1h10 cross a bridge to the S side of the main river,

❏ **Akilpo – Ishinca – Cojup – Quilcayhuanca traverse**
For a really exciting high altitude trek, try this five-day route over three 5000m passes. The section between Ishinca and Cojup involves glacial travel, so hire a guide from Huaraz who's well acquainted with the current condition of the route.

HIKING ROUTES & MAPS

from where it's 1h40, wandering past bus-sized boulders, to the portón and the road.

On guided trips, transport will meet you here. Otherwise, Llupa (L) and Marian (R) are roughly equidistant, 2 hours away (see map p181). It's usually easier to find shared transport back to Huaraz from the latter.

Conchucos

CHACAS – HUARI

This relatively easy trek between two pleasant Conchucos towns is the only multi-day route in this book that doesn't approach the peaks. Follow a wide path through forest before climbing onto the high puna with its green, ichu grass-covered slopes and folded rock strata. Distant snowy mountain views await near 4500m Paso San Bartolomé, before a gradual descent to Laguna Purhuay, accessible by road from Huari.

CHACAS – HUARI
- **Start** Chacas
- **End** Huari
- **Distance** 39km/24 miles
- **Trekking time** 2 or 3 days
- **Vertical climb** 1500m/4900ft
- **Max altitude** 4520m/14,850ft
- **Navigation** 1
- **Terrain** 1

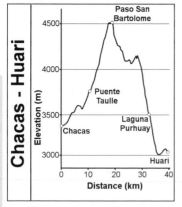

Timing and getting to and from the trailhead

The trek takes two days, or a very leisurely three.

Renzo and El Veloz both have early morning Huaraz to Chacas buses (3h30, S/.16); book a day in advance. Sandoval and Olguita have multiple daily buses from Huari to Huaraz (4h, S/.15), however it's a good option to extend this trek from Huari to Huántar or even Chavín (see following treks in Quebradas Rurichinchay, Rurec and Carhuascancha) for an excellent longer tour of the southern end of the Callejón de Conchucos.

Preparations Supplies can be bought in Chacas, though the selection is much more limited than in Huaraz. The trek passes through PNH; the guardaparque at Laguna Purhuay can sell you a ticket.

Chacas – Paso San Bartolomé – Huari
[Map 24, p130 & Map 25, p131]

Leave Chacas' precious plaza from the SE corner, going one block over to Jr Buenos Aires and turning R. When the paving ends by *Vidrería Milla*, turn L, then R at the end of the street, leaving town. After 30 minutes fork L at a PNH sign – the 4WD track becomes a broad footpath and enters a green quebrada. Easy walking for 1h30 brings you to a bridge over a deep little quebrada – turn L at the adjacent gate and signed junction.

The trail traverses above the main river, through forest alive with bromeliads. Five minutes from the gate, take the middle fork at a trident junction, and 1h15 later cross concrete Puente Taulle which spans a large side river. Soon after, follow Quebrada Asnocohuana signs L at a junction.

Continue up the valley on easy terrain for 1 hour to another signed junction. Go straight/R to Quebrada Empedrado (unless you want to camp, in which case descend L towards Quebrada Pucallullimpa – the first possible **camp spot** since Chacas). The scenery finally opens out as the path curves R into a side valley, away from the triangular rocky hill ahead. In 20 minutes reach another junction and go R, to Paso San Bartolomé, leaving the main valley.

Climb easily by the river; above, waterfalls flash down cliffs to the R/W. After 50 minutes, reach a camp spot – the best of the few sites on the Chacas side of the pass – just before crossing the river.

Behind, the distant Contrahierbas massif appears, followed by Huascarán and Chopicalqui as the path climbs for 40 minutes to a high point, before traversing 20 minutes to modest Paso San Bartolomé. All around, folded rocky layers, some horizontal, others vertical, punctuate the green slopes. Ahead is a spectacular, concertinaed rock formation.

Descend into a valley, passing a good **camp** by a small laguna after 20 minutes. Proceed down the TL/E side for 30 minutes before descending and crossing a pampa to a house, to pick up the path behind, which begins a long traverse towards Laguna Purhuay. Meander in and out of side valleys, climbing and descending for 1h30 to a large side valley with decent **camping**.

Continue for 45 minutes to a pampa (no water) with a stone corral. Pass through a gate – ahead a ribbon of waterfall laces its way down a side valley, while the motorway of a path descends steeply for 45 minutes to a junction near Laguna Purhuay. Go straight (L heads N along the lake shore) and soon hit the road by a bus stop. **Camping**, **toilets**, a guardaparque and boat rides can be found at the lake; possibly also transport to Huari.

If not, follow the road or shortcuts to Acopalca (1 hour). This village, on the Huari to San Luis road, has basic accommodation and many information boards. Notable local sights include the Maria Jiray waterfall (1 hour away) and the roadside cave where unsociable villagers were formerly incarcerated. It's 1 hour on foot, or a 10 minute combi ride to Huari.

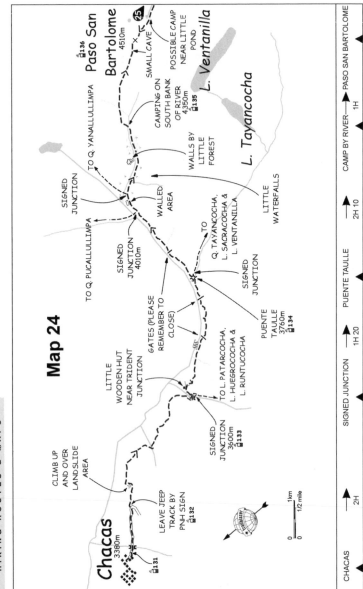

Map 24

Chacas
3380m
🏔131

LEAVE JEEP
TRACK BY
PNH SIGN
🏔132

CLIMB UP
AND OVER
LANDSLIDE
AREA

SIGNED
JUNCTION
3600m
🏔133

TO L. PATARCOCHA,
L. HUEGROCOCHA &
L. RUNTUCOCHA

LITTLE
WOODEN HUT
NEAR TRIDENT
JUNCTION

GATES (PLEASE
REMEMBER TO
CLOSE)

PUENTE
TAULLE
3760m
🏔134

SIGNED
JUNCTION

TO
Q. TAYANCOCHA,
L. SACRACOCHA &
L. VENTANILLA

TO Q. PUCALLULLIMPA

SIGNED
JUNCTION
4010m

SIGNED
JUNCTION

TO Q. YANALLULLIMPA

WALLED
AREA

WALLS BY
LITTLE FOREST

LITTLE
WATERFALLS

CAMPING ON
SOUTH BANK
OF RIVER
4350m
🏔135

SMALL CAVE

POSSIBLE CAMP
NEAR LITTLE
POND

Paso San
Bartolome
4510m
🏔136

L. Ventanilla

L. Tayancocha

0   1km
0   1/2 mile

◀ CHACAS   2H →   SIGNED JUNCTION ◀   1H 20 →   PUENTE TAULLE ◀   2H 10 →   CAMP BY RIVER ◀   1H →   PASO SAN BARTOLOME ◀

HIKING ROUTES & MAPS

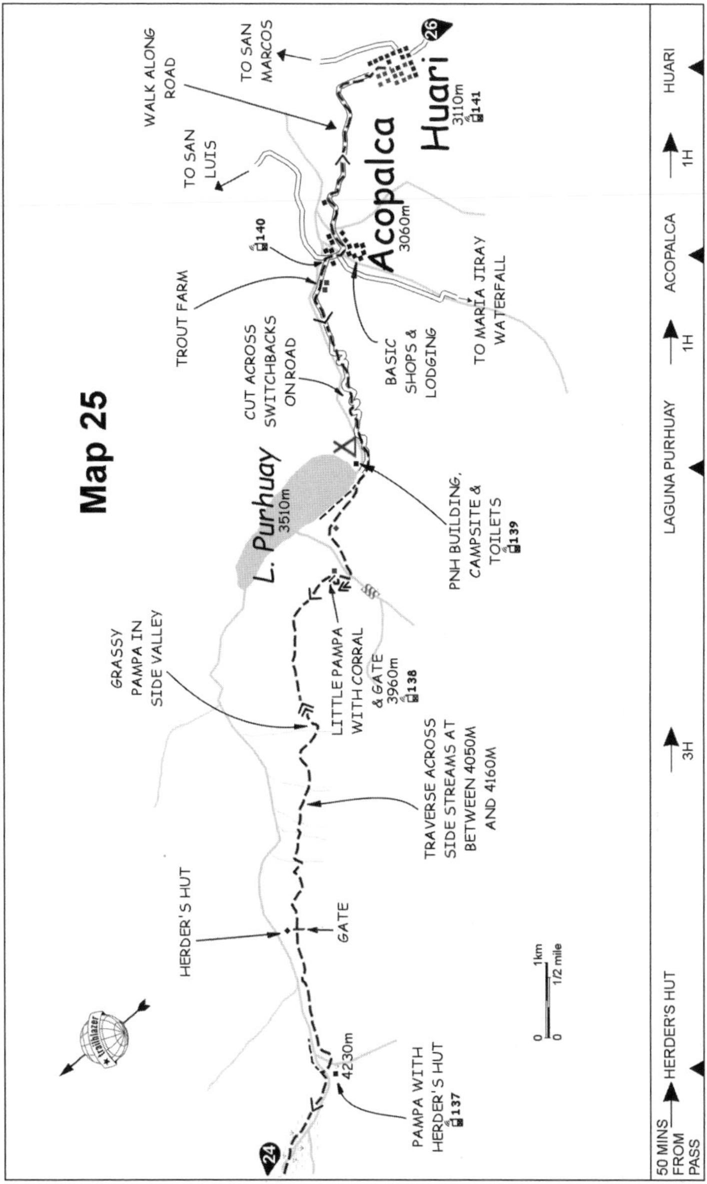

Map 25

TO SAN MARCOS

26

WALK ALONG ROAD

TO SAN LUIS

Huari 3110m ⌂141

HUARI

Acopalca 3060m

⌂140

TROUT FARM

CUT ACROSS SWITCHBACKS ON ROAD

BASIC SHOPS & LODGING

TO MARIA JIRAY WATERFALL

ACOPALCA

1H

L. Purhuay 3510m

PNH BUILDING, CAMPSITE & TOILETS ⌂139

GRASSY PAMPA IN SIDE VALLEY

LITTLE PAMPA WITH CORRAL & GATE 3960m ⌂138

LAGUNA PURHUAY

1H

TRAVERSE ACROSS SIDE STREAMS AT BETWEEN 4050M AND 4160M

3H

HERDER'S HUT

GATE

4230m

PAMPA WITH HERDER'S HUT ⌂137

0 1km
0 1/2 mile

24

50 MINS FROM PASS

HERDER'S HUT

HIKING ROUTES & MAPS

QUEBRADA RURICHINCHAY

The pastoral wander from Huari to Mallas through thriving traditional villages is a delight. There are views of green, eucalyptus-studded hillsides and serrated rocky ridges, and plenty of jovial campesinos to engage in chat. After entering Quebrada Rurichinchay, the route follows a 4WD track to an abandoned mine, before climbing further to some paradise pampas. It's a mission to reach Lagunas Rurichinchay – but persevere and the intermittent cow paths over tricky terrain bring you out at the lakes, beneath Nevado Copap's layered, zebra-striped south face.

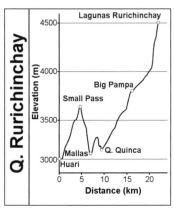

QUEBRADA RURICHINCHAY
- **Start & end** Huari
- **Distance** 56km/35 miles
- **Trekking time** 3 days
- **Vertical climb** 3000m/9800ft
- **Max altitude** 4560m/14,950ft
- **Navigation** 2
- **Terrain** 2

Timing and getting to and from the trailhead

The trek takes at least three days return from Huari (p72), though can be shortened by taking transport to or from Mallas. There's only one combi a week from Huari to Mallas, on Sundays; best take a taxi (around S/.50). See p60 for details on Huaraz to Huari buses.

Preparations The top part of Quebrada Rurichinchay is within PNH, however there's no checkpost. The 4WD road to the abandoned mine camp half way up the valley is almost all rideable, making this a good trip to do as a biking/hiking combination. Buy all supplies in Huari.

Huari – Lagunas Rurichinchay – Huari   **[Map 26, pp134-5]**

From Huari's Plaza de Armas, head to the Mallas road in the SW corner of town. At a bridge (15 minutes) take a footpath signposted 'Buenos Aires' which climbs above the road. Follow the next BsAs sign, continuing straight/L at a BsAs/Cushin signpost (30 minutes), on a rising traverse towards Yakya. In 1 hour, the path meets the road to Yakya by a wooden cross – go R. The road forks (15 minutes) at the far end of this large village – go R, to a small pass (30 minutes) by a water channel.

Don't take the trail that leads R just before the channel, instead continue over the pass, and take the R fork immediately after. After 15 minutes, go L onto a large path, leaving the 4WD track, and continue the descent to Mallas (25 minutes). Turn R on hitting the road and continue through the village for 20 minutes to the trailhead behind the football pitch.

The path for Quebrada Rurichinchay leaves to the R of a row of houses (one a basic **shop**), then climbs and descends to avoid rocky outcrops on the steep N slopes of the quebrada. There's a possible **camp** just before crossing the side stream in Quebrada Quinca (1 hour), and 10 minutes later the path joins the 4WD road to the abandoned mine camp. Follow the road for 1 hour to a decent **campsite**, after which there are many **water sources** but no good camp spots for the 1h30 walk to the bridge by the mine camp.

Leave the scarred area surrounding the mine behind and continue on the TL/N side of the river on a footpath, climbing to a large pampa (45 minutes). Here, cross the bridge to the TR/S side. Excellent **camping** opportunities abound on the way to crossing the river (20 minutes) from Laguna Yuraccocha (Chalhuacocha on the *Alpenvereinskarte*). It's apparently possible to clamber up to this lake, but there's no path and any route would be steep and overgrown.

Continue up the main valley, crossing pampas for 1 hour on indistinct paths, to the river emanating from gorgeous, fluted Nevado Chinchey Norte (which is to the L/W). Hop this, then stay low to the end of the pampa (10 minutes). At first sight, the existence of a route forward would seem unlikely, however head L for the base of a small grassy ramp. Here a tiny path snakes its way steeply up through woods, to emerge onto a higher plateau by the roaring river (50 minutes).

Proceed up valley on draining terrain – a mix of vegetated pampa and rocky moraine – over small ridges and false tops. There's no real path, just start-stop trails made by cattle which somehow have penetrated into this part of the valley. It's 1 hour to a high point overlooking Lagunas Rurichinchay; a good spot for a picnic and well-earned rest.

Descending takes 2h45 to the mine camp, a further 1h45 to the junction where the footpath to Mallas leaves the 4WD track and 3h30 more to Huari.

Alternative ending: link to Quebrada Rurec and Huántar

Continue down the 4WD road after ignoring the Mallas path turn-off and in 40 minutes reach the Mallas-Huántar road. Turn R for Quebrada Rurec (see below).

QUEBRADA RUREC (CONCHUCOS)

This trek explores Quebrada Rurec, a little visited valley in southern Conchucos (not to be confused with the valley of the same name near Olleros) which is quilted with wild, verdant forest. The route only has views of a few snowy peaks, however those craving way-off-the-beaten-path trekking will be in their element; peace and tranquillity will be your

QUEBRADA RUREC (CONCHUCOS)
● **Start & end** Huántar
● **Distance** 32km/20 miles
● **Trekking time** 2 days
● **Vertical climb** 1200m/3900ft
● **Max altitude** 4220m/13,850ft
● **Navigation** 2
● **Terrain** 1

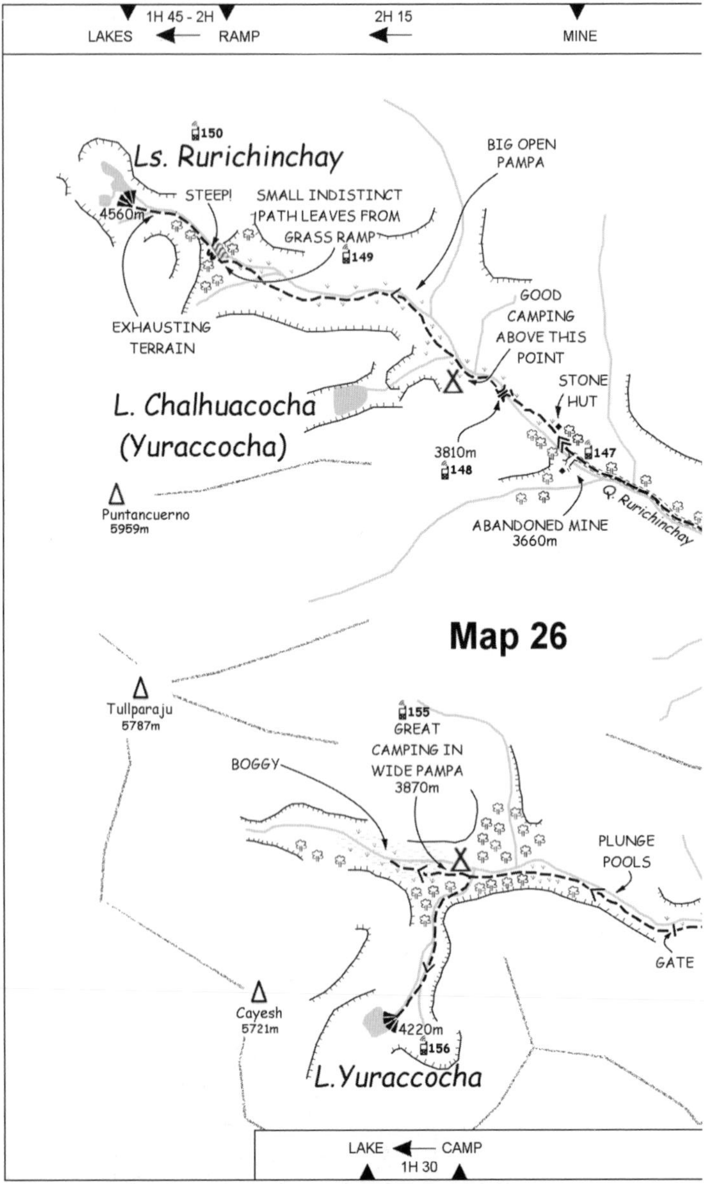

1H 45 - 2H
LAKES ◄— RAMP

2H 15
◄— MINE

🏕150
Ls. Rurichinchay

BIG OPEN PAMPA

STEEP!
4560m

SMALL INDISTINCT PATH LEAVES FROM GRASS RAMP
🏕149

GOOD CAMPING ABOVE THIS POINT

EXHAUSTING TERRAIN

STONE HUT

L. Chalhuacocha (Yuraccocha)

3810m
🏕148

🏕147

Q. Rurichinchay

△ Puntancuerno 5959m

ABANDONED MINE 3660m

Map 26

△ Tullparaju 5787m

🏕155
GREAT CAMPING IN WIDE PAMPA 3870m

BOGGY

PLUNGE POOLS

GATE

△ Cayesh 5721m

4220m
🏕156

L.Yuraccocha

LAKE ◄— CAMP
1H 30

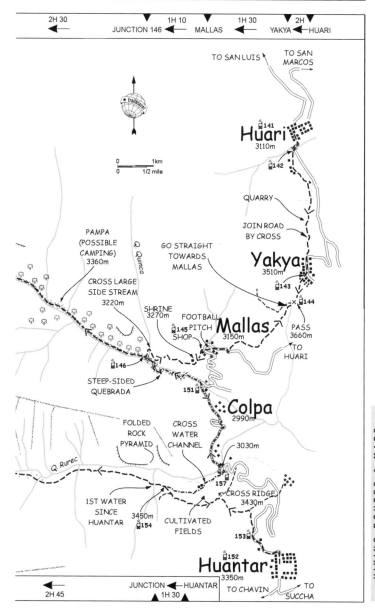

HIKING ROUTES & MAPS

only companions. Venturing into a well-guarded side valley deep in the heart of the main quebrada, it's possible to reach Laguna Yuraccocha, under the towering gaze of Nevado Cayesh. As one of the Blanca's lowest altitude multi-day treks, this is a good acclimatization option, though it's also the central part of a wonderful longer route from Olleros or Carpa to Chacas.

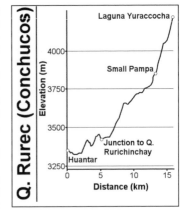

Timing and getting to and from the trailhead
The trek takes two days, with a camp on the pampa near the head of Quebrada Rurec. To reach Huántar from Huaraz, first head to San Marcos on a combi/colectivo (3h/2h30, S/.20/25, from the Chavín stop on Jr Bolognesi) then find a combi (1h, S/.5) onwards to Huántar. Usually it's necessary to change in Succha (which can also be reached from Huaraz on a Huari-bound bus (4h, S/.12)) and wait there for transport up the hill to Huántar.

Preparations Supplies, basic restaurants and accommodation can be found in Huántar. The trek is within PNH, but there's no checkpost.

Huántar – Laguna Yuraccocha – Huántar   [Map 26, pp134-5]
From the cute Plaza de Armas in Huántar, wander N along the road to Mallas. After 10 minutes pass the 'welcome to Huántar' sign, and 10 minutes later leave the road, turning L onto a wide path at the end of a long line of eucalyptus (which are R of the road).

Meet a larger path at a hairpin (15 minutes) and turn L, heading towards the quebrada on a slow rising traverse. Stay straight, on the lower main trail at a high point and junction (50 minutes); then 5 minutes later reach another junction on a ridge. Stay straight here too – R/down is the path which connects to Quebrada Rurichinchay (see Alternative route opposite).

Descend slightly to the first possible **camp** (10 minutes), with **water**, since Huántar. The quebrada is vertical here, with the river far, far below. Over on the N side is an amazing folded triangle of rocky layers.

Continue up valley, passing many pampas carpeted with daisy-like *werneria nubigena*. Red bromeliads cling to the western faces of cliffs on both sides of the valley and there are plenty of side streams and forested sections of trail. Stay on the S side of the valley, ignoring small bridges over the main river, and in 2 hours arrive at a large pampa with views of Nevado Cayesh. From here it's a 30 minute climb to reach the river flowing down from Laguna Yuraccocha.

Shortly after crossing the last branch of this river is a small pampa. It's possible to continue up the main valley a bit further, but the views don't really improve and the way is boggy. A better alternative is to **camp**, then climb to Laguna Yuraccocha in the morning. The path to this lovely lake heads up the grassy slope just after the last branch of river, slicing through forest on a good trail before emerging onto more open ground. Follow the path of least resistance, veering R/W, towards Nevado Cayesh's snow and ice pockmarked E face, to reach the lake (1h30).

It takes 45 minutes back to the main valley, 2h15 more to the trail junction to Quebrada Rurichinchay and a further 1h20 to Huántar.

Alternative route: connecting to Quebrada Rurichinchay

From the trail junction on the ridge, descend on a good, often steep, path. After 30 minutes cross a water channel and continue down for 15 minutes to the virtually unused road. Turn L and follow this, or shortcuts, for 1 hour to the bridge over Río Rurichinchay. Immediately after, take the 4WD track which heads up into the quebrada. It's 45 minutes to the junction where the footpath from Mallas joins (see map p135).

QUEBRADA CARHUASCANCHA

Carhuascancha flaunts an embarrassment of riches: more than 20 lakes, many water-falls and a gaggle of snowy peaks which include mighty Huantsan, the highest peak in the southern Cordillera Blanca. It's a spectacular quebrada and probably the finest rarely-trekked trek in the range. At the business end of the valley the hike can feel like a procession from one amazingly-sited camp to the next, but the walking really makes you work for those views.

> **QUEBRADA CARHUASCANCHA**
> - **Start** Chavín
> - **End** San Marcos
> - **Distance** 55km/34 miles +
> - **Trekking time** 4-5 days
> - **Vertical climb** 2300m/7500ft
> - **Max altitude** 4780m/15,700ft
> - **Navigation** 3
> - **Terrain** 3

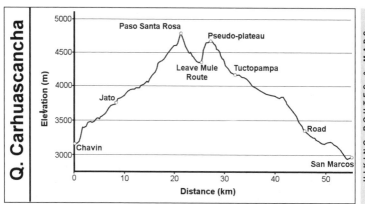

There are several route options, the best of which is a four- to five-day loop from Chavín to San Marcos, via Paso Santa Rosa. This is a demanding route, with tricky navigation in places and many sections over challenging terrain with no paths. The main alternative is an easier there-and-back three day walk up the valley which still offers excellent lake and peak views.

Timing and getting to and from the trailhead

See p60 for getting to Chavín/San Marcos from Huaraz.

Beginning in Chavín, the trek to San Marcos will take most people five days, though it's possible to lop off a day by taking a taxi to Chichucancha or Jato (30 minutes, S/.40), then by finding transport to San Marcos from Yurayacu or Acopara at the end of the walk.

Sticking to the there-and-back Carhuascancha trek takes three days; hire a taxi from San Marcos to the quebrada entrance (40 minutes, S/.40), if you want to avoid walking this section both ways.

As there are so many lakes and viewpoints in the valley, it's easy to while away extra days visiting all of these. It's also easy to link this trek with others in southern Conchucos such as Quebradas Raria or Rurec, or Olleros – Chavín.

Preparations Most of the trek is within PNH, but there's nowhere on the route to buy a ticket. There are basic shops in the villages from Chavín to Chichucancha and also in Acopara, but nothing higher up – it's best to bring all supplies with you.

Chavín – Paso Santa Rosa – San Marcos   [Map 27, pp140-1]

From Chavín's plaza, head S, passing the ruins, then turn R/W (15 minutes) up a wide path that cuts through Barrio La Florida. After 40 minutes reach the road and follow this into Quebrada Huachecsa. Pass through Nunupata (30 minutes, **homestays** possible – enquire at the tourist office in Chavín) and Lanchan (a further 1 hour) to Chichucancha (30 minutes), where the route to Olleros leads off. Ignore this, sticking to the road awhile before climbing the footpath to Jato (20 minutes).

Keep to the main path through the village, and take the R fork immediately after crossing a wooden bridge over a side river (15 minutes). Cross a bridge over the main river 1h20 later, onto the TL/N side (the main path continues on the TR/S side, but it's not always possible to cross the river safely higher up – one slip and you'd be over a waterfall and far below). The path isn't always clear as it makes its way up valley to Huantsanpampa (40 minutes), an idyllic meadow with excellent camping and mountain views.

Stay on cow paths traversing the N slopes of Quebrada Alhuina, always keeping below queñuales which cram the side valleys, aiming for the far R/N of the ridge that juts into the valley forming a large waterfall. Zigzag tightly up through queñuales to the top of this ridge (1 hour), at which point the good path ends and navigation becomes problematic.

Continue, crossing a small stream in a side valley with a lake (10 minutes), then climb slightly, but remain in grassy areas, not the rocky slabs higher up.

Skirt round rocky protuberances until Nevados Rurec and Huantsan appear in full (15 minutes); here turn up a rock rib on a faint path which climbs N into a side valley towards the pass. The path traverses high above the river and soon Paso Santa Rosa comes into view ahead. It's the low point in the serrated ridge, and from this viewpoint looks more fearsome than it actually is!

After 15 minutes, pass above a large rock shelter and descend via an ablation valley towards a lake in a bowl (15 minutes). Just before reaching the lake, turn R, climbing steeply up a faint path. The path soon disappears and the undulating route weaves between small lakes and boggy *bofedales* (marshy wetlands), aiming at the pass. **Camp spots** in this area (Gitaqok) all come with outstanding views of Huantsan's terrifying E face, which looms large to the W. It's 1 hour from the bowl-lake to the base of the pass and a steep 150m, 30 minute climb on mud and rock shavings to the pass.

❑ **Bovine byways**

Cow paths spring up out of nowhere in most quebradas and disappear equally suddenly. Be wary of following them unthinkingly: the cattle aren't necessarily doing the same trek as you.

The route continues to be pathless on the descent – stick to the TL/W side of the valley, crossing plenty of boggy areas. After 1h15 reach a grassy pampa and a first comfortable campsite, at the base of a large rock turret which is to the L/W.

At the far end of the turret join a path that traverses the L/W slopes; then comes a route choice. For best views turn up the very steep ichu slopes to the L/W upon reaching a boulder perched on an even larger boulder (described here, though going this way there is no path until Tuctopampa). Alternatively follow the mule route, which continues downhill for 1 hour to the main valley. A tough ascent (1h30) brings you to a pseudo-plateau with many small lakes and fantastic mountain views. Huantsan, San Juan and Cayesh dominate the western skyline.

Continue heading W, over hummocks, for 30 minutes to a high point. The ground in this area is covered in ichu grass, but it is just possible to find somewhere to **pitch a tent**, and all sites come with wonderful panoramas.

The easiest way to get down to Tuctopampa is to head NW to a pampa, skirting round and down without crossing the river from Laguna Tumarina. But to visit this lake and Laguna Tumagarañon, stay L/SW. It takes 1 hour of rough walking to reach the moraine overlooking Laguna Tumarina – behind are steep rock walls and the immense, glaciated Huantsan. The way becomes even rougher to reach the slopes (50 minutes) below Laguna Tumagarañon, from where the lake is a round trip of 1 hour away.

HIKING ROUTES & MAPS

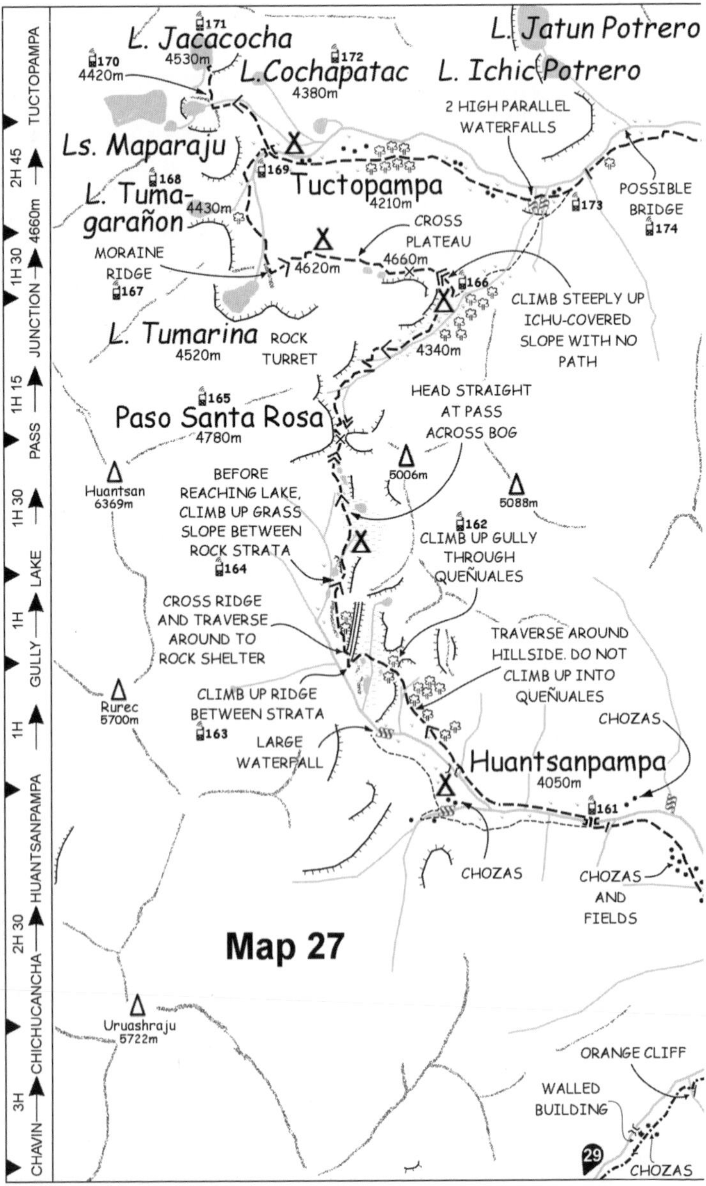

TUCTOPAMPA

2H 45 — 4660m

1H 30 — JUNCTION

1H 15 — PASS

1H 30 — LAKE

1H — GULLY

1H — HUANTSANPAMPA

2H 30 — CHICHUCANCHA

3H — CHAVIN

L. Jacacocha
4530m
▯171
▯170
4420m
L. Cochapatac
4380m
▯172
Ls. Maparaju
L. Tuma-garañon
4430m
▯168
MORAINE RIDGE
▯167
L. Tumarina
4520m
ROCK TURRET
✕169
Tuctopampa
4210m
4620m
CROSS PLATEAU
4660m
4340m
▯166
CLIMB STEEPLY UP ICHU-COVERED SLOPE WITH NO PATH
L. Jatun Potrero
L. Ichic Potrero
2 HIGH PARALLEL WATERFALLS
POSSIBLE BRIDGE
▯173
▯174
HEAD STRAIGHT AT PASS ACROSS BOG
Paso Santa Rosa
4780m
▯165
5006m
Huantsan
6369m
BEFORE REACHING LAKE, CLIMB UP GRASS SLOPE BETWEEN ROCK STRATA
▯164
5088m
▯162
CLIMB UP GULLY THROUGH QUEÑUALES
CROSS RIDGE AND TRAVERSE AROUND TO ROCK SHELTER
Rurec
5700m
CLIMB UP RIDGE BETWEEN STRATA
▯163
LARGE WATERFALL
TRAVERSE AROUND HILLSIDE. DO NOT CLIMB UP INTO QUEÑUALES
CHOZAS
Huantsanpampa
4050m
▯161
CHOZAS
CHOZAS AND FIELDS
Map 27
Uruashraju
5722m
ORANGE CLIFF
WALLED BUILDING
29
CHOZAS

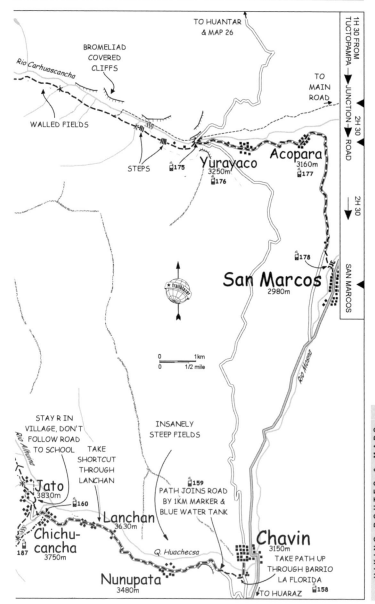

TO HUANTAR
& MAP 26

BROMELIAD
COVERED
CLIFFS

Rio Carhuascancha

TO
MAIN
ROAD

1H 30 FROM
TUCTOPAMPA →

JUNCTION →

2H 30

ROAD

WALLED FIELDS

STEPS

🏠175

Yurayaco
3250m

🏠176

Acopara
3160m

🏠177

2H 30

🏠178

San Marcos
2980m

SAN MARCOS

trailblazer

0   1km
0   1/2 mile

Rio Mosna

STAY R IN
VILLAGE, DON'T
FOLLOW ROAD
TO SCHOOL

TAKE
SHORTCUT
THROUGH
LANCHAN

INSANELY
STEEP FIELDS

Rio Alfonso

Jato
3830m

🏠160

Lanchan
3630m

🏠159

PATH JOINS ROAD
BY 1KM MARKER &
BLUE WATER TANK

🏠187

Chichu-
cancha
3750m

Q. Huachecsa

Chavin
3150m

TAKE PATH UP
THROUGH BARRIO
LA FLORIDA

Nunupata
3480m

TO HUARAZ

🏠158

HIKING ROUTES & MAPS

Continuing down the main valley, jump the side river from Laguna Tumagarañon after 10 minutes, at which point the walking finally becomes easy to the good camp spot at Tuctopampa (15 minutes).

Side trip to Laguna Maparaju and Jacacocha (2h30)
It's well worth hiking the side trip up to the lower of the Lagunas Maparaju (45 minutes, no path) – this turquoise lake in a deep bowl, backdropped by Nevado San Juan, is probably the most picturesque of all the lakes in the valley. Cross the outflow by the lake and continue, sometimes on a path, for another 35 minutes to shallow Jacacocha, which wallows beneath the glaciers on Nevado Cayesh. Either return the same way or loop round via Laguna Cochapatac, on very overgrown and challenging terrain, back to Tuctopampa (1 hour).

Cross the bridge at Tuctopampa to the TR/S side, and pass to the R of all the chozas. Descend the slope after the last of these huts and link up with a path (30 minutes) which heads down valley, between the river and some thick stands of queñuales. The route is now clear all the way to the end of the trek.

Pass pampas where **camping** is possible (though ask any campesinos first) en route to where the direct trail from Paso Santa Rosa joins (1 hour), just before a gate. After 20 minutes you'll reach the turnoff to Lagunas Ichic and Jatun Potrero. If the bridge is rebuilt, or the river wade-able, these beautiful lakes are only a short detour away.

From this turnoff it's 1h20 to a junction, by a '2+800' rock marker. It's slightly quicker to stay straight here, crossing a water channel (25 minutes), to reach the road at the entrance to the quebrada in a further 25 minutes. No traffic plies this route, leaving three options for getting back to civilization.
• Cross the road bridge and follow the road to Huántar (2 hours, for Quebrada Rurec).
• Cross the bridge, then turn off R, down a 4WD track that leads downhill to the main road (1h30).
• Turn R and almost immediately L, passing Yurayaco and Acopara en route to San Marcos (2h30). There are occasional colectivos from these two villages to San Marcos (S/.3.50).

❏ Apus and Apachetas
For thousands of years Andean mountains have been revered as mountain spirits known as **Apus**. Each mountain is believed to have its own spirit that protects and punishes those in the valleys below who are supplied by water from the mountain's slopes.

You may see stone cairns known as **apachetas** ('source where the flow begins') on ancient paths in the Cordillera. Often located on passes and places with beautiful views which were considered sacred, individual stones were carried up from the valleys by travellers, as offerings to the apus for protection.

Southern Cordillera Blanca

OLLEROS – CHAVÍN

Also known as the Llama Trek, this three-day crossing of the Cordillera Blanca on an old pilgrimage route will appeal to those who are looking for a more cultural trekking experience. At either end, the route passes through small villages, and Chavín has the most important ruins in the area, making it worthwhile spending the day after the trek exploring these and the museum at the opposite end of town (both closed Mondays).

Few of the Blanca's usual snow, ice and lakey treats exist on this puna trail, however there are still many weird and wonderful rock formations to entertain the eye and a certain thrill in knowing that Andean feet have trodden this route for thousands of years.

Timing and getting to and from the trailhead

The route takes three days, though it can be shortened to two by taking transport past Olleros, or from Chichucancha. It can also be lengthened, by linking with treks in Quebrada Rurec (Huaylas) or Carhuascancha.

Olleros is only a couple of kilometres off the main road; combis leave from Jr 27 de Noviembre in Huaraz, when full, throughout the day (30 minutes, S/.2.50). See p66 for Chavín information.

Peru Llama Trek (Agustin Loli 463, Huaraz, ☎ 421266, 🖳 info@perullamatrek.com.pe) runs Olleros – Chavín treks (and extensions into Carhuascancha), using llamas as pack animals. They operate out of Canrey Chico near Olleros and also have an office in Huaraz. RESPONS (p59) is one of the few other agencies to offer this trek with llamas.

Preparations The trek is within PNH – tickets can be bought at Sacracancha or Shongo if a guardaparque is there. Olleros has a couple of basic accommodations and restaurants, well

> **OLLEROS – CHAVÍN**
> - **Start** Olleros
> - **End** Chavín
> - **Distance** 44km/27 miles
> - **Trekking time** 3 days
> - **Vertical climb** 1300m/4300ft
> - **Max altitude** 4680m/15,350ft
> - **Navigation** 1
> - **Terrain** 1

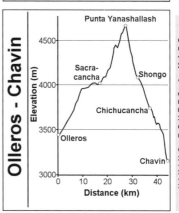

stocked shops and many houses with lovely old wooden doors. Between Olleros and Chichucancha there's nowhere to buy supplies. Please use the official campsites at Sacracancha and Shongo; both have toilets and guardaparque huts.

Olleros – Punta Yanashallash – Chavín
[Map 28, Map 29 & Map 27, pp140-1]

From Olleros' Plaza de Armas, continue E on paving for a couple of minutes, to a dirt road which descends R, past a crumbling bullring. Cross the bridge and continue on the track to a PNH sign in Agocancha (1h20). Leave the main 4WD track here, heading L, past the sign. Leave this 4WD track when it switches

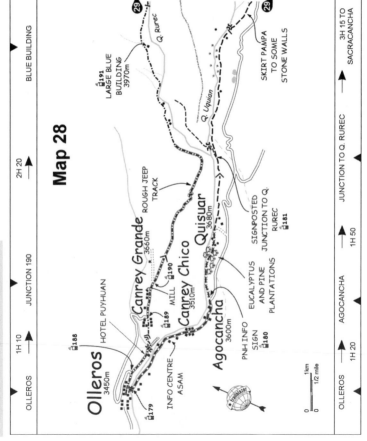

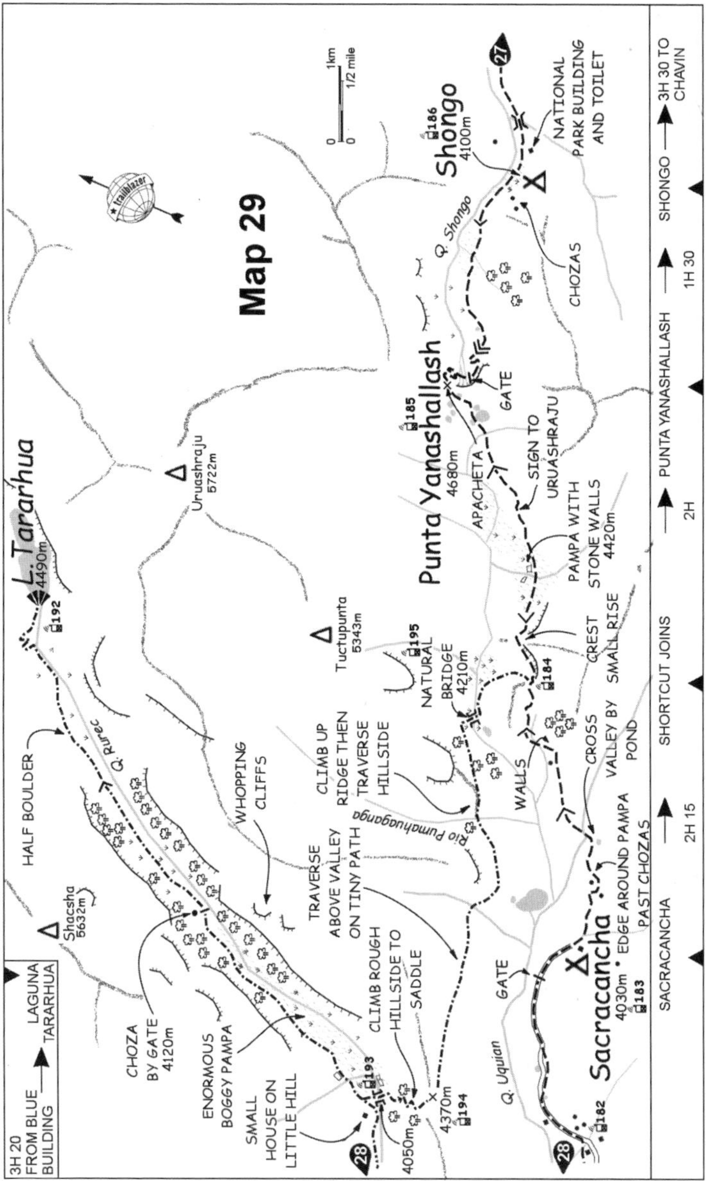

Map 29

0 1km
0 1/2 mile

Tararhua ⃤ 4490m 📷192

Uruashraju ⃤ 5722m

Shacsha ⃤ 5632m

HALF BOULDER

Q. Rurec

CHOZA BY GATE 4120m

ENORMOUS BOGGY PAMPA

SMALL HOUSE ON LITTLE HILL

📷193

4050m

4370m 📷194

WHOPPING CLIFFS

TRAVERSE ABOVE VALLEY ON TINY PATH

CLIMB UP RIDGE THEN TRAVERSE HILLSIDE

CLIMB ROUGH HILLSIDE TO SADDLE

Tuctupunta ⃤ 5343m

📷195

NATURAL BRIDGE 4210m

Río Pumahuaganga

Rio Pumahuaganga

WALLS

CROSS VALLEY BY POND

📷184

CREST SMALL RISE

Shongo 4100m 📷186

NATIONAL PARK BUILDING AND TOILET

Q. Shongo

CHOZAS

GATE

Punta Yanashallash 4680m 📷185

APACHETA

SIGN TO URUASHRAJU

PAMPA WITH STONE WALLS 4420m

Sacracancha 4030m 📷182

EDGE AROUND PAMPA PAST CHOZAS

GATE

Q. Uquian

28

28

27

3H 20 FROM BLUE BUILDING

LAGUNA TARARHUA

SACRACANCHA

2H 15

SHORTCUT JOINS

2H

PUNTA YANASHALLASH

1H 30

SHONGO

3H 30 TO CHAVIN

back (50 minutes), heading L onto a wide path. There are good views of impossibly-steep Shacsha's spiky crown to the L/NE.

After 1 hour of easy walking, pass a PNH sign and continue into Quebrada Uquian. The climb flattens off in a further 25 minutes, and there are good views of the meandering river and Pucaraju. Keep heading upriver, either by descending to the pampa, or by traversing the slopes above a water channel – after 1 hour the two meet. Rejoin the 4WD track in a further 40 minutes and go L, following this track or shortcuts for 1h10 to Sacracancha camp.

Traverse the hillside, past chozas, on the TL/S side of the main river. In 45 minutes, pass to the L of a pond, and immediately cut L, on a path that crosses the river in Quebrada Araranca and climbs to a wide path on a ridge. The climb steepens briefly 1h30 later, as the path rounds a rocky outcrop by a small cascade. At this point the shortcut from Quebrada Rurec joins (see opposite). There are some brief sections on ancient stones worn smooth by the soles and hooves of time, en route to cresting a small rise (30 minutes).

From here, the path is visible ahead in the main, left-hand valley, as is Uruashraju, the snowy peak to the N with the monochrome S face. There are fascinating rock faces and strata all around on the easy 1h30 climb to Punta Yanashallash.

The large path descends the TR/S side of the quebrada to Shongo Camp (1h30). Fifteen minutes later, cross a bridge at a confluence of rivers, then continue down to a tri-junction (1 hour). Take the left-hand of the two paths ahead for Chavín (or, if continuing your trek to Quebrada Carhuascancha, go back L, down to the bridge over the main river and the shortcut path to Jato – see p138).

Hit the quiet road (20 minutes) at the far end of Chichucancha and follow it R, taking shortcuts through Lanchan after 20 minutes, to Nunupata (a further 45 minutes). Rounding a right hand bend with a conspicuous rock (15 minutes) daubed in political graffiti, the Chavín ruins appear in the Río Mosna valley below. Leave the road 5 minutes later by a blue water tank onto a footpath that descends to the road by the ruins. Turn L for Chavín's pleasant Plaza de Armas (30 minutes), passing the entrance to the famous ruins on the way.

QUEBRADA RUREC (HUAYLAS)

Not to be confused with its namesake valley in Conchucos, this Quebrada Rurec, with its towering rock walls and surrounding of 5000m peaks, is one of the Blanca's hidden gems. Little visited other than by adventurous rock climbers, it makes an excellent three (or two, with private transport) day getaway from the hustle and bustle of Huaraz. It's also possible to trek from Olleros to Quebrada Rurec, then over Paso Yanashallash to Chavín in three or four days – a good way to spice up the scenery on the traditional Olleros – Chavín puna route.

Olleros – Quebrada Rurec   [Map 28, p144 & Map 29, p145]

From Olleros' plaza, head E on paving until the main road doubles back (10 minutes). Go straight here on a 4WD track signed 'A Puyhuan'. In 15 minutes, cross a wooden bridge over a side river and immediately go L, climbing on a wide path to the village green in Canrey Grande (25 minutes).

Go over the green and continue up the 4WD track, going R in 20 minutes when it divides. Enter Quebrada Rurec, sticking to the track on the N side of the wide valley. An hour and a half from the split, the 4WD track becomes an unmotorable path, which in 50 minutes leads to a large blue building. Graffiti scrawled on the side states this is now a *'Sala de Porno de Sexo'*, though we suspect this wasn't the original reason for its construction.

Up valley a further 35 minutes, the path turns a corner to reveal a giant pampa and 500m-high rock walls on the S side which resemble some kind of *Lord of the Rings* death slide. Below, at the SW corner of the pampa, is a small bridge – the shortcut over to Chavín (see below).

Continue into the heart of the valley for 2 hours to a small hut; there

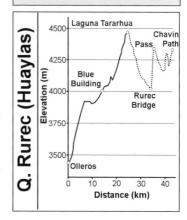

QUEBRADA RUREC (HUAYLAS)
- **Start & end** Olleros
- **Distance** 48km/30 miles
- **Trekking time** 3 days
- **Vertical climb** 1150m/3800ft
- **Max altitude** 4490m/14,750ft
- **Navigation** 1
- **Terrain** 1

are plenty of possible **camp** sites around so just choose your spot. Beyond the hut is an incredible 'half boulder' just above the path, 10m high and with one side sliced clean off – as though by a swift blow from Pachamama's sharpest samurai sword.

With luck you'll see wildlife up here – deer, vizcacha and plenty of birds. Reach the top of the moraine encasing Laguna Tararhua 45 minutes from the hut. It's possible to **camp** at this lovely spot with peaks at all intercardinal directions: Rurec to the NE, Uruashraju (SE), Shacsha (SW) and Cashan (NW).

Returning, it's 2h15 back to the bridge and shortcut to Chavín and a further 3h30 to Olleros.

Quebrada Rurec – Quebrada Uquian Link (4h)

Linking Quebrada Rurec with Quebrada Uquian and the Olleros – Chavín trek is this fun shortcut, which requires some navigation skills and cross-country walking over terrain with no, or only faint, paths.

Cross the precarious bridge at the SW corner of the pampa in Quebrada Rurec and climb the grassy slopes to the S to a pass (1 hour). Follow a tiny path that leads off L/E along the steep N slopes of Quebrada Uquian; after 30 minutes the slope gradients ease and the trail becomes harder to follow. Continue up the valley as best you can to Río Pumahuaganga (1 hour). Cross the river and

HIKING ROUTES & MAPS

ascend the grassy ridge on the far side. Don't go too high, crossing the ridge after 25 minutes and continuing up valley to a natural bridge over the main river (30 minutes). Cross and make your way up easy slopes to the main trail (30 minutes) on the S side of the valley.

QUEBRADA RARIA

- **Start** Carpa
- **End** Machac
- **Distance** 39km/24 miles
- **Trekking time** 3 days
- **Vertical climb** 900m/3000ft
- **Max altitude** 4800m/15,750ft
- **Navigation** 2
- **Terrain** 2

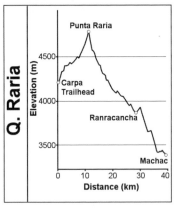

QUEBRADA RARIA

The varied three-day trek in the quiet valleys of Raria and Ranracancha is way off most trekkers' radars. Beginning at Carpa, stray *Puya raimondii* tower over the trail, which eases its way into Quebrada Raria, passing lakes and spiky snowy peaks. There's cross-country walking either side of Punta Raria, but the terrain is not difficult, and the long descent traverses the green slopes of Quebrada Ranracancha past tumbling waterfalls and contorted rock.

The path eventually hits a motorable road near Machac, a short ride from Chavín, making this a more scenically exciting alternative to the Olleros – Chavín route. Linking up with Quebrada Carhuascancha makes for a superb week of off-the-beaten-path hiking.

Timing and getting to and from the trailhead

The route takes three days; to complete it in two is tough and means crossing Punta Raria on the first afternoon.

The trailhead is in Quebrada Pumapampa, 3.5km after the Carpa PNH office, on a road which sees little traffic except for tourist buses heading to Pastoruri. One option for reaching here is to book on a Pastoruri tour from Huaraz (2 hours, S/.30), and ask to be let out at the trailhead. If there's a group of you, it makes better economic sense to take a taxi from Huaraz (1h15) or Catac (40 minutes).

The trek ends in Machac, near Chavín. Flag down transport for the 20 minute journey to Chavín, or a combi/bus (2h30/3 hours, S/.20/12) back to Huaraz. It's possible to avoid Machac and the main road and walk all the way to Chavín on ancient trails, in 3 hours from Pichíu.

Preparations The start of the trek is at 4200m and the first good camp at 4400m, so ensure sufficient acclimatization before beginning. You can buy a PNH ticket at Carpa; bring all supplies.

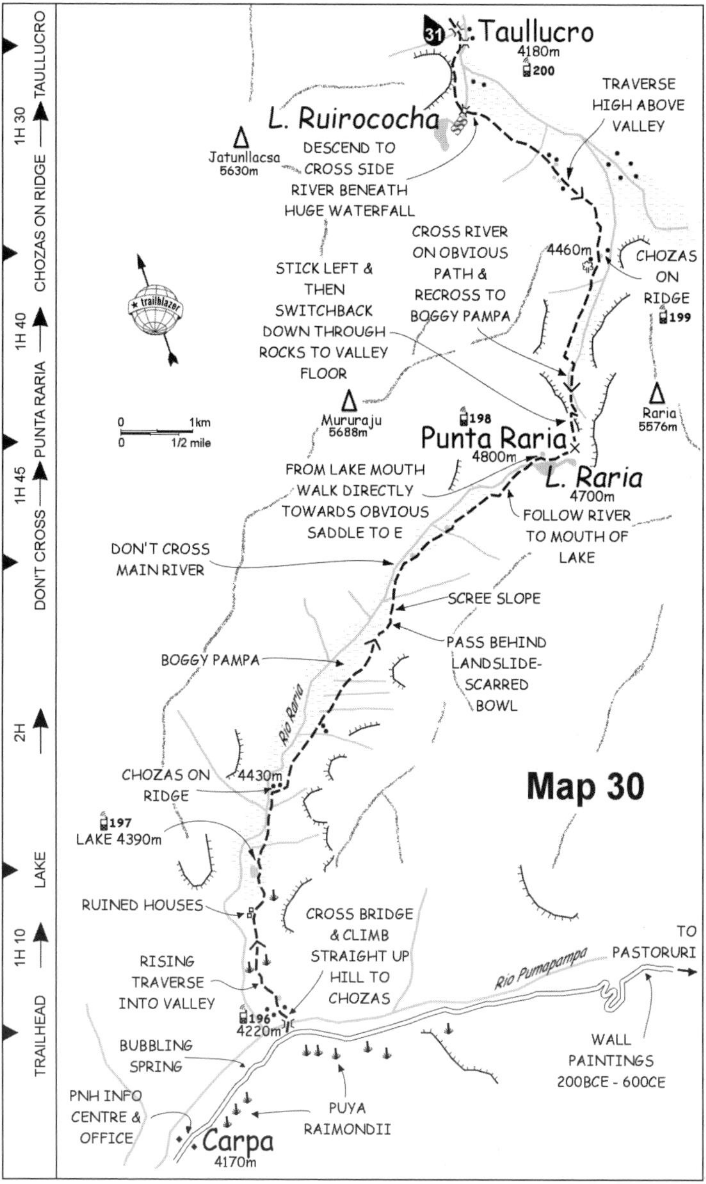

31 ☼ Taullucro
4180m
🏠200

TRAVERSE
HIGH ABOVE
VALLEY

L. Ruirococha

△ Jatunllacsa
5630m

DESCEND TO
CROSS SIDE
RIVER BENEATH
HUGE WATERFALL

CROSS RIVER
ON OBVIOUS
PATH &
RECROSS TO
BOGGY PAMPA

4460m

CHOZAS
ON
RIDGE
🏠199

STICK LEFT &
THEN
SWITCHBACK
DOWN THROUGH
ROCKS TO VALLEY
FLOOR

★ trailblazer

0   1km
0   1/2 mile

△ Mururaju
5688m

🏠198

Punta Raria
4800m

△ Raria
5576m

L. Raria
4700m

FROM LAKE MOUTH
WALK DIRECTLY
TOWARDS OBVIOUS
SADDLE TO E

FOLLOW RIVER
TO MOUTH
OF LAKE

DON'T CROSS
MAIN RIVER

SCREE SLOPE

PASS BEHIND
LANDSLIDE-
SCARRED
BOWL

BOGGY PAMPA

Rio Raria

Map 30

CHOZAS ON
RIDGE

4430m

🏠197
LAKE 4390m

RUINED HOUSES

CROSS BRIDGE
& CLIMB
STRAIGHT UP
HILL TO
CHOZAS

TO
PASTORURI

RISING
TRAVERSE
INTO VALLEY

🏠196
4220m

Rio Pumapampa

WALL
PAINTINGS
200BCE - 600CE

BUBBLING
SPRING

PNH INFO
CENTRE &
OFFICE

PUYA
RAIMONDII

Carpa
4170m

TAULLUCRO
1H 30
CHOZAS ON RIDGE
1H 40
PUNTA RARIA
1H 45
DON'T CROSS
2H
CHOZAS ON RIDGE
LAKE
1H 10
TRAILHEAD

HIKING ROUTES & MAPS

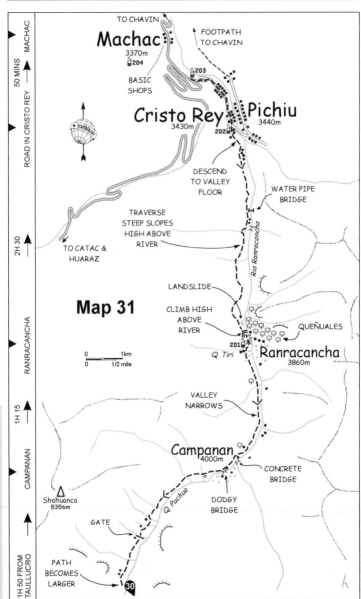

Carpa – Punta Raria – Machac [Map 30, p149 & Map 31]

From the road, and brown stump of a broken 'Quebrada Raria' signpost, head NE for 2 minutes to a well-hidden bridge. Cross, then climb up the hillside beyond, passing some chozas before linking up with a path that traverses into Quebrada Raria (the large quebrada to the N of that housing the road).

Rock swirls adorn the N side of the valley, and after 30 minutes come the first views of the impressive triangle of Nevado Mururaju (Pongos on the *Alpenvereinskarte*), as the trail eases up the quebrada's S slopes, far above the river. The first **water** source in the valley is just before a lake (35 minutes), the shores of which make for a good **camp**.

Continue on the S side – the path becoming ever smaller and eventually disappearing at the river's edge (2 hours). Do not cross; instead continue making progress up the valley for 50 minutes to a flat, green, boggy pampa. In another 25 minutes is the lower of the Lagunas Raria, dominated by its namesake peak, where there's just about room for a spectacular, high **camp**.

Punta Raria is the low point in the ridge ahead and is easily reached 30 minutes after crossing the lake's outflow. Stay L initially on the descent before dropping to the valley floor (25 minutes). Follow traces of paths, but no real trail, as you make your way down to a boggy pampa (25 minutes), best traversed on the slopes to the L/W, then to some chozas on a ridge jutting into the valley (50 minutes).

Follow a good path for 15 minutes before veering NW into the larger Ranracancha valley. The route stays in this valley to Machac – stick to the TL/W side, without crossing the main, raging river. After 1 hour, jump the side stream which roars down from Laguna Ruirococha and in a further 20 minutes reach a choza at Taullucro.

Twenty minutes from here the path becomes clear and remains so until the end of the trek. Gentle downhill walking for 1h30 brings you to the few scattered buildings of Campanan, in the environs of which **camping** is possible.

Downriver, the valley narrows and the hillsides steepen, making for an interesting, undulating walk out. It's 1h15 to the bridge over the river in Quebrada Tiri at Ranracancha and a further 2h15 to a junction above the large village of Pichíu. Go R and descend to the village if you wish to walk all the way to Chavín (3 hours), or else continue straight for 10 minutes, hitting a road in Cristo Rey. Turn L for the 30 minute walk to the main road near Machac.

❏ Hats

Hats in the Peruvian Cordillera are a sign of status and designate people's town of origin – as you lap the Blanca you'll notice the continually-changing headwear. Near Huaraz women wear elongated trilby-type hats with an elaborate fan of ribbon on one side. In Pomabamba look out for heavy white felt numbers with domed tops, while in Caraz and Carhuaz the women flaunt expensive, handmade, oversized, wide-brimmed straw sombreros. Look out for sombrererías to get your hands on, and head into, a fabulous souvenir.

Cordillera Huayhuash

HUAYHUASH CIRCUIT

Only 30km long by 15km wide, the compact Cordillera Huayhuash (pronounced 'why-wash', with the second syllable rhyming with 'rash') really

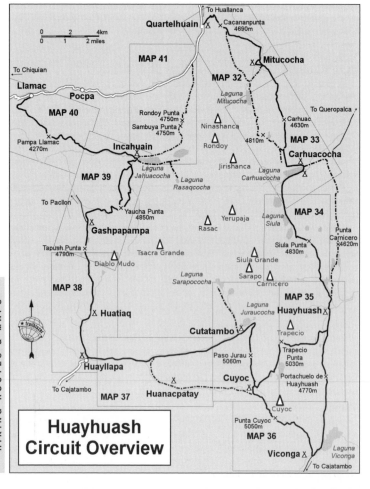

To Huallanca
Quartelhuain × Cacananpunta
4690m

MAP 41

× **Mitucocha**

MAP 32

To Chiquian
Llamac
Pocpa
Laguna Mitucocha

To Queropalca
× Carhuac 4630m

MAP 40
Rondoy Punta 4750m ×
Sambuya Punta 4750m ×
Ninashanca △
× 4810m
MAP 33

Pampa Llamac × 4270m
Incahuain
Rondoy △
Carhuacocha ×

Laguna Jahuacocha
Laguna Rasaqcocha
Jirishanca △
Laguna Carhuacocha
×

MAP 39

To Paclion
Yaucha Punta × 4850m
Yerupaja △
Laguna Siula
MAP 34

Gashpapampa
Rasac △
Punta Carnicero × 4620m

Tapush Punta × 4790m
Tsacra Grande △
Diablo Mudo △
Siula Punta × 4830m
Siula Grande △

MAP 38
Laguna Sarapococha
Sarapo △
Carnicero

× **Huatiaq**
Laguna Juraucocha
MAP 35
Huayhuash ×

Cutatambo ×
Trapecio ×

Paso Jurau × 5060m
Trapecio Punta 5030m ×

× **Huayllapa**
Cuyoc
Portachuelo de × Huayhuash 4770m

To Cajatambo
MAP 37 **Huanacpatay** ×
Cuyoc △

Huayhuash Circuit Overview
Punta Cuyoc 5050m ×
MAP 36

Viconga ×
Laguna Viconga
To Cajatambo

0   2   4km
0   1   2 miles

punches above its weight. Packed into this small region are three major summits over 6000m, countless other razor-sharp peaks, bejewelled alpine lakes, chaotic ice falls, gargantuan rock faces and fascinating contorted strata. Magnificent scenery awaits at every turn: it's not surprising this circuit has many peoples' vote for the best trek on the continent.

HUAYHUASH CIRCUIT
- **Start** Quartelhuain
- **End** Llamac
- **Distance** 110km/68 miles +
- **Trekking time** 7-14 days
- **Vertical climb** 5700m/18,700ft +
- **Max altitude** 5060m/16,600ft
- **Navigation** 2
- **Terrain** 2

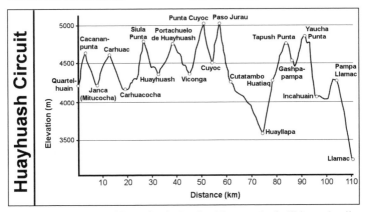

Nine local communities maintain the circuit's campsite facilities and trails, charging tourists for the privilege. Please stay at these official campsites – all of which have toilets – both to help the cleanliness of the trails, and also for your own safety. At the time of writing it costs S/.205 to buy all the community tickets needed to trek the whole circuit.

Safety
The Huayhuash circuit is currently considered safe, and we are not aware of any robberies in recent years. This was not always the case, however. Until the early '90s the Sendero Luminoso was active in the region and in the early 2000s, a number of nasty armed incidents against trekking groups occurred. The current ticketing system has helped improve safety, and by paying fees and camping at community campsites, you are in effect being given the protection of the local community.

Timing
Depending on route selection and side trips, the circuit can take anything from seven to fourteen days. Most people take about ten days, and almost all walk the route in a clockwise direction. Those with less time can get a taster by tackling the still-impressive four-day 'Mini Huayhuash' (a loop from Llamac over Rondoy Punta and Pampa Llamac).

Getting to the start of the trek The vast majority of people begin in Quartelhuain (often called Matacancha), a 4 hour drive from Huaraz. There is no public transport to this campsite however, which means independent trekkers have the following options:

• Take an early morning bus with El Rápido or Nazario from Huaraz to Chiquián (05:00 & 14:00, 2h, S/.10); catch Nazario's 08:00 service from Chiquián to Pocpa (2h, S/.12) and spend the rest of the first day walking (or hitching) along the road to Quartelhuain (12km, 4h);

• Arrange with one of the trekking agencies in Huaraz to take you;

• Catch a morning bus from Huaraz to Huallanca (3h30, S/.12, El Rápido and others), then try hitching (wait on the south side of the bridge in Huallanca for a lift) to Quartelhuain with one of the morning mine trucks (1h30, S/.tip appropriate) heading to Mina Mitsui. If you don't get lucky hitching, or the mine is closed, a taxi from Huallanca to Quartelhuain costs upwards of S/.120.

If trekking the circuit with a reputable agency, transport to and from the trek will almost certainly be included in the price.

The trek can also be started or finished in Huayllapa on the south-west side of the circuit, taking transport from Lima via Barranca and Cajatambo (one bus daily). From Cajatambo (basic accommodation, restaurants and shops; unreliable internet, no ATM) there's a daily combi to Huayllapa (2h, S/.15) which leaves around midday.

Queropalca (a half day walk from Carhuacocha) has basic facilities and is reachable by public transport from Huallanca via La Unión and Baños. This is an adventurous entry point, rarely used by foreign trekkers.

Getting from the end of the trek The majority of trekkers end in Llamac. If you are not being met with private transport, the last bus leaves Llamac for Chiquián at around 11:30. The scenery makes it worthwhile walking out over Rondoy Punta, but unless you are being picked up this means an extra day, or hitching with one of the few mine vehicles, as you miss this bus.

Preparations The only place to buy provisions during the trek is Huayllapa. This is six or seven days from Quartelhuain for most people, though can be rushed in four. Buy sufficient supplies to reach Huayllapa before beginning.

It's perfectly feasible to walk independently if you can carry enough food, but most people choose to go on a guided tour with an agency, or simply hire an arriero. Arrieros can be found in Llamac, Pocpa, Queropalca and Huayllapa; it's a good idea to get a recommendation from a fellow hiker or to consider organizing through a reputable agency. See Chiquián (p68), Huaraz (p59) and Guided or independent (p19) sections for more information.

Note that though the distance and altitude gain per day appear moderate, the trek is strenuous due to the many high passes and fact that almost all the route is above 4000m.

Ticketing system
The full circuit passes through nine communities' lands. Each charges a fee just to pass through – it's irrelevant how long you stay. The Pocpa fee only applies if

you travel through the village; the Cutatambo fee is only applicable for those entering the higher part of the Río Calinca valley; if you go via Trapecio Punta, the Uramaza ticket is not necessary. A Llamac ticket bought at the start of your trek is valid when you pass through again at the finish. Keep all tickets until the end of your trek and check 🖳 blancahuayhuash.com for any changes in ticketing arrangements and prices.

Comunidad campesina	S/.
Llamac	20
Pocpa	10
Queropalca	40
Quishuarcancha	25
Túpac Amaru (Huayhuash)	20
Uramaza (Viconga)	20
Huayllapa	40
Cutatambo	10
Pacllón	20

❏ Ticketing tricks

Although most *cobradores* (ticket sellers) are honest, making the process of buying your ticket straightforward and good-natured, some aren't averse to trying to earn extra cash by cheating tourists, or more commonly, their own communities.

Some cobradores wear waistcoats with the name of their community on, but most have nothing but a ticket book to prove who they are, which can make it confusing, particularly for independent trekkers. Added to this, there is no standardization of tickets – all nine look different.

Scams include:
● Being sold a ticket which is actually a carbon copy of one sold to a previous trekker; later, you are asked to buy another ticket as yours is not valid.
● A random person with a receipt book trying to sell you a 'ticket' even though they are not an official cobrador.
● Being told there's a need for a second ticket for the same community, even though you have already bought one.

Always get your paper ticket before handing over cash, checking that: 1) any date and nationality details are correct (so that you're not buying a copy of a 'used' ticket); 2) everyone in your group has an identical looking ticket from each community (carbon copies of tickets are a different colour); and 3) every trekker has their own ticket (don't allow more than one name to be written on the same ticket).

If you suspect someone is trying it on with you, remain cheery but firm. We've noted in the route description where each cobrador usually hangs out.

Day 1: Quartelhuain – Mitucocha camp [Map 32, p157]

● **Duration** 4h-4h30
● **Summary** Begin the circuit with a relatively short day which provides a taster of the delights to come. Take it easy on the unrelenting climb to Cacananpunta, then descend gently down the colourful Quebrada Caliente. Camp below Laguna Mitucocha, with great views of Jirishanca to the south-west.

If arriving at Quartelhuain via Llamac and Pocpa, a cobrador will board your bus in the former and meet you at the bridge in the latter to sell you community tickets. Arriving via Huallanca, a cobrador will usually sell you a Llamac ticket at the Quartelhuain campsite. It's not a bad idea to camp at Quartelhuain to aid acclimatization, as once you cross Cacananpunta it is more complicated escaping to lower altitudes.

Day 1 (cont'd) From the road bridge at Quartelhuain, head NE through camp, past the toilets and corrals. The clear path crosses a stream, begins zigzagging up a grassy ridge and, but for a short traverse, climbs continuously to Cacananpunta (2h-2h30). Behind to the N is the Cordillera Huallanca, while to the W is Mina Mitsui, the company responsible for building the Chiquián to Huallanca road.

This first pass is an oft-windy spot and has views down kaleidoscopic Quebrada Caliente. The path descends steeply on zigzags for 10 minutes to a junction where a small path (the alternative route to Laguna Mitucocha – see below) goes off R. Continue descending on the main trail for 10 minutes to a metal cross which commemorates a young Polish explorer who died in 1998 trying to locate the source of the Marañon.

From the cross, traverse down the R/W side of the valley to Jancahuayi (1 hour), a small collection of dwellings near the junction of Ríos Caliente and Janca. Here the path curves R/SW into the Río Janca valley for the 30 minute walk to the **toilet block** at Mitucocha **campsite**. The cobrador for Queropalca is normally to be found in this area. If you have time, it's well worth walking up the valley to Laguna Mitucocha (45 minutes each way).

Groups with rushed itineraries often continue directly to Carhuacocha this first day, but this is not a particularly good idea as it leaves many trekkers shattered right at the beginning of the trek.

Day 1 alternative route: Cacananpunta – Mitucocha camp   [Map 32]

● **Duration** 4h30-6h30 from Quartelhuain to Mitucocha Camp

A more interesting alternative to the mule route is to go R at the small junction just after Cacananpunta and traverse southwards on a faint path. Keep the rocky cliffs to your R and don't lose much ground on the way to crossing a small ridge (35 minutes). Continue on the same bearing to a second ridge (25 minutes), all the time heading at Jirishanca. From here either descend the small river valley, to reach the terminal moraine (50 minutes) in the main valley below Mitucocha, from where it's possible to wander S to the lake, or N to the official campsite (30 minutes); or continue high above the main valley, undulating southwards to lap Mitucocha before returning northwards to the campsite (2 hours from ridge).

Day 2: Mitucocha camp – Carhuac – Carhuacocha   [Map 33, p158]

● **Duration** 3h30
● **Summary** The rewards for climbing to Carhuac are revealed on the descent, as the largest peaks in the Huayhuash gradually appear. Arrival above Carhuacocha is greeted by Siula Grande, Yerupajá and Jirishanca – all huge, resplendent peaks dominating the skyline to the west – while near the lake's shore, two idyllic campsites await.

From the Mitucocha camp, cross the footbridge and head for the large path which makes its way up the side valley to the E. The walk to Carhuac (1h40) is reasonably sheltered from views until the peaks begin appearing to the SW on

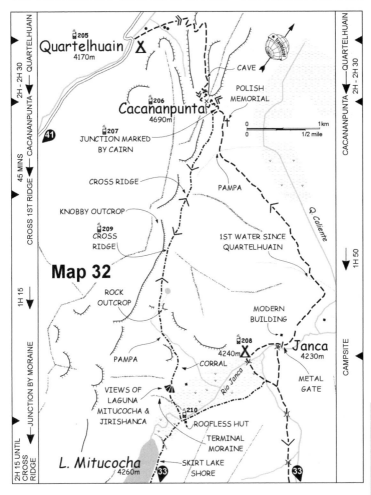

the descent to the valley floor in Quebrada Yanayana. Cross the river to meet the Alternative route from Alcaycocha, next to Artuberto's chozas (50 minutes).

Follow the river down on the TR/W side, and after 20 minutes reach a cliff overlooking Laguna Carhuacocha. The peak views here are superb. Head L/E, passing some adobe buildings on the way to the **camp** (20 minutes) above the NE corner of the lake. Either **pitch your tent** on this patch of grass, or else continue round to the SE corner of the lake and another **campsite** (10 minutes), by the lake's outflow, with equally exquisite views. The

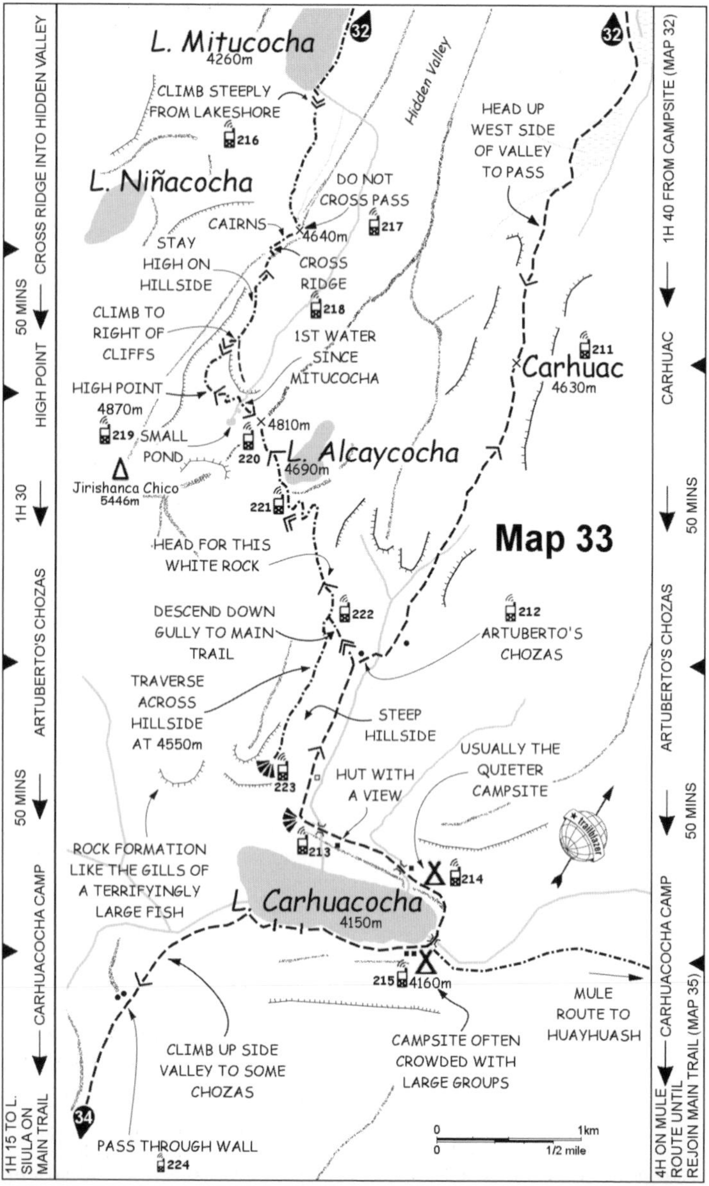

CROSS RIDGE INTO HIDDEN VALLEY
50 MINS
HIGH POINT
1H 30
ARTUBERTO'S CHOZAS
50 MINS
CARHUACOCHA CAMP
1H 15 TO L. SIULA ON MAIN TRAIL
1H 40 FROM CAMPSITE (MAP 32)
CARHUAC
50 MINS
ARTUBERTO'S CHOZAS
50 MINS
CARHUACOCHA CAMP
4H ON MULE ROUTE UNTIL REJOIN MAIN TRAIL (MAP 35)
L. Mitucocha
4260m
Hidden Valley
CLIMB STEEPLY FROM LAKESHORE
216
HEAD UP WEST SIDE OF VALLEY TO PASS
L. Niñacocha
DO NOT CROSS PASS
217
CAIRNS
4640m
STAY HIGH ON HILLSIDE
CROSS RIDGE
218
CLIMB TO RIGHT OF CLIFFS
1ST WATER SINCE MITUCOCHA
211
Carhuac
4630m
HIGH POINT 4870m
4810m
219
SMALL POND
220
L. Alcaycocha
4690m
Jirishanca Chico
5446m
221
Map 33
HEAD FOR THIS WHITE ROCK
222
212
DESCEND DOWN GULLY TO MAIN TRAIL
ARTUBERTO'S CHOZAS
TRAVERSE ACROSS HILLSIDE AT 4550m
STEEP HILLSIDE
USUALLY THE QUIETER CAMPSITE
223
HUT WITH A VIEW
trailblazer
ROCK FORMATION LIKE THE GILLS OF A TERRIFYINGLY LARGE FISH
213
214
L. Carhuacocha
4150m
215
4160m
MULE ROUTE TO HUAYHUASH
CLIMB UP SIDE VALLEY TO SOME CHOZAS
CAMPSITE OFTEN CROWDED WITH LARGE GROUPS
34
32
32
PASS THROUGH WALL
224
0
1km
0
1/2 mile

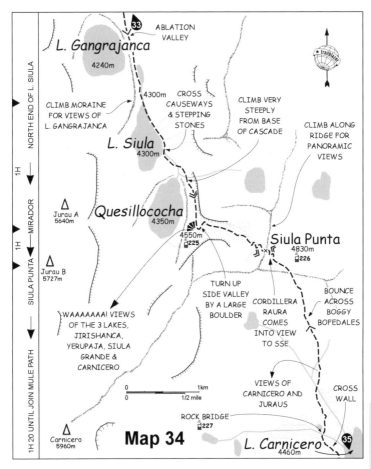

Map 34

0   1km
0   1/2 mile

L. Gangrajanca
4240m

ABLATION
VALLEY

33

NORTH END OF L. SIULA

CLIMB MORAINE
FOR VIEWS OF
L. GANGRAJANCA

4300m   CROSS
CAUSEWAYS
& STEPPING
STONES

CLIMB VERY
STEEPLY
FROM BASE
OF CASCADE

CLIMB ALONG
RIDGE FOR
PANORAMIC
VIEWS

L. Siula
4300m

1H

MIRADOR

△
Jurau A
5640m

Quesillococha
4350m

4550m
225

Siula Punta
4830m
226

1H

SIULA PUNTA

△
Jurau B
5727m

TURN UP
SIDE VALLEY
BY A LARGE
BOULDER

CORDILLERA
RAURA
COMES
INTO VIEW
TO SSE

BOUNCE
ACROSS
BOGGY
BOFEDALES

WAAAAAAA! VIEWS
OF THE 3 LAKES,
JIRISHANCA,
YERUPAJA, SIULA
GRANDE &
CARNICERO

1H 20 UNTIL JOIN MULE PATH

VIEWS OF
CARNICERO AND
JURAUS

CROSS
WALL

ROCK BRIDGE
227

△
Carnicero
5960m

L. Carnicero
4460m

35

HIKING ROUTES & MAPS

Quishuarcancha community fee is collected at this second camp and the
Queropalca fee at the first camp, if you haven't already paid it.

Day 2 alternative route: Mitucocha – Alcaycocha – Carhuacocha
[Map 32, p157 & Map 33]

• **Duration** 6-7h
• **Summary** The early morning views at Laguna Mitucocha are exceptional and remain so
as you climb on indistinct and often non-existent trails. This strenuous route is frequently
steep and requires more navigational skills than any other part of the circuit, as it climbs to
a high point beneath Jirishanca Chico, then descends to a pass above precious Alcaycocha.

If you have time, continue to a viewpoint with lake and peak views, before rejoining the main route near Carhuacocha.

From the campsite, cross the bridge to the TR/E side of Río Janca, and make your way up valley to Laguna Mitucocha (45 minutes). Round the E shore, aiming for the grassy ramp that can be seen rising from Mitucocha's SE corner. Cross the streams that drop down from the heights to the L, turning L up the small path after the last stream (25 minutes).

This soon peters out into a series of cow paths – continue heading SSE, gaining altitude rapidly on grassy slopes. The spot you're aiming for is the pass (1h15) into 'Hidden Valley' to the E, which is the obvious point to the R/S of the cliffs above.

The pass affords good views, but don't cross it and descend into Hidden Valley. Instead, continue S on a vague path up another grassy ramp, following cairns to the R/W of the ridge. After 20 minutes, meet a clear path traversing across the slope – turn L/E on this, continuing to climb steeply. In a few minutes, cross the ridge into Hidden Valley. Follow the path S, up valley, aiming for the angled rock strata of Jirishanca Chico, staying as high as possible on the western slopes. There's still some inevitable descending.

Eventually the route climbs up R/W, to a high point (50 minutes) under Jirishanca Chico, to avoid the cliffs directly ahead.

Descend on loose rocks and a small path, to the black scree pass (25 minutes) which can be seen to the E, just L/N of a small pond. Beautiful Alcaycocha comes into view, its dark blue waters set off against the surrounding green slopes. Descend these grassy slopes past the S end of the lake, linking fragments of paths as best you can to a dry gully and junction (50 minutes).

If you have the time and inclination, it's worth traversing (see Mirador side trip below), otherwise descend down the easy angled gully to the main route in the valley (15 minutes).

> ### Side trip to Mirador overlooking Carhuacocha (50 minutes return)
> From the junction, continue traversing S on a small path, to reach a little pampa. At the far end is a mirador with great views of the three lakes as well as Siula Grande and Yerupajá. Return to the gully via the same route.

Day 3: Carhuacocha – Huayhuash
[Map 33, p158; Map 34, p159 & Map 35, pp162-3]

• **Duration** 5-6h
• **Summary** Today provides some of the best views of the whole circuit. From the moment you leave camp, until arrival at Siula Punta, you are treated to fabulous vistas of jagged peaks, tumbling ice falls and shimmering lakes.

By the wall at the back of the second Carhuacocha camp, the mule route turns L (see Alternative Route), while the main trekking route turns R and follows the southern shore of Carhuacocha. After the end of the lake (25 minutes), the path begins heading L/SW, passing some thatched stone huts and continuing along the bed of an ablation valley.

Go to the R/W of a small lake in the valley to ethereal Laguna Siula (50 minutes), crossing its outflow on a stone bridge. Skirt round the eastern shore before climbing to the moraine (30 minutes) by Laguna Quesillococha.

From the base of a cascade, a clear path starts climbing steeply up the precipitous slopes to the L/E and in 35 minutes reaches the Huayhuash's classic mirador of the three lakes backdropped by superlative mountain scenery.

The going becomes easy for a while as the path turns L/E up a side valley, climbing gently towards the base of the pass (30 minutes). The final 25 minutes to the top are on steep zigzags. At the Punta la Cordillera Raura comes into view to the SSE. The most northerly of the glaciated peaks, locally called 'Leon Dormido', really

❏ **The highest bar in Peru?**

Maria Muñoz Flores and/or sons climb up to 4830m Siula Punta in trekking season to offer cans of beer and bottles of pop to trekkers. The drinks are bought in La Unión, taken to Queropalca on public transport and continue on mules to Maria's house near the pass. There are worse places to spend an hour, sipping a cold *Pilsen*...

does look like a reposed cat. Descend 10 minutes to a lower pass, and enter the valley to the south.

Traverse the L/E slopes, before descending to a flat marshy area and crossing a rock bridge over the river (45 minutes). Pass over a stone wall, en route to joining the mule path by a river (25 minutes). It's a 20 minute descent to Huayhuash camp, where a cobrador usually collects money early each morning.

Day 3 alternative route: via Punta Carnicero
[Map 33, p158 & Map 35, pp162-3]

• **Duration** 4h
• **Summary** Views-wise there's no reason to take this alternative, however pack animals use this path from Carhuacocha to Huayhuash, and they are often joined by any clients who are too tired to tackle the main, higher route.

From the camp by Carhuacocha's outflow, head briefly down valley before beginning the gentle climb up Quebrada Atocshayco to Punta Carnicero (3h). It takes about 1 hour to descend to the main trekking route, joining S of Laguna Carnicero.

Day 4: Huayhuash to Viconga   [Map 35, pp162-3 & Map 36, p165]

• **Duration** 4h-4h30
• **Summary** Nevado Trapecio's photogenic pyramid of rock and ice is a constant companion for the climb to Portachuelo de Huayhuash, while at the pass the Cordillera Raura makes another entrance. The path drops steadily past Laguna Viconga to a camp with steaming hot springs.

HIKING ROUTES & MAPS

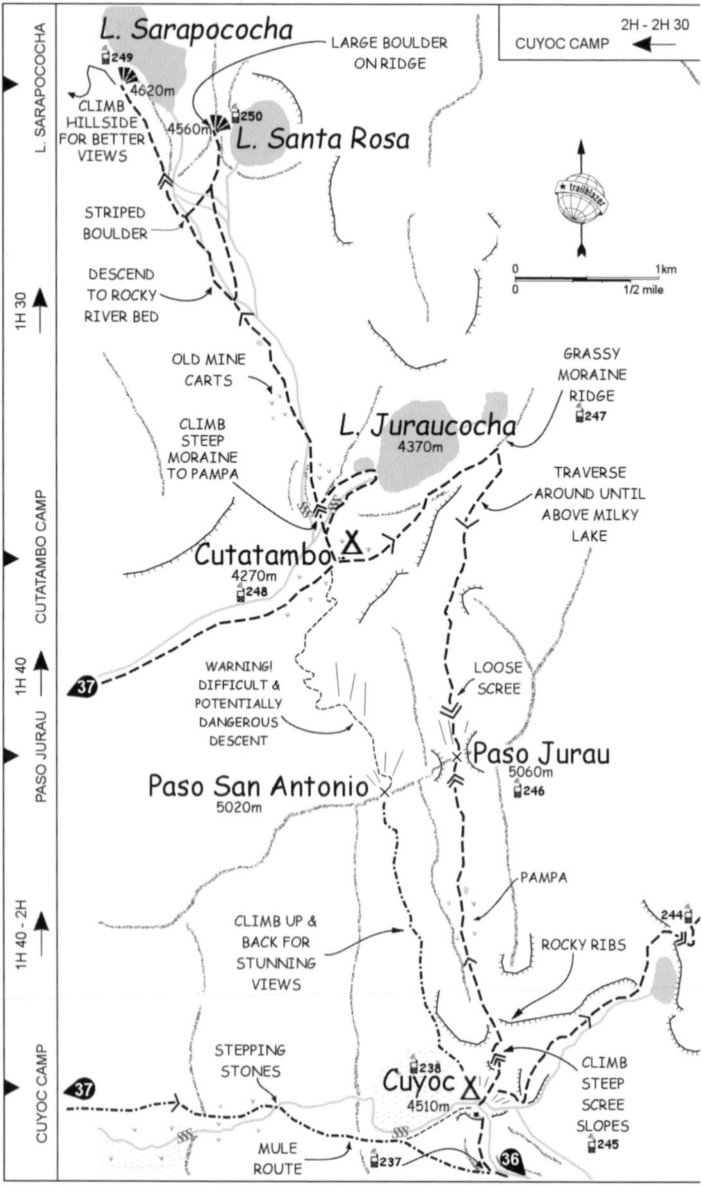

L. Sarapococha
LARGE BOULDER
ON RIDGE

2H - 2H 30
CUYOC CAMP

🏕249
4620m

CLIMB
HILLSIDE
FOR BETTER
VIEWS

4560m
🏕250
L. Santa Rosa

trailblazer

0   1km
0   1/2 mile

STRIPED
BOULDER

DESCEND
TO ROCKY
RIVER BED

GRASSY
MORAINE
RIDGE
🏕247

OLD MINE
CARTS

L. Juraucocha
4370m

TRAVERSE
AROUND UNTIL
ABOVE MILKY
LAKE

CLIMB
STEEP
MORAINE
TO PAMPA

Cutatambo
4270m
🏕248

LOOSE
SCREE

37

WARNING!
DIFFICULT &
POTENTIALLY
DANGEROUS
DESCENT

Paso Jurau
5060m
🏕246

Paso San Antonio
5020m

PAMPA

CLIMB UP &
BACK FOR
STUNNING
VIEWS

ROCKY RIBS
244

STEPPING
STONES

🏕238
Cuyoc
4510m

CLIMB
STEEP
SCREE
SLOPES
🏕245

37

MULE
ROUTE

🏕237

36

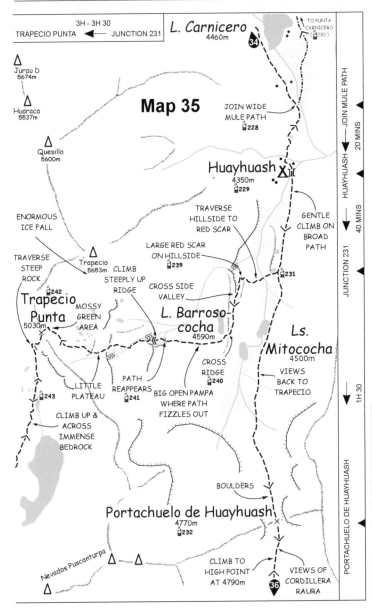

3H - 3H 30

TRAPECIO PUNTA ◄──── JUNCTION 231

L. Carnicero
4460m
34

TO PUNTA
CARNICERO
(🏠230)

△
Jurau D
5674m

△
Huaraca
5537m

△
Quesillo
5600m

Map 35

JOIN WIDE
MULE PATH
🏠228

Huayhuash ✕
4350m
🏠229

ENORMOUS
ICE FALL

TRAVERSE
HILLSIDE TO
RED SCAR

GENTLE
CLIMB ON
BROAD
PATH

TRAVERSE
STEEP
ROCK

△
Trapecio
5653m

CLIMB
STEEPLY UP
RIDGE

LARGE RED SCAR
ON HILLSIDE
🏠239

🏠231

CROSS SIDE
VALLEY

🏠242
**Trapecio
Punta**
5030m

MOSSY
GREEN
AREA

L. Barroso-
cocha
4590m

Ls.
Mitococha
4500m

VIEWS
BACK TO
TRAPECIO

CROSS
RIDGE
🏠240

🏠243

LITTLE
PLATEAU

PATH
REAPPEARS
🏠241

BIG OPEN PAMPA
WHERE PATH
FIZZLES OUT

CLIMB UP &
ACROSS
IMMENSE
BEDROCK

BOULDERS

Portachuelo de Huayhuash
4770m
🏠232

CLIMB TO
HIGH POINT
AT 4790m

VIEWS OF
CORDILLERA
RAURA

36

Nevados Puscanturpa △ △

△

JOIN MULE PATH

20 MINS | HUAYHUASH

40 MINS | JUNCTION 231

1H 30

PORTACHUELO DE HUAYHUASH

HIKING ROUTES & MAPS

From Huayhuash camp, cross the stone bridge to the E bank and climb southwards. The wide pre-Inca path climbs gently, passing a couple of ponds, on the way to the lower Laguna Mitococha (1 hour).

It takes a further 1h10 to reach the pass proper, at the circuit's closest point to the rarely-visited Cordillera Raura. The path climbs a bit higher, before descending down the R/W of the valley. Cross a boggy valley floor 40 minutes from the pass and merge with a path on the far side for the 30 minute descent to Laguna Viconga's shores. Take either fork when the trail splits and climb briefly to a gate above the SW corner of the lake (20 minutes), which is manned by the Uramaza community's cobrador.

Descend, turning R soon after crossing a water channel, then L/down at a fork (10 minutes) just before the Estación Viconga buildings. In a further couple of minutes is another junction, just before reaching a pampa. R is the direct route to Punta Cuyoc (bypassing the Aguas Termales); continue L/straight for these hot springs. Cross a concrete bridge (15 minutes) over the main river (either roaring or sedate, depending on the dam operators – see box) and continue for another 10 minutes to the lovely Viconga **camp**. The two **thermal pools** here are genuinely hot: only asbestos skin can tolerate the smaller one.

> ❏ **A raging river**
> Beware the narrow but deep river by Viconga camp. At times it's a sedate little stream, but when the dam workers open the sluice gates it transforms into a raging torrent. Run if you're by the gentle stream, hear a roar and suspect the gates have just been opened!

Day 4 alternative route: via Trapecio Punta   [Map 35, pp162-3]

• **Duration** 5-6h, skips day 5
• **Summary** This route shaves a day off the longer route round via Portachuelo de Huayhuash, getting you away from most groups and up close to Nevado Trapecio. On the climb there are marvellous glacier and rock views, while descending from the pass to Cuyoc camp is through an otherworldly landscape of turquoise moraine lakes and the spiky Puscanturpa peaks.

Look S from Huayhuash camp and memorize the position of the red earthy scar on a ridge in the valley, under the largest of the peaks on the southern skyline. Head along the main trail for 40 minutes from camp before cutting across to the scar (a further 10 minutes). Climb the ridge path behind the scar, and eventually follow this over the ridge to the W (30 minutes).

Continue W, going S of Barrosococha, over easy ground. Aim for the faint path which can just be seen ahead, cutting diagonally up the slope between cliffs and a small gully. The pass can also be seen on the skyline ahead – the point where light and dark rock meet. After 20 minutes cross a stream, then climb steeply on a path, passing between a waterfall and the cliffs in a further 45 minutes. Soon reach and cross a plateau studded with moraine lakes and loomed over by Nevado Trapecio, before climbing to Trapecio Punta (40 minutes).

The scenery on the descent is equally impressive, as the distinct path slides down the valley, past many turquoise lakes. After 40 minutes begin a short climb to the R of a small lake, on a trail to the R/W of the largest lake

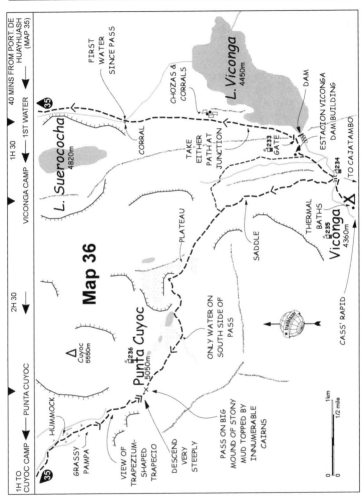

in the valley. It takes a further 1h30 to descend to Cuyoc **camp**.

Day 5: Viconga – Cuyoc camp   [Map 36 & Map 35, pp162-3]

● **Duration** 3h30-4h
● **Summary** The climb to Punta Cuyoc has excellent views of Nevados Puscanturpa, and at the pass Nevado Cuyoc's glacier seems almost close enough to touch. The initial part of the descent is on an awkward, stony surface, but lower down the going eases as you cross pampas to a campsite with views of the dramatic north-west face of Nevado Cuyoc Norte.

HIKING ROUTES & MAPS

From the hot springs, return to the concrete bridge. Cross and continue straight/L on a path heading N, aiming at the spiky rock tower at the E end of Nevados Puscanturpa. Climb to a high pampa (50 minutes) with lovely peak views.

After a brief flat period, climb again up the slopes on the L/W. The direct route from Laguna Viconga joins on the way to the first of a series of lakes (1 hour). The clear path heads L, climbing to the S of the lake to Punta Cuyoc (40 minutes).

The initial part of the descent, on a hard-packed path covered in small stones, is like walking on marbles. After 30 minutes the surface finally improves as you approach a pampa carpeted in sage-like *anqush (Senecio canescens)*. Cross the pampa, and descend between two streams to a junction (25 minutes). Go R/down for Cuyoc **camp** (10 minutes) and the main route over Paso Jurau. Going straight is for the Alternative (traditional) route to Huayllapa.

Day 6: Cuyoc camp to Cutatambo [Map 35, pp162-3]

- **Duration** 3h30
- **Summary** If the weather and your legs are cooperating, the route over Paso Jurau is a must. A far more exciting option than following Quebrada Huanacpatay down to the Río Calinca, the panoramas which greet you at the highest pass on the circuit are phenomenal. The descent is long and taxing and traverses towards the Jurau glaciers, far above brilliant Juraucocha. Mules are not allowed to cross the pass, but can take the long way round via the Alternative route. Some maps mark the more westerly Paso San Antonio rather than Paso Jurau. It is worth climbing up to Paso San Antonio for the views, but the descent from there towards Cutatambo is very steep and far more difficult. 'One slip,' as they say round here, 'and you're food for the condors!'

Cross the river from Cuyoc camp and head NE across the pampa. The valley to aim for is the very steep, shallow one to the L/W of rocky ribs. (The deeper grassy valley further L/W goes to Paso San Antonio.) After 5 minutes leave the pampa and start zigzagging steeply up a path in a small gully. Soon traverse L across grassy terrain, to the base of a scree slope (10 minutes). Follow the path over into a steep valley and climb up to emerge onto a large pampa (35 minutes). The pass, which can be seen ahead, is 50 minutes away.

Paso Jurau is an unforgettable spot, with Yerupajá and Sarapo foremost among the wonderful snowy peaks to the N. Lower down, in the valley below lies dazzling Juraucocha. The path of descent is clear, dropping sharply down the R/E scree slopes, before the trail swings R/NE, and traverses straight at the Juraus' snowy peaks and vertiginous glaciers. Reach the moraine and terra firma past the E end of Juraucocha (1 hour), then double back along the moraine. Drop down via an ablation valley to Cutatambo **camp** (40 minutes).

Day 6 alternative route: Cuyoc camp – Q. Huanacpatay – Río Calinca [Map 35, pp162-3 & Map 37]

- **Duration** 2h30 to Río Calinca, making it possible to reach Huatiaq in the afternoon.
- **Summary** As with the Alternative day 3, this route bypasses some amazing scenery and there is little point taking it unless you wish to save a day or are not feeling strong enough to tackle Paso Jurau.

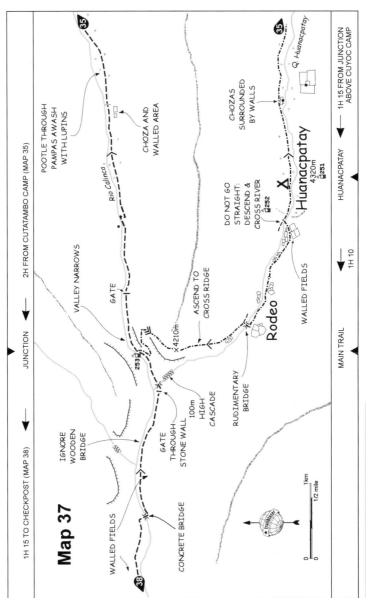

Map 37

From the junction above Cuyoc camp, continue down valley, crossing the main river after 25 minutes and reaching Huanacpatay **camp** 50 minutes later. Less than 10 minutes after the camp, descend at a junction, sticking to the main path which crosses the river on stones. Recross 25 minutes later, following a good path that heads away from the river, then climbs N to a high point with views down the Río

> ❏ **Touching the Void**
> In 1985, after a first ascent of Siula Grande's west face, Joe Simpson fell and broke a leg while descending with climbing partner Simon Yates. His extraordinary escape back to basecamp from the bottom of a crevasse (popularized by both a book and film) has become the stuff of mountaineering legend.

Huayllapa valley. Descend steeply to the main trail by the Río Calinca (35 minutes).

Side trip into Quebrada Sarapococha   [Map 35, pp162-3]

● **Summary** This side trip explores the beautiful valley where Joe Simpson's epic escape from Siula Grande unfolded (see box above). Lagunas Sarapococha and Santa Rosa could be tacked on in the afternoon after a morning crossing of Paso Jurau, but with more time it's better done as a day trip from Cutatambo. The energetic can continue up to Cerro Gran Vista (marked 5152m on the *Alpenvereinskarte*) for unbeatable views of the Huayhuash's most magnificent peaks.

Head N from Cutatambo camp, aiming for the steep path to the R/E of the waterfall that can be seen from camp. After 25 minutes, cross the main river at an island and pick up faint trails heading up the valley to a striped boulder (35 minutes). From here, it's a further 30 minutes to reach the moraine top overlooking Sarapococha. For best views, climb the hillsides to the W.

The really keen will want to head up towards Cerro Gran Vista, the most outrageous trekking viewpoint in the valley. This takes around 3 hours return from the mirador overlooking Sarapococha.

From the striped boulder, it's also 30 minutes to the moraine top overlooking Laguna Santa Rosa; on the return to Cutatambo, it's possible to detour via Juraucocha.

Day 7: Cutatambo to Huatiaq
[Map 35, pp162-3; Map 37, p167 & Map 38]

● **Duration** 5-6h

● **Summary** Today contrasts greatly with others on the circuit. Leave the big peaks behind and descend below 4000m for the first time, down the pleasantly verdant Río Calinca valley to Huayllapa. If needed, detour to restock in the village, before tackling the longest climb on the circuit, breaking it by camping at Huatiaq.

From Cutatambo, head down valley on the TL/S side, reaching the junction where the mule route joins after 2 hours. Continue down, crossing a concrete bridge over the main river after 45 minutes. Stay straight at a junction (30 minutes) and soon reach a gate manned by the cobradores for Huayllapa and Cutatambo. There's no point puzzling over how the Cutatambo cobradora knows you've been in her valley; she has magic powers and just does.

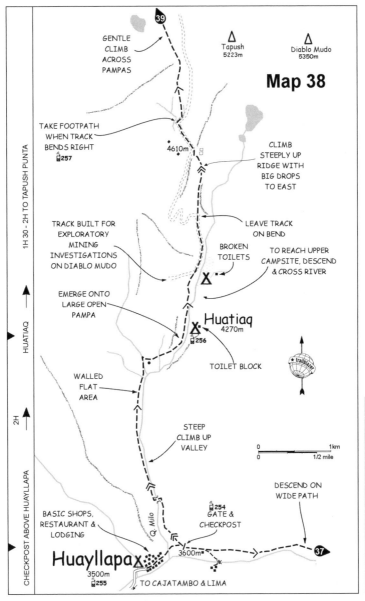

39

GENTLE
CLIMB
ACROSS
PAMPAS

△ Tapush 5223m

△ Diablo Mudo 5350m

Map 38

TAKE FOOTPATH
WHEN TRACK
BENDS RIGHT
🏕257

4610m

CLIMB
STEEPLY UP
RIDGE WITH
BIG DROPS
TO EAST

TRACK BUILT FOR
EXPLORATORY
MINING
INVESTIGATIONS
ON DIABLO MUDO

LEAVE TRACK
ON BEND

BROKEN
TOILETS

TO REACH UPPER
CAMPSITE, DESCEND
& CROSS RIVER

EMERGE ONTO
LARGE OPEN
PAMPA

X Huatiaq
4270m
🏕256

TOILET BLOCK

★ trailblazer

WALLED
FLAT
AREA

STEEP
CLIMB UP
VALLEY

0   1km
0   1/2 mile

DESCEND ON
WIDE PATH

37

BASIC SHOPS,
RESTAURANT &
LODGING

🏕254
GATE &
CHECKPOST

Q. Milo

Huayllapax
3500m
🏕255

3600m

TO CAJATAMBO & LIMA

1H 30 - 2H TO TAPUSH PUNTA

HUATIAQ

2H

CHECKPOST ABOVE HUAYLLAPA

HIKING ROUTES & MAPS

Immediately after the gate is another junction. The biggest trail goes to Huayllapa (20 minutes), while the trekking circuit turns R, climbing relentlessly towards Tapush Punta. It's a 2 hour slog to the lower Huatiaq **camp**; if this is too congested, continue 5 minutes to the higher camp on a larger meadow.

Huayllapa is a pleasant adobe and tin roof village with reasonably well-stocked **shops**, some basic **restaurants** and **accommodation** (S/.10 per bed). A combi leaves for Cajatambo (2h, S/.15) daily in the morning, returning in early afternoon. There's no internet.

Day 8: Huatiaq – Incahuain   [Map 38, p169 & Map 39]

● **Duration** 6h
● **Summary** The circuit nears its end with a bang! Climb to and cross Tapush Punta, then descend and climb to Yaucha Punta. At this second pass there are good views, and these improve if you detour from the pack trail for a stunning ridge walk to Cerro Huacrish. Snowy peaks from Ninashanca to Tsacra Grande light up the horizon to the east, before the twin lakes Jahuacocha and Solteracocha put in an appearance. Descending from the mirador feels like you're falling off the end of the earth, but makes for a rapid journey to another picturesque campsite, on the shores of Jahuacocha.

From the upper camp, climb for 15 minutes to a 4WD track and continue northwards. Leave at the first switchback, onto a footpath which rejoins the track after 30 minutes. Cross easy ground for 50 minutes to Tapush Punta.

The descent leads past Susucocha to a basic **campsite** at Gashpapampa (40 minutes), before turning R/E into Quebrada Angocancha. Pass some chozas where you may encounter the Pacllón cobrador; if not here, he'll find you at Incahuain. The route crosses the river (25 minutes), then climbs continuously to Yaucha Punta. Keep R of a small N-S cliff ahead, skirting round to reach the S end of a hidden pampa. Continue across the S side of this, heading E, and climb to a higher, parallel pampa. Turn L/N here, crossing the pampa to a scree slope (50 minutes) from where it's a further 30 minutes to the pass.

At Yaucha Punta, the trail splits. The wider mule path goes down (for 1h15 to the rejoining of routes), while a walking route heads off L on a small path that traverses N, then climbs NE to a high point (25 minutes) with fabulous views of the Huayhuash's main peaks. The path continues northwards along a ridge to Cerro Huacrish (30 minutes).

From the mirador, descend directly to Jahuacocha. Ignore any minor paths traversing across the slope – the one you want goes straight down. After 20 minutes go R of a rocky outcrop, continuing the vertical descent for 20 minutes to the pack trail.

Descend to the pampa in the Río Jahuacocha valley, swinging E to Incahuain (30 minutes), a lovely **camp** by the western shores of Jahuacocha with views Rondoy, Jirishanca and the Yerupajás. The camp is run by the Pacllón and Llamac communities – if you already have these tickets you don't need to pay again.

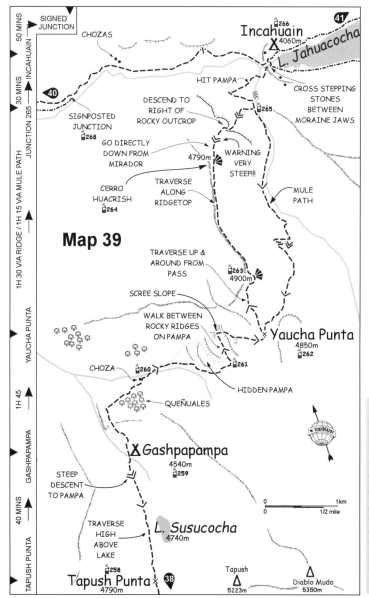

SIGNED JUNCTION

CHOZAS

266
Incahuain
4060m

41

L. Jahuacocha

50 MINS

INCAHUAIN

HIT PAMPA

30 MINS

40

CROSS STEPPING STONES BETWEEN MORAINE JAWS

JUNCTION 265

SIGNPOSTED JUNCTION
268

DESCEND TO RIGHT OF ROCKY OUTCROP

265

GO DIRECTLY DOWN FROM MIRADOR

4790m

WARNING VERY STEEP!!!

CERRO HUACRISH
264

TRAVERSE ALONG RIDGETOP

MULE PATH

1H 30 VIA RIDGE / 1H 15 VIA MULE PATH

Map 39

TRAVERSE UP & AROUND FROM PASS

263
4900m

SCREE SLOPE

YAUCHA PUNTA

WALK BETWEEN ROCKY RIDGES ON PAMPA

Yaucha Punta
4850m
262

CHOZA
260

261

HIDDEN PAMPA

1H 45

QUEÑUALES

trailblazer

X Gashpapampa
4540m
259

GASHPAPAMPA

STEEP DESCENT TO PAMPA

0   1km
0   1/2 mile

40 MINS

TRAVERSE HIGH ABOVE LAKE

L. Susucocha
4740m

TAPUSH PUNTA

258
Tapush Punta
4790m

38

Tapush
△
5223m

Diablo Mudo
△
5350m

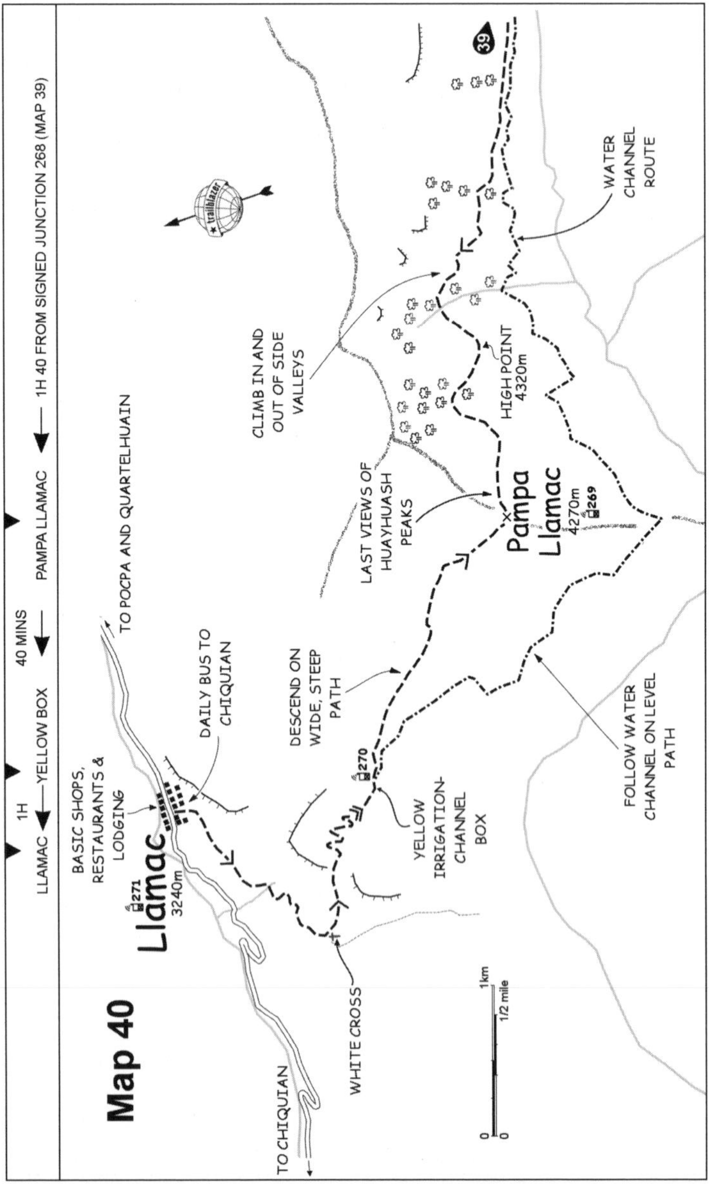

Map 40

LLAMAC ◀— 1H —▶ YELLOW BOX ◀— 40 MINS —▶ PAMPA LLAMAC ◀— 1H 40 FROM SIGNED JUNCTION 268 (MAP 39)

WATER CHANNEL ROUTE

CLIMB IN AND OUT OF SIDE VALLEYS

HIGH POINT 4320m

LAST VIEWS OF HUAYHUASH PEAKS

Pampa Llamac
4270m
▲269

DESCEND ON WIDE, STEEP PATH

▲270

YELLOW IRRIGATION-CHANNEL BOX

FOLLOW WATER CHANNEL ON LEVEL PATH

TO POCPA AND QUARTELHUAIN

DAILY BUS TO CHIQUIAN

BASIC SHOPS, RESTAURANTS & LODGING

Llamac
▲271
3240m

WHITE CROSS

TO CHIQUIAN

39

1km
1/2 mile

0
0

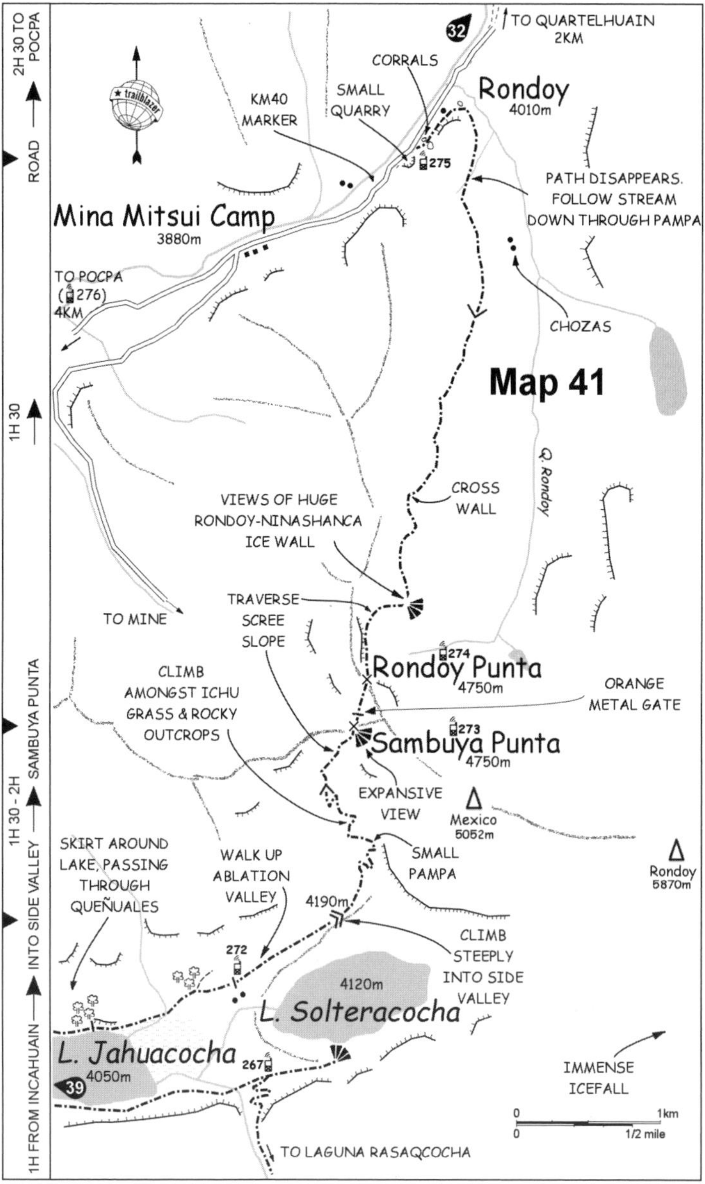
TO QUARTELHUAIN
2KM
32
CORRALS
Rondoy
4010m
KM40
MARKER
SMALL
QUARRY
275
PATH DISAPPEARS.
FOLLOW STREAM
DOWN THROUGH PAMPA
Mina Mitsui Camp
3880m
TO POCPA
(276)
4KM
CHOZAS
Map 41
Q. Rondoy
CROSS
WALL
VIEWS OF HUGE
RONDOY-NINASHANCA
ICE WALL
TRAVERSE
SCREE
SLOPE
TO MINE
274
Rondoy Punta
4750m
CLIMB
AMONGST ICHU
GRASS & ROCKY
OUTCROPS
ORANGE
METAL GATE
273
Sambuya Punta
4750m
EXPANSIVE
VIEW
Mexico
5052m
SMALL
PAMPA
Rondoy
5870m
SKIRT AROUND
LAKE, PASSING
THROUGH
QUEÑUALES
WALK UP
ABLATION
VALLEY
4190m
CLIMB
STEEPLY
INTO SIDE
VALLEY
272
4120m
L. Solteracocha
L. Jahuacocha
4050m
39
267
IMMENSE
ICEFALL
0 1km
0 1/2 mile
TO LAGUNA RASAQCOCHA
2H 30 TO POCPA
ROAD
1H 30
1H 30 - 2H
SAMBUYA PUNTA
INTO SIDE VALLEY
1H FROM INCAHUAIN

Side trip from Incahuain to Solteracocha (2h) and/or Rasaqcocha (3h30)   [Map 39, p171 & Map 41, p173]

From Incahuain camp take the trail on the S side of the lake to a junction (45 minutes) where a path turns R/up to Rasaqcocha (1 hour away). Go straight at the junction on a smaller path in an ablation valley for 15 minutes to the moraine top and great views of Solteracocha and Rondoy's W face.

Day 9: Incahuain – Pampa Llamac – Llamac
[Map 39, p171 & Map 40, p172]

● **Duration** 4-4h30

● **Summary** Most trekkers end their circuit with an easy walk to Llamac. If you're relying on public transport you'll need to set off early though, as the last bus from Llamac to Chiquián/Huaraz leaves around 11:30 (confirm with the cobrador). From camp the trail leads down valley, before climbing a low pass and dropping 1000m to Llamac.

Leave Incahuain via the path on the N side of the river, to reach a signposted junction (50 minutes). The main trail heads R/up here (signed 'To Llamac'), though it's possible to go straight on and follow a water channel. The two routes meet up before Llamac, by the yellow box described below. Following the canal is slightly longer (2h30 from signed junction to yellow box), but avoids any climbing.

The main trail climbs in and out of side valleys full of queñuales and bromeliads, reaching a high point after 1h15; then undulates before descending to the Pampa Llamac pass (25 minutes, Macrash Punta on the *Alpenvereinskarte*). Forty minutes into the descent, the water channel route joins from the L, just before a ridge and yellow concrete box. Continue down for a further 1 hour to Llamac.

Llamac has some **shops**, simple **restaurants** and a couple of basic places to stay – *Hostal Los Andenes* and *Alojamiento Santa Rosa*. **Camping** is also possible. The Nazario bus stop is one block south of the main street.

Day 9 alternative exit: to the road at Rondoy
[Map 39, p171 & Map 41, p173]

● **Duration** 4h

● **Summary** This route boasts better panoramas than the standard final day, so if transport can meet you at the road in Rondoy, or you don't mind walking down the road to Pocpa/Llamac and spending an extra night there, this is a good option. Climbing to Sambuya Punta there are fantastic views of Jirishanca and Yerupajá, and on the descent from Rondoy Punta the Rondoy-Ninashanca ice wall is in your face.

Head E from Incahuain, on the N side of the lakes, and after 1 hour begin climbing L/N out of an ablation valley. It takes 1h30 to reach Sambuya Punta, longer if you can't resist pausing every few minutes to look back at the snow and ice treats on show. At the pass a few stray peaks in the Cordilleras Blanca and Huayllanca come into view to the N, while the path traverses NE for 10 minutes to the slightly higher Rondoy Punta. The up-close views of Nevado Rondoy from here are simply superb. The trail traverses down valley, losing height gradually. It takes 1h20 to reach the road, emerging by a small waterfall and aggregate quarry. Pocpa is 2h30 away on foot.

CYCLE TOURING ROUTES & MAPS

Introduction

Cycling in the Cordilleras Blanca and Huayhuash is simply spectacular – many of the classic biking routes in the region are also the most picturesque and exciting on the continent. As in days of old, when Wari and Inca civilizations constructed a vast network of mountain trails, modern day Peruvians are still the master road builders of the Andes. Roads cut through the mountains in the most unlikely of locations, providing a rare opportunity to pedal through territory more used to condors than bicycles.

The only prerequisite for enjoying a tour here is a love of climbing: flat routes simply do not exist. Almost all routes have significant vertical ascents, but the rewards for tackling these scenic mountain roads are great.

Though roads in the area aren't as high as some in the Himalaya, they rise far above anything in Europe or North America, and the short distances between valley towns and 4500m+ passes means that acclimatization must play an important part in trip planning.

Routes described are all a mixture of tarmac and dirt roads. There are currently no circuits which can be done all on paving; likewise it's possible to spend most, but not all of your time chewing up dirt. See p23 for kit planning suggestions. Unpaved surfaces are generally reasonably good – there's no sand or corrugations, though some routes are bumpy and can be muddy in rainy season. Gradients are rarely over 10%, with 4-5% being the norm on most climbs.

Cyclists shouldn't expect to be able to average more than 40-50km a day. The vertical terrain means you'll climb at least 1000m in this time, which, combined with the high altitude, makes for energy-sapping riding.

Trailblazer's *Adventure Cycle-Touring Handbook* (see p235) is a good resource to help prepare for any kind of multi-day biking tour.

PRACTICAL INFORMATION

Bikes on transport

Airline policies for carrying bicycles vary greatly. Some charge, others don't, but almost all insist the bike is boxed or bagged. Read conditions of carriage carefully before buying your flight, and take a printout copy in case you need to show check-in staff.

Most buses from Lima to the Cordillera Blanca and between towns in the Cordillera will carry bikes. More upmarket companies have set fees, while drivers at others will size you up before deciding what to try and charge. This is almost always lower than set fees, but don't be afraid to haggle good naturedly (the bike fare should be less than the price for your seat). For a trip from Huaraz to a town in Conchucos, expect to pay a bike fee of around S/.10.

It's equally easy to throw a bike on smaller forms of transport if you need to shorten or access a route. Most taxis are estate cars (station wagons) with room for a few bikes; old combis have roof racks – you're usually charged an extra fare ('*pasaje*') to put your bike up top – and newer combis are able to fold down the back row of four seats (for which you must pay) to make room for bikes.

Bike spares and mechanics
Bikers in Huaraz are relatively well catered for in terms of spares, with an eclectic assortment of Shimano components to be found, as well as more common disc pads and rotors. Expect high price tags, and don't rely on finding the latest gear. Although there are plenty of 26" rims and tyres available (especially downhill), 29er riders will need to have spares sent up from the capital.

Of the Huaraz **bike shops**, Montañas Mágicas Bike Center by Plaza Ginebra, and Reyes, by the Río Quilcay, have the widest selection of spares. For **repairs**, hunt down Arturo Corpus – a skillful and reliable mechanic with over 20 years of bici-tinkering experience who is proudly equipped with a collection of Park Tools (Av Atusparia 851, ☎ 763753, ☎ 943 164000). All three can order parts to be delivered from better-stocked Lima shops (see p51); mountain biking agencies (p214) may also be able to help in the event of mechanical problems.

Outside of Huaraz, many towns have mechanics and very basic bike shops. Don't expect more than 26" tyres, tubes, rims and puncture repair kits in the way of spares, and don't be surprised if local mechanic techniques involve brute force and a mallet.

Renting bikes
If cycling is the main purpose of your trip, it makes sense to bring your own bike – you'll be more familiar with its foibles, and it's likely to be more comfortable. Added to this, finding suitable bikes to rent for a multi-day tour in Huaraz is difficult – try asking at Riders (p214). Those who are primarily trekking, but who wish to squeeze in a few day rides, will find it easy to rent

---

❑ **Gringooooo!**
Cyclists will find themselves referred to as gringo/gringa at regular intervals. In the vast majority of cases it's a descriptive rather than derogatory moniker, so don't take offense. If not gringo, you'd be *gordito* (fatty), *flaquito* (skinny), *chino* (Chinaman) or one of the many other nicknames Peruvians call one another.

bikes in Huaraz (see p214) or Caraz (p64), saving the considerable hassle of transporting your steed from home.

Dangers and nuisances

Ride defensively at all times. In towns, combi and colectivo drivers have an annoying habit of swerving right in front of cyclists to pick up clients, which puts the onus on you to avoid an accident. Stay alert for potholes, missing manhole covers, ice cream sellers, fruit carts, escaped guinea pigs and other obstacles.

Especially in populated centres which rarely see cyclists, **dogs** can be a nuisance. You should remain particularly alert during day rides in the vicinity of Huaraz, as though Peruvian dogs aren't generally that large, they can be aggressive. Simply stopping normally shuts them up; if it doesn't, bending down to pick up a rock usually works. Occasionally you may need to throw the rock, like the locals do. See p44 for advice in the unlikely event that you are bitten.

All routes described are on quiet roads, except for the sections on the paved road by the Río Santa. It's still a good idea to bring a helmet as not only can you pick up huge speeds on the descents, but the standard of driving is questionable and in rainy season there's a slight danger from rock fall.

When wild camping, always ensure you are out of sight of the road.

Route tables

The route tables in this section show cumulative **distances (km)**, **GPS waypoints**, **altitudes** (m) and include **directions** – left (←), right (→), straight on (↑) – and **local information**.

The GPS waypoints can be downloaded from ▣ **blancahuayhuash.com** (no charge).

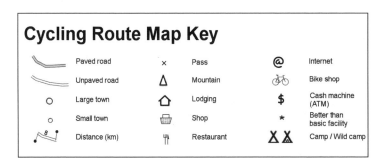

Cycling Route Map Key

〰	Paved road	×	Pass	@	Internet
〰	Unpaved road	△	Mountain	🚲	Bike shop
○	Large town	⌂	Lodging	$	Cash machine (ATM)
∘	Small town	🛒	Shop	★	Better than basic facility
⟋⁸⟍	Distance (km)	🍴	Restaurant	⚑ ⚑	Camp / Wild camp

Routes

DAY RIDES NEAR HUARAZ

The first four of these rides from Huaraz are good ways to acclimatize before heading out to tackle some of the high passes, and the better acclimatized you are, the more enjoyable your multi-day riding will be. Most villages in the hills around Huaraz have a basic shop selling fizzy drinks and biscuits; it's a good idea to bring water and other snacks with you from town.

Huaraz Ruins Loop

This half-day loop into the hills above Huaraz makes a good first ride in the Blanca. The route climbs steadily out of town to the Recuay and Wari period ruins at **Wilcahuaín** (S/.5, open 09:00-17:00 Mon-Sat, to 14:00 Sun/hols) and **Ichic Wilcahuaín** (same ticket and timetable). Beyond, the scenery opens out and it's a quiet ride with sweeping views of the Negra and the Blanca's southern quebradas and peaks. Pastoral rural life continues sedately – it's a world away from Ancash's busy capital.

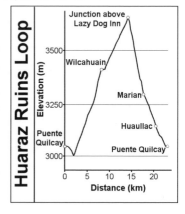

At the beginning of the steep and bumpy descent, pass *Café Yurac Yacu* (open daily 11:00-16:00, early/mid-June – September), which serves up local organic produce and makes a great lunch spot. All proceeds from the café benefit the community centre housed there. Before arriving back in Huaraz, the road skirts a third set of Wari ruins at Huaullac.

It's possible to avoid most of the climbing on this loop by catching a combi (30 mins, S/.1.50 plus S/.1.50 for a bike) to Wilcahuaín (see map p54); bikes are carried on the roof rack.

🚲 HUARAZ RUINS LOOP   [map pp180-1]
- **Start & end**   Huaraz, Puente Quilcay
- **Riding time** 2½-3 hrs
- **Paved/Unpaved %** 20/80
- **Distance** 23km/14 miles
- **Vertical climb** 650m/2100ft
- **Max altitude** 3660m/12,000ft

KM	GPS	ALT (M)	INFO	DESCRIPTION
0	277	3060	Start	**Huaraz**, Puente Quilcay. Head 2 blocks N on Av Centenario until it becomes one way.

Kм	GPS	Alt (m)	Info	Description
0.2		3060	→, ←	R on Víctor Velez, then 1st L on Fco de Zela.
0.9		3050	←, →	L on Fco Araos, at the end of Fco de Zela, then 1st R onto Av Centenario.
1.7	278	3020	→	R to Wilcahuaín (signposted), off main highway. Paving is soon replaced by bumpy dirt road – stick to the largest route as it climbs up behind Huaraz.
6.3		3290		Start of steep km in Paria.
7.5	279	3410	Ruins	Entrance to **Wilcahuaín ruins**. Just after, the route flattens off and the surface becomes good.
8.4	280	3410	Ruins	**Ichic Wilcahuaín ruins**.
8.9	281	3440	↑	Go straight. R descends to Uquia and Huanchac.
13.8	282	3650	→	Junction by Km12 marker. Go R, descending towards Marian. (See Blanca Acclimatization Loop p183 for route that continues straight). Soon reach **The Lazy Dog Inn** and **Café Yurac Yacu**.
17.2	283	3290	↑	Straight at junction in **Marian**. R descends to El Pinar (see p185).
20.2	284	3140	Ruins	**Huaullac ruins**, R of road, just before a bridge. Descend paving to the town centre.
22.5	277	3060	End	**Huaraz**, Puente Quilcay.

Negra Acclimatization Loop

This trip in the Cordillera Negra is another ideal introduction to cycling in the thin air of the Callejón de Huaylas. The route never goes above 3300m, though as it climbs nearly 400m above the valley floor there are great views across to the snowy peaks of the Cordillera Blanca.

After leaving the none-too-clean outskirts of town, the route begins a lovely rising traverse, high above the river, through small villages, patchwork fields, *agave cordillerania* and eucalyptus. Reach a high point before Huanja, then descend swiftly to the main, paved, road and climb back up valley to town. The circuit can be shortened, if desired, by descending to the paving at earlier junctions.

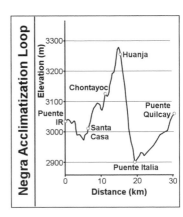

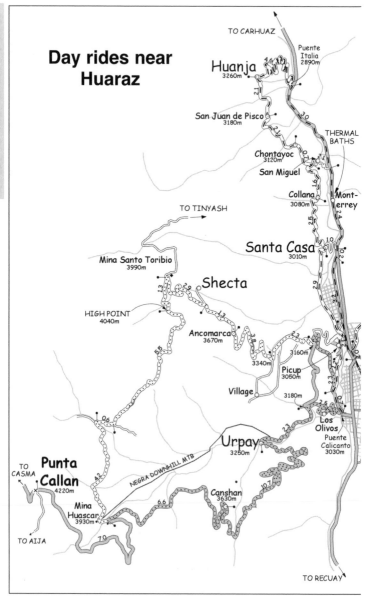

Day rides near Huaraz

TO CARHUAZ

Puente Italia 2890m

Huanja 3260m

4.6

2.1

San Juan de Pisco 3180m

3.0

2.1

THERMAL BATHS

Chontayoc 3120m

San Miguel

1.6

2.1

Collana 3080m

Mont-errey

2.4

2.5

Santa Casa 3010m

1.0

0.2

TO TINYASH

Mina Santo Toribio 3990m

Shecta

2.9

1.3

2.9

HIGH POINT 4040m

1.3

Ancomarca 3670m

3.8

5.5

2.3

3340m

3160m

Picup 3050m

3.0

Village

3180m

0.6

2.6

Los Olivos

Puente Calicanto 3030m

Urpay 3250m

2.3

NEGRA DOWNHILL MTB

4.4

TO CASMA

Punta Callan 4220m

Canshan 3630m

10.7

6.6

Mina Huascar 3930m

TO AIJA

7.9

TO RECUAY

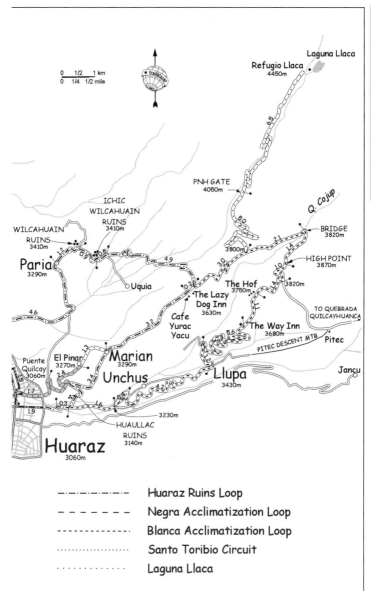

	Huaraz Ruins Loop
	Negra Acclimatization Loop
	Blanca Acclimatization Loop
	Santo Toribio Circuit
	Laguna Llaca

🚲 NEGRA ACCLIMATIZATION LOOP   [map pp180-1]
- **Start** Huaraz, Puente Interoceánico Raimondi
- **End** Huaraz, Puente Quilcay
- **Distance** 29km/18 miles   • **Riding time** 3 hrs   • **Paved/Unpaved %** 40/60
- **Vertical climb** 650m/2100ft   • **Max altitude** 3280m/10,750ft

Km	GPS	Alt (m)	Info	Description
0	285	3030	Start	**Huaraz**, Puente Interoceánico Raimondi.
			→	Cross the Río Santa and go R immediately after this new bridge (which is 0.2km north of Puente Calicanto), on paving.
0.5	286	3040	→	Turn R onto rough dirt road at concrete dip in road.
1.7		3050	→	R onto paving in Picup.
1.9	287	3050	→	Descend on dirt road.
2.3		3020	→	Continue descent on dirt.
2.9		2990	←	Stay on W side of the Río Santa. (R crosses Puente Santo Toribio.)
5.2		2990		Marcac.
5.8	288	3010	←	L in **Santa Casa**. (Going straight here descends 1km to the main road.) Be alert for the many dogs on the next section.
8.3		3080		**Collana**.
9.9	289	3080	←	L to Chontayoc. (R descends for 2.1km, through San Miguel, to the main road.)
10.6		3120		**Chontayoc**.
12.7		3180		**San Juan de Pisco**. Stay L, traversing, at the village junction.
14.4		3280	Top	High point.
14.8	290	3260	→	**Huanja**. Go R on reaching the plaza and immediately R again, following a good dirt surface back to the main road.
19.1		2890	Bridge	Puente Italia.
19.4	291	2920	→	R on paved main road at Km578 (between Puente Mullaca and a Pecsa gas station).
22.4		2940	↑	Road from shortcut via San Miguel joins from R.
24.8		2980	↑	Road from shortcut via Santa Casa joins from R.
25	292	2980	→	Turn R, signed 'Hospital II Huaraz', to avoid the main road into town.
28.2		3030	↑	Straight at traffic lights, on Av Centenario.
29.4	277	3060	End	**Huaraz**, Puente Quilcay.

Blanca Acclimatization Loop

For more of a workout than the half-day rides already described, whilst still remaining below 4000m, try this route in the hills above Huaraz. The mountain views are superior to those on the Ruins Loop, and from the high point there are tantalizing glimpses of snow and ice in quebradas Llaca and Cojup. At the beginning of the bumpy descent feast your eyes on Nevados Shacsha and Cashan, and if you wish to descend on singletrack, detour to the Pitec Descent (p215).

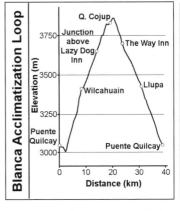

Those lucky enough to be riding at the beginning of the dry season in May and June will find the road-side wildflowers are a riot of colour – purple lupins and yellow asters foremost among them.

To the junction at 13.8km, it's possible to take the more direct and much steeper road via El Pinar and Marian – see Laguna Llaca ride (p185).

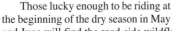

🚲 BLANCA ACCLIMATIZATION LOOP [map pp180-1]

- **Start & end** Huaraz, Puente Quilcay
- **Distance** 39km/24 miles
- **Riding time** 4-5 hrs
- **Vertical climb** 900m/3000ft
- **Paved/Unpaved %** 10/90
- **Max altitude** 3870m/12,700ft

Km	GPS	Alt (m)	Info	Description
0	277	3060	Start	**Huaraz**, Puente Quilcay. Follow Huaraz Ruins Loop to junction at 13.8km.
13.8	282	3650	↑	Junction by Km12 marker. Continue straight, climbing gently.
16.8	293	3800	↑	Go straight, ignoring turn-off L to Laguna Llaca.
18.9		3820	Bridge	Cross Río Cojup.
20.3		3870	Top	High point with good views of Nevados Cashan and Shacsha.
21.3	294	3820	→	Stay R on main route. L is for Quebrada Quilcayhuanca and also the singletrack Pitec Descent.
22.7		3750		Pass entrance to *The Hof* (see p62).
23.8		3680		Pass *The Way Inn Lodge*.
29.4		3470	↑	Road from Yarush joins from the R.
30.6		3430		**Llupa**.
34.8	295	3230	←	Go L at the 4-way junction in **Unchus** for the most direct route back to Huaraz.

Km	GPS	Alt (m)	Info	Description
35.2		3200	↑	Roads rejoin. Go straight for Huaraz. (L goes towards Jancu.)
36.8		3110	↑	Huaraz Ruins Loop joins. Go straight for Huaraz, R for **Huaullac ruins** (0.5km away).
38.7	277	3060	End	**Huaraz**, Puente Quilcay.

Santo Toribio Circuit

This route climbs more than a thousand vertical metres from Huaraz into the Cordillera Negra, on the paved road which leads to the sea at Casma. The climb is not particularly taxing as the gradients are gentle, and it makes an excellent warm-up for the high passes on the Huascarán Circuit.

Just below 4000m, turn off the tarmac onto a traversing dirt track that bumps its way north to the abandoned Santo Toribio mine. Here, point your bike downhill and roll all the way back to town.

If you're feeling energetic, consider continuing on the paving to Punta Callán before returning to cycle the dirt section – the pass is 7km past the dirt road turn-off and tops out at 4220m.

Mountain bikers can make a thrilling loop of it by plummeting down the Negra Downhill (p218) route soon after leaving the paving near Mina Huascar.

🚲 SANTO TORIBIO CIRCUIT [map pp180-1]

- **Start & end** Huaraz, Puente Calicanto
- **Riding time** 4-6 hrs
- **Paved/Unpaved %** 50/50
- **Distance** 47km/29 miles
- **Vertical climb** 1100m/3600ft
- **Max altitude** 4040m/13,250ft

Km	GPS	Alt (m)	Info	Description
0	296	3030	Start ↑	**Huaraz**, Puente Calicanto. Go straight at the junction immediately after the bridge and snake steeply up the paving through Los Olivos.
2.6	297	3180	←	Turn L on Casma road, just S of Puente Cochac, and continue climbing towards Punta Callán on paving.
22.2	298	3930	→	Turn R through a gap in the safety barriers, on a hairpin bend after the Km121 marker. Soon pass the turn-off for the Negra Downhill,

Km	GPS	Alt (m)	Info	Description
				then traverse on a sometimes bumpy and rocky surface.
26.4		3960	↑	Straight at junction by bridge.
27		3960	←	Go L and continue traverse, reaching 4040m high point just before next junction.
33.8	299	3990	→	R at junction by **Mina Santo Toribio**. Begin a long, rattling descent to town.
38		3670		**Ancomarca**.
41.8		3340	←	Stay on main route, rounding a left-hand hair-pin, then stay straight at 3 junctions in quick succession.
44.1	300	3160	←	Rejoin paved Punta Callán road.
46.9		3040		Puente Interoceánico Raimondi – cross for Av Raimondi.
47.1	296	3030	End	**Huaraz**, Puente Calicanto.

Laguna Llaca

For the acclimatized, this long climb into a steep-sided quebrada above Huaraz makes for an enjoyable, though challenging day trip. The road ends at Refugio Llaca, just five minutes' walk from Laguna Llaca, a milky green lake nestled under the impressive peaks of Ocshapalca and Ranrapalca.

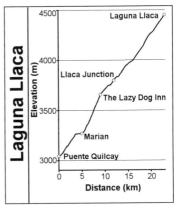

Leaving the tarmac at El Pinar, the dirt road climbs through villages where local women herd cows and sheep to pastures. The final 12km to Laguna Llaca are on a rocky surface which is a battle to climb in places: suspension makes for a faster and more comfortable descent. It's possible to camp high in the valley if you wish to break the ride into two days, but the refugio is for the use of Casa de Guías (see p60) clients only.

There are options for getting to the Llaca turn-off at 3800m. Here we describe the most direct route, which is the quickest and by far the steepest. It's also possible to pedal via Wilcahuaín (see p178) or Llupa (see p183). In theory you need a PNH ticket to enter Quebrada Llaca, so take cash in case you meet a guardaparque.

🚲 LAGUNA LLACA   [map pp180-1]

- **Start & end** Huaraz, Puente Quilcay
- **Riding time** 5-6 hrs
- **Paved/Unpaved %** 15/85

- **Distance** 47km/29 miles (return)
- **Vertical climb** 1400m/4600ft
- **Max altitude** 4450m/14,600ft

KM	GPS	ALT (M)	INFO	DESCRIPTION
0	277	3060	Start	**Huaraz**, Puente Quilcay. Go one block N.
0.1		3060	→	Turn R onto Jr Manco Capac and remain on this through town.
1.7	301	3150	→	Turn R, signposted 'El Pinar'.
4.1		3270	→	Turn R onto unpaved road at **El Pinar**, a gated community for Antamina mine workers.
5.4	283	3290	←	L at T-junction in **Marian**. Soon begin a series of very steep climbs. Pass *The Lazy Dog Inn* and *Café Yurac Yacu* just before reaching the next junction.
8.8	282	3650	→	Go R on meeting road from Wilcahuaín. Climb gently on good surface.
11.8	293	3800	←	Turn off L to Laguna Llaca, before main route enters Quebrada Cojup.
16.8		4050		**PNH gate** as you enter Quebrada Llaca. Ocshapalca and Ranrapalca in view ahead.
23.3	302	4450	Top	*Refugio Llaca* and road end. For best views, lock up your bike and walk up the footpath to Laguna Llaca, before beginning the long descent.
46.6	277	3060	End	**Huaraz**, Puente Quilcay.

HUASCARÁN CIRCUIT

The circuit of Huascarán is a classic Andean cycle route, providing a visual and cultural treat to all intrepid cyclists willing to accept the challenge. The loop crosses the spine of the Cordillera twice, at Punta Olímpica (4890m) and Portachuelo de Llanganuco (4710m), passes cut through rocky ridges in the 1980s, for roads which soar high among glaciers and are towered over by the Blanca's largest peaks.

Six or seven riding days is the ideal amount of time to spend on encircling Peru's highest mountain. You'll need to camp a couple of times and will probably also want to add in a day or two for resting in one of the towns, or for exploring Quebradas Llanganuco or Ulta, in order to soak up some of the most spectacular natural beauty in the whole of the Andes.

It makes little difference which way you cycle the loop; here we describe it in an anticlockwise direction so as to start with an easier, paved climb.

Much of the route is in PNH – buy the S/.65 ticket at the Llanganuco post if you overnight in the park.

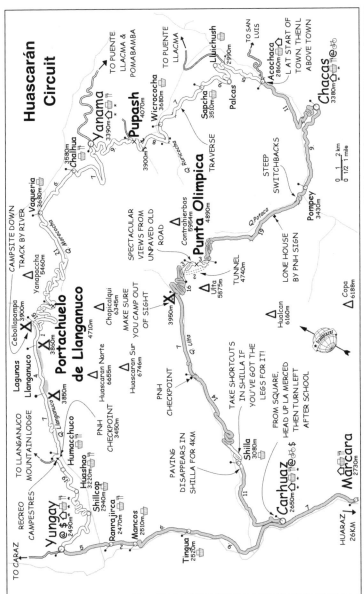

Huascarán Circuit

TO CARAZ

TO LLANGANUCO
MOUNTAIN LODGE

RECREO
CAMPESTRES

Yungay
@ $ 2490m

Ranrajirca
2470m

Shillcop
2940m

Huashao
3220m

Humacchuco

Mancos
2510m

Tingua
2520m

Lagunas
Llanganuco
3850m

Portachuelo
de Llanganuco
3860m

Chopicalqui
6345m

Huascaran Norte
6655m

Huascaran Sur
6746m

Cebollapampa
3900m

CAMPSITE DOWN
TRACK BY RIVER

Yanapaccha
5460m

Vaqueria
3680m

Chalhua
3680m

Yanama
3390m

Pupash
4070m

TO PUENTE
LLACMA &
POMABAMBA

Wicrococha
3680m

3900m

Sapcha
3510m

Palcas

Lluichush
2990m

Acochaca
2860m

Chacas
3380m

TO PUENTE
LLACMA

TO SAN
LUIS

L AT START OF
TOWN, THEN1
ABOVE TOWN

3580m

6

7

21

15

16

8

9

11

9

11

TRAVERSE

STEEP
SWITCHBACKS

Pompey
3430m

19

Q. Potaca

Copa
6188m

Q. Runtococha

PNH
CHECKPOINT
3450m

Q. Llanganuco

SPECTACULAR
VIEWS FROM
UNPAVED OLD
ROAD

MAKE SURE
YOU CAMP OUT
OF SIGHT

Contrahierbas
5954m

Punta Olimpica
4890m

Ulta
5875m

LONE HOUSE
BY PNH SIGN

TUNNEL
4740m

3950m

Q. Ulta

Huaican
6160m

PNH
CHECKPOINT

TAKE SHORTCUTS
IN SHILLA IF
YOU'VE GOT THE
LEGS FOR IT!

FROM SQUARE,
HEAD UP LA MERCED
THEN TURN LEFT
AFTER SCHOOL

PAVING
DISAPPEARS IN
SHILLA FOR 4KM

Shilla
3080m

Carhuaz
2650m

Marcara
2730m

HUARAZ
26KM

5

6

7

14

11

6

1

0   1   2 km
0 1/2 1 mile

trailblazer

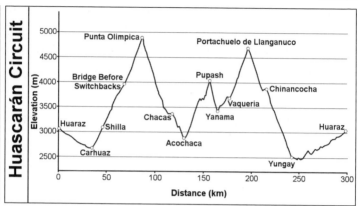

Huascarán Circuit

Route description

Begin leisurely enough with a cruise downhill from Huaraz to Carhuaz. Initially traffic is quite heavy, but it thins the further you travel from the Ancash capital. In Carhuaz, turn off onto the newly paved road to Chacas and the long, beautiful haul to Punta Olímpica. There's great camping in Quebrada Ulta, on a pampa surrounded by splendid peaks – Ulta and Contrahierbas, Huascarán and Chopicalqui – before the zigzags to the top begin.

In 2013 Túnel Olímpica, the highest road tunnel in the world, was opened, offering the chance to circumvent the uppermost 200m of switchbacks to the pass, but this is still the Daddy of Andean road passes. It may be too bold to state that it's the best on the continent; but it's in the top one.

The advent of the tunnel makes it a race against time for cyclists wishing to cross the true pass – the road's upper reaches are prone to avalanches and landslides and if it ceases to be maintained the elements will render it impassable. Rumour has it that local mayors have agreed to keep the pass proper open for visiting tourists, but it remains to be seen whether this will be the case.

The descent into the Callejón de Conchucos is almost equally exciting. As you fly down the tarmac make sure to avert your gaze from the mountains and lakes to the road just long enough to avoid overshooting the switchbacks which funnel you out at the quaint town of Chacas.

After Acochaca comes a route choice. The recommended way to Yanama is over 4070m Pupash pass, on a road built at the beginning of the century. This route doesn't climb any more than the lower alternative which drops to the bridge at Llacma, before ascending to Yanama. The quiet towns and villages on this eastern side of the Blanca can feel a world away from the Callejón de Huaylas, and the lack of vehicular traffic means you're more likely to be held up by herds of animals than hear the roar of a 4x4.

From Yanama comes the bumpy climb past a scattering of small lakes to the fabulous Portachuelo de Llanganuco. The pass is surrounded by majestic glaciated peaks, and the switchback descent down to Cebollapampa and the Lagunas de Llanganuco is unforgettable. The shores of turquoise Chinancocha and Orgoncocha, flanked by steep granite walls, both make excellent camp sites, and it's possible to do day walks to Laguna 69 (see p107) or Pisco Basecamp from the valley.

Exit the quebrada and continue apace to Yungay, before returning on the main road to Huaraz.

CYCLE TOURING ROUTES & MAPS

🚲 **HUASCARÁN CIRCUIT**   **[see maps p187, p198 & p200]**
- **Start & end** Huaraz
- **Riding time** 6-7 days
- **Paved/Unpaved %** 60/40
- **Distance** 299km/186 miles
- **Vertical climb** 6300m/20,700ft
- **Max altitude** 4890m/16,050ft
  (4740m/15,550ft via tunnel)

KM	GPS	ALT (M)	INFO	DESCRIPTION
0	303	3060	Start	**Huaraz**, Plaza de Armas. Take main road heading N (see p178 for detail from Puente Quilcay).
2.5	278	3020	←, →	Turn L, opposite the Wilcahuaín turn, then R at the end to follow a quieter, parallel road past Hospital II. (You could stick to the main road, but it's busy.)
5.5	292	2980	←	Turn L, rejoining main road.
7		2940		Pass turn-off to the **Monterrey** baths (p61).
17	304	2820	→	Go R (signed 'Pariahuanca'), leaving the main road before Puente Jangas. This gets you away from the traffic, but is mostly unpaved. Sticking to the main road is 0.5km longer.
17.5		2810	↑	Pass entrance to **Taricá**, a village famous for its pottery artisans.
21		2770	↑	Go straight (R goes to Pariahuanca), pedalling past fields and giant agaves.
25.5	305	2730	↑	Rejoin main road in **Marcará**.
33	306	2650	→	**Carhuaz** (p64). Leave main road, turning R just before the welcome arch, onto Av Santa Rosa. Pass through town to link up with Punta Olímpica road. Views of Huascarán, Copa, Hualcán on the climb.
43.5		3060	→	Go R at the junction near the start of **Shilla**, then zigzag up through town. The other three shortcuts save a km, but are super steep.
45		3120		Top of last shortcut. Once the paving restarts in 1km, remain on it to the tunnel.
57.5		3700		**PNH checkpoint** (often unmanned).
60.0		3810		Start of **pampa**. Views of Contrahierbas and later Ulta.

🚲 HUASCARÁN CIRCUIT [cont'd]

Km	GPS	Alt (m)	Info	Description
65.5		3950	Bridge Wild Camp	Cross bridge and begin zigzagging climb with views of Huascarán and Chopicalqui. There's good, hidden camping if you push your bike a couple of minutes upriver on the S side of the bridge.
81		4740	← Tunnel	Turn L onto an unpaved road at the tunnel entrance. (If you go via the paved tunnel, it's 2km to where the routes meet.)
83.5	307	4890	Pass	**Punta Olímpica**. Waaah! Give yourself a pat on the back, before descending amazingly tight switchbacks to the paving.
87		4660		Rejoin **paving**, below tunnel entrance. There are no stand-out campsites on the descent.
106		3430		**Pompey**.
114.5		3380		**Chacas** (p71), Plaza Mayor. Continue N on tarmac.
126	308	2860	←, ←	Junctions in **Acochaca**. Go L, then L again 0.1km later, onto an unpaved road (R at either of these junctions goes to San Luis).
130.5	309	2990	←	Go L for Pupash at a fork before some woods. R goes to Cunya (see p205) and is the alternative low way to Yanama, via Puente Llacma.
133		3150		**Lluichush**. It's well worth detouring for a minute to compare the old (adobe) and new (brick) churches in the plaza.
140		3510	←	Plaza in **Sapcha**. Turn L at the church.
146.5		3680		**Wicrococha**. There are some wild camping opportunities between this village and the pass.
148		3680		Cross **river** in Quebrada Ruricocha. Contrahierbas visible up valley.
152.5		3920	↑	Continue straight – L is a small track to Mina Cajavilca.
154.5	310	4070	Pass ←	**Pupash**. From the pass are views of Nevado Cajavilca, and as you descend Chacraraju appears ahead. Soon after the pass, go L at a junction (R goes to Cunya).
164	311	3390	←	**Yanama** (p71), Plaza de Armas. Head L for Llanganuco.
171.5		3580		**Chalhua**. Ignore road off R which goes to Colcabamba.

🚲 HUASCARÁN CIRCUIT [cont'd]

Km	GPS	Alt (m)	Info	Description
177		3680		**Vaquería** – trailhead for Santa Cruz trek (p88).
178.5		3720		**Upper Vaquería**. Road surface deteriorates.
184		3850	Wild Camp	Km60+600 marker by a pampa – the best hidden camp this side of the pass.
193.5		4470		Km50 marker and the highest possible camp before the pass. There's an old toilet block, but the site is in view of the road, so is not recommended.
198	312	4710	Pass	**Portachuelo de Llanganuco** and fabulous peak views. The awesome, zigzag descent is bumpy.
212.5	313	3930		Access to **Cebollapampa camp** and Laguna 69 (see p107).
214		3860		**Yuraccorral camp**, near the east end of Laguna Orgoncocha.
218.5		3850		**Zona de Recreación Chinancocha** with PNH station, boating, picnic tables and camping.
225.5		3450		Llanganuco **PNH checkpoint**. Tickets and drinks available for purchase.
226.5	314	3400	←	Go L at junction by Recreo Campestre Llanganuco. R takes a quieter (2km longer) route to Yungay, passing near Keushu ruins and lake and Llanganuco Mountain Lodge (see p62).
229.5		3220		**Huashao**. Ignore road which goes R to Yuracoto.
235		2970	←	Stay L on main road, ignoring track off R to Atma.
235.5		2940		**Shillcop**.
244	315	2490	←	**Yungay** (p70). Go L on main road, passing Campo Santo memorial (to those who died in the 1970 aluvión, entry S/.5) after 1km.
266	306	2640		**Carhuaz**.
299	303	3060	End	**Huaraz**, Plaza de Armas.

CYCLE TOURING ROUTES & MAPS

Huayhuash & Puya Raimondii

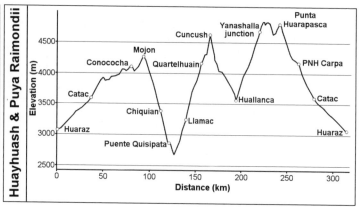

HUAYHUASH AND PUYA RAIMONDII LOOP

For panoramas of the Cordillera Huayhuash and up-close encounters with *Puya raimondii* in the southern Cordillera Blanca, this circuit from Huaraz (or Catac) can't be bettered. Most people need six or seven days to cycle the 315km route as long stretches are at high altitude and there are four 4000m passes to negotiate.

Cycling either of the sections from Llamac to Huallanca or Huallanca to Catac in a day is beyond most mortals, so bring camping equipment. The communities in Llamac and Pocpa charge fees to pass through (S/.20 and S/.10 respectively – see p154). Though this is really meant for the Huayhuash Circuit trek, cyclists have to pay even if they don't leave the road. The puna stretch over

❏ **Ruta de los Dinosaurios**

During construction of the paving to Antamina, Peru's biggest mine, workmen were somewhat surprised to uncover dinosaur footprints in the bedrock being excavated – these incredible discoveries can twice be seen right by the road. To visit, detour from the circuit at the junction above Huanzala. It's possible to continue past the prints to Antamina mine (46km from the junction) and on for a further 60km to San Marcos. A shorter, rougher way to Conchucos is to turn off the paving 30km after the junction above Huanzala and cut straight down to Chavín (26km away).

Additionally, you could take the earlier part of the Antamina road from Conococha to Yanashalla. This is an easier and shorter alternative to going via Chiquián and Cuncush. Conococha to Yanashalla is 61km.

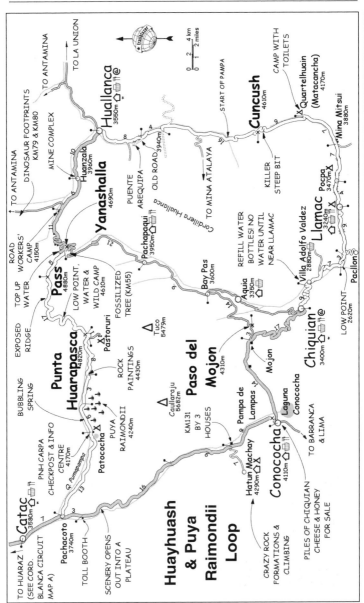

Huayhuash & Puya Raimondii Loop

TO HUARAZ
(SEE CORD.
BLANCA CIRCUIT
MAP A)

Catac 3580m
Pachacoto 3740m
TOLL BOOTH
SCENERY OPENS OUT INTO A PLATEAU
PNH CARPA CHECKPOST & INFO CENTRE 4170m
BUBBLING SPRING
Patococha
PUYA RAIMONDII 4240m
Q. Pumapampa
ROCK PAINTINGS 4430m
Punta Huarapasca 4820m
Pastoruri
Tuco 5479m
Caullaraju 5682m
KM131 BY 3 HOUSES
CRAZY ROCK FORMATIONS & CLIMBING
Hatun Machay 4290m
Pampa de Lampas
Paso del Mojon 4310m
Conococha 4110m
Laguna Conococha
PILES OF CHIQUIAN CHEESE & HONEY FOR SALE
TO BARRANCA & LIMA
Mojon
Aquia 3350m
Bay Pas 3600m
Chiquian 3400m
LOW POINT 2620m
REFILL WATER BOTTLES! NO WATER UNTIL NEAR LLAMAC
Villa Adolfo Valdez 2880m
Llamac 3240m
Pocpa 3470m
Pacllon
Cordillera Huallanca
TO MINA ATALAYA
EXPOSED RIDGE
TOP UP WATER
Pass 4880m
LOW POINT, WATER & WILD CAMP 4610m
FOSSILIZED TREE (KM55)
Yanashalla 4690m
Pachapaqui 3960m
PUENTE AREQUIPA
OLD ROAD 3940m
ROAD WORKERS' CAMP 4150m
Huanzala 3960m
Huallanca 3550m
MINE COMPLEX
DINOSAUR FOOTPRINTS KM79 & KM80
TO ANTAMINA
TO LA UNION
START OF PAMPA
KILLER STEEP BIT
Cuncush 4610m
Quartelhuain (Matacancha) 4170m
CAMP WITH TOILETS
Mina Mitsui 3880m

Punta Huarapasca is within PNH – you can buy a ticket at the Carpa checkpost.

The circuit is described here in an anti-clockwise direction, as this leaves the highest passes until the end. If you're already acclimatized, it makes more sense to reverse the route to avoid the tough 2000m climb from below Puente Quisipata to Cuncush. Those with less time can complete a shorter and easier loop in four days by continuing on the paving from Conococha to Yanashalla before joining the dirt road to Punta Huarapasca.

Route description

Cycle south from Huaraz on the main road to Catac, passing through the pleasant town of Recuay en route. Above Catac the valley opens out, the traffic thins and Nevado Caullaraju dominates the peaks at the southern end of the Blanca. On a clear day the views of the Cordillera Huayhuash near Mojón are superb and it's worth overshooting the turn-off to Chiquián and continuing a few minutes on the road to Bay Pas, before returning, in order to get the best panoramas of the range.

Descend at speed on tarmac to Chiquián, an energetic town that marks the end of the easy riding. Follow a dirt road into the bowels of the earth, before eventually beginning the long, tiring, but virtually traffic-free climb to Cuncush. It's possible to stay in Llamac or camp in Pocpa, but as these are both short days from Chiquián, some prefer to put in a big (1600m climb) day to the campsite at Quartelhuain.

As you near Cuncush (4600m), the snowy peaks of the Huayhuash again appear, to be replaced by the less impressive Cordillera Huallanca on the descent. There's a long flat pampa section before reaching the paving at Huallanca.

Climbing the green valley towards Yanashalla is a wonderful ride, and despite some huge mines in the area, there's only a vehicle every few minutes. On reaching the Antamina turn-off, we highly recommend detouring briefly from the main route for 9km to the dinosaur prints (see box p192).

Just before Yanashalla pass, turn off the paving onto a road that continues climbing gently, through a wild Andean landscape. The Cordilleras Huallanca, Huayhuash and Blanca are all in view as the route clings to an exposed ridge on either side of a 4880m high point. There's decent camping on the descent, before a short climb brings you to 4820m Punta Huarapasca, the final pass of the trip. The hills are a palette of colours – greens, oranges, browns – while above black rock meets icy glacier on Nevados Cajap, Huarapasca and Pastoruri.

The Pastoruri junction marks a deterioration in the road surface as the route has been churned up by vehicles bringing tourists to gape at Quebrada Pumapampa's most impressive residents: the magnificent *Puya raimondii* (see box p30 and colour panel C5, p18). These bromeliads tower like sentinels above a road which eases its way down valley to the main road at Pachacoto. Turning north, Huaraz's pizzerias are but two short hours away.

Hatun Machay sidetrip
At 4290m and only 7km off the main road south of Catac is this incredible stone forest. It's a rock-climbing and bouldering paradise, with many ancient paintings adorning the weird rock formations. **Andean Kingdom**, an agency in Huaraz, runs the site and organizes daily transport from town. Day entry costs S/.5, while overnighting is S/.20 to camp and S/.30 for a bed in the refugio.

Pastoruri sidetrip
The 7km-return trip, up a very rough 4WD track on Nevado Pastoruri, is the highest rideable road in the Cordillera Blanca. It terminates at a camp area with a lofty altitude of 4950m, from where it's a 20-minute walk to a 5000m viewpoint overlooking the mountain's fast-retreating glaciers.

🚴 HUAYHUASH & PUYA RAIMONDII LOOP   [maps p193 & p198]
- **Start & end** Huaraz
- **Riding time** 6-7 days
- **Paved/Unpaved %** 55/45
- **Distance** 315km/196 miles
- **Vertical climb** 5500m/18,000ft
- **Max altitude** 4880m/16,000ft

Km	GPS	Alt (m)	Info	Description
0	303	3060	Start	**Huaraz**, Plaza de Armas. Take the main road S.
24.5		3410	←	Turn off to **Recuay** and continue right through the town. This is more interesting than sticking to the main road, and doesn't add any distance or time.
28		3440	↑	Rejoin main road.
30		3470		**Ticapampa**.
35.5		3580	↑	**Catac**. Continue straight (L goes to Chavín).
42.5	316	3740	↑	Remain on the paving in **Pachacoto**, a near ghost-village with no facilities. L goes to Pastoruri and is the road by which this loop returns (at 273km, see p197).
71		4060	↑	Km131 marker and **turn-off to Hatun Machay**.
80	317	4110	←	**Conococha village**. Turn L towards La Unión/Chiquián.
93.5	318	4260	→	Turn R at the few houses of **Mojón** and descend to Chiquián. (For even better views of the Huayhuash, continue straight on the main road for a few minutes – detouring onto the track up a tiny hill to the R for best panoramas – before returning).
111		3400		**Chiquián** (see p68). Leaving town, take the road heading E to Llamac, descending on a bumpy surface.
119.5		2870	Bridge	Cross Puente Quisipata.
120		2880		**Villa Adolfo Valdez**.
122	319	2870	→	Stick R, on the main route at a fork, by a Km0 marker and 'Nicanor Cerrate' sign.

🚲 HUAYHUASH & PUYA RAIMONDII LOOP [cont'd]

Km	GPS	Alt (m)	Info	Description
127		2620		Start the lengthy climb to Cuncush.
130	320	2770	←	Keep L at a fork. R is the road to Pacllón (8km).
139		3240		**Llamac** (see p174). Pay S/.20 fee.
143.5		3470		**Pocpa**. Pay S/.10 fee.
150		3880		In the **Mitsui Mine** complex.
157		4170	Camp	**Quartelhuain** camp (often referred to as **Matacancha**) – the usual start point for the Huayhuash Circuit trek. Climb, often steeply, to the pass.
165.5	321	4610	Pass	**Cuncush**. Cordillera Huallanca comes into view and the interminable climb transforms into a bumpy descent.
182		3940	↑	Ignore large mine road leading off L.
193.5	322	3550	← Bridge	Turn L, crossing a bridge by the Raul Cordova Alvarado School.
194		3550		**Huallanca**, Plaza de Armas. There's transport to Lima and Huaraz; *Hostal Milan* has hot water and hearty meals; *Hotel El Pueblo Huallanca* is the smartest place in town. Take the Huaraz road, past the bullring, out of town. Easy, paved climb up a quebrada with many one-man mines in the hillsides.
204		3960		**Huanzala mine**.
209.5	323	4150	↑	Junction with the Antamina road. Go straight (or, better, head R towards Antamina and climb to the **dinosaur prints**, before returning and continuing the route below. The first set of prints is after 8km, the second set is 1km further).
220.5	324	4670	→	Turn off R to Pachacoto (signed 'Huaraz'), on a little-used dirt road with a good surface. (Yanashalla pass is 0.5km further on the paving).
226	325	4880	Pass	**High point**, on either side of which are possible, though exposed, camp spots with water sources.
236		4610		Low point.
237		4630		Good camping, with clear water in small side rivers.
243.5	326	4820	Pass	**Punta Huarapasca**.
244.5		4770	↑	Continue straight. L is short **detour to Pastoruri**.

🚲 HUAYHUASH & PUYA RAIMONDII LOOP [cont'd]

Km	GPS	Alt (m)	Info	Description
252		4430		**Pintura rupestre** – paintings dating from 200 BCE – 600 CE, on a rock face by the road.
255		4240		The main stand of *Puya raimondii* in Quebrada Pumapampa.
259.5		4170	PNH	**Carpa PNH checkpost**; ticket sales, toilets, Visitor Centre and possible camping.
273	316	3740	➔	Turn R upon meeting main, paved, road in **Pachacoto**.
315	303	3060	End	**Huaraz**, Plaza de Armas.

CORDILLERA BLANCA CIRCUIT

This encircling of the Cordillera Blanca is a great choice for those who wish to see and experience traditional rural Ancash life. Adobe and tile buildings, animal herding, colourful woven clothing and wonderful hats all abound. It doesn't go as high as, or pass as close to, the snowy peaks as other routes, but there are still fabulous views and plenty of climbing, as the quiet rollercoaster of a road darts in and out of side valleys and crosses three 4000m passes. Cyclists with enough time will find it easy to tack on the Huascarán Circuit or Huayhuash Loop for an even more comprehensive, varied and exciting ride.

It makes sense to cycle the circuit in an anti-clockwise direction, thus avoiding a 3000m climb to Abra Cahuacona near the beginning. If you're willing and able to put in long days, it's possible to go without camping gear, overnighting in basic village accommodation along the way. Though there are a few good spots to roll out your sleeping mat, wild camping is tricky for the most part due to frequent homesteads and the vertical terrain. Water and supplies are easy to find.

Route description

Climb up the main road from Huaraz to the attractive town of Recuay, where there is a minor route choice. Either take the lovely dirt road shortcut, saving 7km, which crosses the Río Santa and meets the paving above Catac; or, stick to the paving as far as Catac before turning east. Laguna Querococha, backed by hills pitted with deep, wrinkled valleys, makes a good camp spot part way into the

(continued on p202)

❏ **Pastoruri**

In Huaraz you'll see many Pastoruri day tours advertised. These are something of a hangover from the days when there were ice-caves to visit and the mountain's glaciers were far larger; in fact, nowhere is glacial retreat in the Blanca more in evidence than on this peak. The tours are still popular with backpackers and local tourists as they visit the *Puya raimondii* near Carpa en route to depositing you within a short walk of Pastoruri's glaciers.

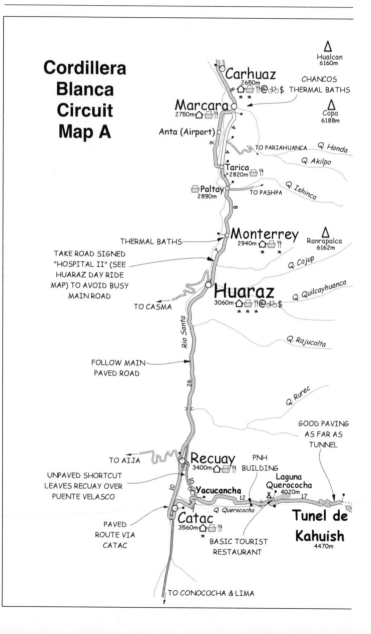

Cordillera Blanca Circuit Map A

△ Hualcan 6160m

Carhuaz 2650m

CHANCOS THERMAL BATHS

Marcara 2750m

△ Copa 6188m

Anta (Airport)

TO PARIAHUANCA

Q. Honda

Q. Akilpo

Tarica 2820m

TO PASHPA

Q. Ishinca

Paltay 2890m

THERMAL BATHS

Monterrey 2940m

△ Ranrapalca 6162m

Q. Cojup

TAKE ROAD SIGNED "HOSPITAL II" (SEE HUARAZ DAY RIDE MAP) TO AVOID BUSY MAIN ROAD

Huaraz 3060m

Q. Quilcayhuanca

TO CASMA

Rio Santa

Q. Rajucolta

FOLLOW MAIN PAVED ROAD

26

Q. Rurec

GOOD PAVING AS FAR AS TUNNEL

TO AIJA

Recuay 3400m

PNH BUILDING

UNPAVED SHORTCUT LEAVES RECUAY OVER PUENTE VELASCO

Yacucancha

Laguna Querococha 4020m

Q. Querococha

12

17

PAVED ROUTE VIA CATAC

Catac 3560m

Tunel de Kahuish 4470m

BASIC TOURIST RESTAURANT

TO CONOCOCHA & LIMA

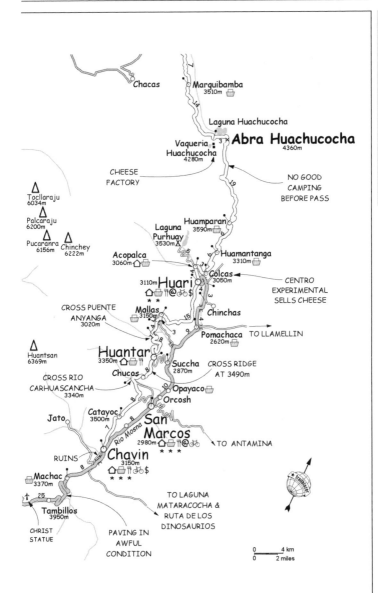

Chacas

Marquibamba
3510m

Laguna Huachucocha

Abra Huachucocha
4360m

Vaqueria
Huachucocha
4280m

3

CHEESE
FACTORY

NO GOOD
CAMPING
BEFORE PASS

9

Tocllaraju
6034m

Palcaraju
6200m

Pucaranra
6156m   Chinchey
6222m

Huamparan
3590m

Laguna
Purhuay
3530m

Huamantanga
3310m

Acopalca
3060m

Colcas
3050m

CENTRO
EXPERIMENTAL
SELLS CHEESE

3110m Huari
@ $

4

CROSS PUENTE
ANYANGA
3020m

Mallas
3150m

Chinchas

16

Pomachaca
2620m   TO LLAMELLIN

3   9

Huantsan
6369m

Huantar
3350m

CROSS RIO
CARHUASCANCHA
3340m

Chucos

8

Succha
2870m

CROSS RIDGE
AT 3490m

Opayaco

8

Orcosh

Catayoc
3500m

Jato

Rio Mosna

San
Marcos
2980m   @

TO ANTAMINA

RUINS

Chavin
3150m
@ $

Machac
3370m

25

TO LAGUNA
MATARACOCHA &
RUTA DE LOS
DINOSAURIOS

Tambillos
3950m

CHRIST
STATUE

PAVING IN
AWFUL
CONDITION

0   4 km
0   2 miles

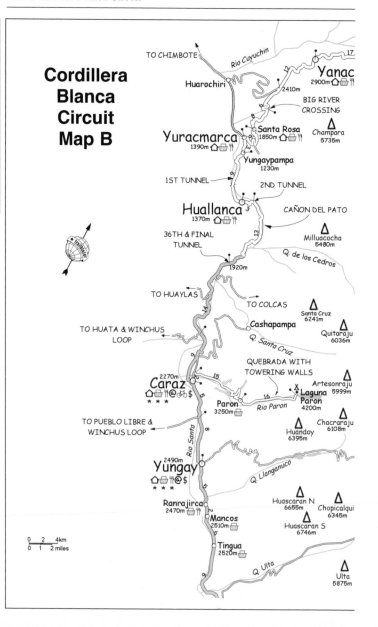

Cordillera Blanca Circuit Map B

TO CHIMBOTE

Rio Cuyuchin

17

Yanac 2900m

Huarochiri

2410m

BIG RIVER CROSSING

Santa Rosa 1850m

Champara 5735m

Yuracmarca 1390m

Yungaypampa 1230m

1ST TUNNEL

2ND TUNNEL

Huallanca 1370m

CAÑON DEL PATO

Milluacocha 5480m

36TH & FINAL TUNNEL

Q. de los Cedros

1920m

TO HUAYLAS

TO COLCAS

Santa Cruz 6241m

Cashapampa

TO HUATA & WINCHUS LOOP

Quitaraju 6036m

Q. Santa Cruz

QUEBRADA WITH TOWERING WALLS

Caraz 2270m

Artesonraju 5999m

Laguna Paron 4200m

Paron 3250m

Rio Paron

TO PUEBLO LIBRE & WINCHUS LOOP

Chacraraju 6108m

Huandoy 6395m

Rio Santa

Yungay 2490m

Q. Llanganuco

Ranrajirca 2470m

Huascaran N 6655m

Chopicalqui 6345m

Mancos 2510m

Huascaran S 6746m

Tingua 2520m

Q. Ulta

Ulta 5875m

0   2   4km
0   1   2 miles

PAVING ENDS

Rio Sihuas

Abra Cahuacona
4200m

Tarica
3370m

TO SIHUAS

Pasacancha
3630m

Pariashpampa
3610m

Rio Rupac

Andaymayo
3090m

3190m

Cilindre
3090m

Rio Andaymayo

TO TAURIBAMBA & SIHUAS

Yacupampa
3250m

TO LAGUNA
SAFUNA

TO PAROBAMBA

Palo Seco
3770m

Shiulla
3280m

Tayapampa
5675m

Alpamayo
5947m

Pucajirca
6046m

Taulliraju
5830m

Pomabamba
2960m

Huayllan
2870m

Rio Pomabamba

TO HUANCHACBAMBA

Rio Lucma

Huaycho
3110m

Piscobamba

Portachuelo
de
Llanganuco
4710m

DESCEND TO
RIVER AT 2820m

Lucma
3070m

Masqui
3100m

VIEWS OF
TAULLIRAJU
& PUCAJIRCA

Llumpa
2860m

Yanama

Rio Yurma

Puente Llacma
2460m

TO YAUYA & SAN
NICOLAS

Pupash
4070m

Alpabamba
2900m

Cochaocro
3240m

Rio Chucpin

INTRICATELY
CARVED WOODEN
STATIONS OF THE
CROSS

Cunya
3000m

Pomallucay
2780m

Contrahierbas
5954m

Punta
Olimpica
4890m

Acochaca
2860m

San Luis
3150m

Cordillera Blanca Circuit

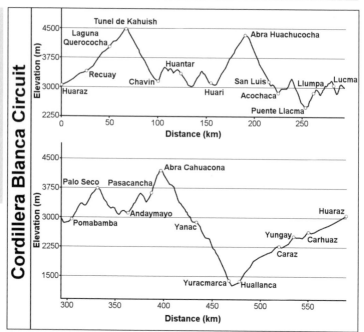

ascent, before the route passes through Túnel de Kahuish and descends to the verdant Callejón de Conchucos and Chavín. It's worth spending a day here visiting the most important archaeological site in the region before continuing.

There are two route options from Chavín to Huari. We recommend the more scenic high, unpaved way through Huántar, though this is more strenuous than the main road which descends the Río Mosna valley and passes through San Marcos before climbing to Huari.

From Huari comes a long ascent over Abra Huachucocha to San Luis, where again the road divides. The high route via Cunya offers better views and the chance to linger in untouched villages which rarely see a foreigner. The low route has the advantage of fewer vertical metres to ascend and the opportunity for a quick detour to the pilgrimage site of Pomallucay. The routes rejoin near Puente Llacma and zigzag up to the village of Llumpa. The main, though still very quiet, way to Pomabamba is via Piscobamba; however it's better to take the shortcut via Lucma as the surface and panoramas are superior.

The northern sector from Pomabamba to Yuracmarca is the least impacted by the modern world. Interactions with welcoming poncho-clad villagers, out tending fields or knitting whilst herding animals, are a highlight as the road undulates upwards to Abra Cahuacona. The descent down a large valley from the pass is phenomenal, with huge drops down to the river and pampas below.

Chuckle at the gall of Peruvian road engineers as you cut down a near-vertical slope en route to Yuracmarca, then marvel again after hitting the main road and climbing up to Caraz through the Cañón del Pato. The route passes through 36 tunnels cut into the steep-sided canyon walls. Bring good lights – there is some traffic and the unlit tunnels are as much as 250m long.

Caraz makes a good place to rest and recuperate before continuing for a day up the paving by the Río Santa, through Yungay and Carhuaz to Huaraz.

🚲 CORDILLERA BLANCA CIRCUIT   [maps pp198-9 & pp200-1]

- **Start & end** Huaraz
- **Riding time** 10-14 days
- **Paved/Unpaved %** 30/70
- **Distance** 589km/366 miles
- **Vertical climb** 11,200m/36,700ft
- **Max altitude** 4470m/14,650ft

Kм	GPS	Alt (m)	Info	Description
0	303	3060	Start	**Huaraz**, Plaza de Armas. Take the main road S.
24.5	327	3410	←	L off main road, to Recuay.
25.5		3400	←, →	**Recuay**, Plaza de Armas. Turn L, then R by the river, for the dirt road shortcut. (Continue straight and rejoin the main road for the **alternative route** via Catac – see p208.) *Hostal Pasto Ruri*, S of Recuay's Plaza, has basic en suite rooms and is a decent choice.
26.5	328	3410	← Bridge	Go L across **Puente Velasco** (if it has been rebuilt – it collapsed in the 2014 rainy season) then turn R/S. If the road bridge has not been rebuilt, go over the pedestrian bridge 1km further S. Pass through **Llullucachi** village.
30.5		3470	←	Turn L, climbing up a green side valley. R is a rough track to Ticapampa.
34		3590		**Yacucancha.**
35.5	329	3640	←	Turn L and rejoin paving at the few houses of Buenos Aires. Gentle and easy climb with views of spiky peaks near Quebrada Rurec.
46.5		3960		PNH Querococha Office.
48		4020		**Laguna Querococha** and basic (in season) café. Possible camping.
65	330	4470	Tunnel	Enter 500m-long **Túnel de Kahuish**. On leaving, you're greeted with a wave from a large Cristo de los Andes figure. Road surface is poor and there are no good campsites on the descent.
90		3370		**Machac.**
94.5	331	3220	↑	Stay straight at junction in **Quercos** (thermal baths). R is the unpaved way to Ruta de los Dinosaurios (see box p192).

☂ CORDILLERA BLANCA CIRCUIT [cont'd]

Km	GPS	Alt (m)	Info	Description
95.5		3190	↑	Stay straight on the main road. (L goes to the Chavín ruins on a dirt road and is a pleasant alternative route into town.)
97.5		3150		**Chavín** (see p66), Plaza de Armas. Either take the more interesting high, unpaved route through Huántar (described here), or the **alternative route** (see p208) – the easier, shorter, almost-all-paved main road at the bottom of the valley.
98	332	3140	←	Turn L onto dirt road on Jr Huascar.
105		3500	Top	**Catayoc**. High point.
108.5		3400	↑	Go straight, heading for Huántar. R descends to San Marcos and the main road.
111		3510	Top	High point.
113		3350	↑	Go straight. R descends to Yurayaco, Acopara and San Marcos.
113.5		3340	Bridge	Cross Río Carhuascancha.
114		3360	←	Stay L. R descends to a hamlet.
116		3430		**Chucos**.
118		3490	Top	High point. Huántar comes into view.
120.5	333	3350	↑	Go straight, on paving at S end of Huántar. R descends to Succha.
121		3350		**Huántar**, Plaza de Armas. Known as 'El Balcón del Conchucos', for its stunning location.
126		3150	↑	Keep straight. R goes to Huarac.
129.5		3020	Bridge	Cross Puente Anyanga in Quebrada Rurec.
133		2990	Bridge	Cross Río Rurichinchay.
133.5	334	3010	←	Go L. R descends to the main road.
136		3140	←	Turn L at the start of Mallas.
143.5	335	3420	Top, →	Go R at the junction soon after high point (L goes to Yakya).
146.5		3330	↑	Straight at a junction.
151.5	336	3110		**Huari** (p72), Plaza de Armas.
155		3060	↑	Stay straight at the junction to Maria Jiray waterfall (L) in **Acopalca**. (It's 2km up a sheer-sided valley to the end of the very steep, but rideable road, from where it's a 15 minute walk to the fall.)
155.5		3060	↑	Go straight, when a road leads off L to Laguna Purhuay (5km) and the largest fish farm (*piscigranja*) in the area.

🚲 CORDILLERA BLANCA CIRCUIT [cont'd]

Km	GPS	Alt (m)	Info	Description
158		3050		Centro Experimental, Colcas. Good **cheese** available.
163.5		3310		**Huamantanga**.
170		3590		**Huamparan**, the last village before the pass. Ancient footpaths zigzag up the steep valley sides and there are many houses around until above 4000m. We wouldn't recommend wild camping before San Luis, due to reports of very occasional night robberies on this road.
188.5	337	4360	Pass	**Abra Huachucocha**. Descend past Laguna Huachucocha.
191.5		4280		Stay straight. L goes to Vaquería Huachucocha, a **cheese factory** run by Don Bosco (p71) where it's possible to buy dairy produce and you could ask to camp.
205.5		3510		**Marquibamba**.
213		3150		**San Luis**, Plaza de Armas, which houses a surprisingly large church. *Hospedaje Beker* is OK and cheap; *Hotel Pucayacu* is nicer. Possible to buy Don Bosco **cheese** here too.
215.5	338	2980	←	L to Acochaca/Chacas on paving (described here). **Alternative route** (see p208): descend R on dirt, for the quicker route to Llacma, which passes near Pomallucay.
223.5	308	2860	→, ←	R at junction in S part of **Acochaca** (straight goes to Chacas). In 0.1km turn L, off the paving, onto a dirt road which goes to Yanama and Llacma.
228	309	2990	→	Go R for Cunya at a fork before some woods. L goes to Pupash (see p190).
231.5		2970		Colpa.
233.5		3000		**Cunya**. Larger village with two churches.
237.5		3240	Top →	**Cochaocro**. Village, high point and junction. Go R/down, on the largest track, for Llacma.
243.5		2900		**Alpabamba**. Picturesque village with tile and adobe buildings.
248.5	339	2590	←	Direct low route from San Luis rejoins – go L for Llacma.
253	340	2460	↑ Bridge	**Puente Llacma**: low point and junction (L) to Yanama. Continue straight for Llumpa, climbing zigzags.

CYCLE TOURING ROUTES & MAPS

🚲 CORDILLERA BLANCA CIRCUIT [cont'd]

Km	GPS	Alt (m)	Info	Description
261.5		2860	↑	Stay straight, in the lower part of **Llumpa**, 'Capital de la Chirimoya'. L climbs to the centre. The main river is in a deep and narrow gorge, far below.
268.5	341	2800	←	L to Lucma, on higher road. The lower road is the bus route, via Piscobamba.
277.5		3100		**Masqui**. Climb to 3170m before descending.
282		3070		**Lucma**. Plunge down from the quaint plaza into the depths of the valley, past agave and eucalyptus, to the bridge.
286.5		2820	Bridge	Cross the Río Lucma.
292		3110		**Huaycho**.
301.5		2870		**Huayllán**.
302		2870	↑	Stay straight. L climbs to Huanchacbamba.
307	342	2960		**Pomabamba** (p69), Plaza de Armas. Head N, on road to Sihuas.
319.5		3280		**Shiulla**.
334	343	3770	Top, ↑	Go straight at **Palo Seco** (a junction and pass). R goes to Parobamba. L is for the rough track to Laguna Safuna – the most outrageous place you can reach by road in the Blanca. The scenery near the pass is like a Scottish moor – wild camping is possible above 3600m.
340.5	344	3490	←	Go L. R is for Tauribamba and Sihuas.
342		3400	↑	Stay straight. R descends to Chulcana.
350		3250		**Yacupampa**.
352.5		3160	←	Go L. (R descends to Chinchabamba). The next few kilometres can become unmotorable in rainy season.
357		3090		**Cilindre**. Climb to 3190m, before descending.
365.5		3090		**Andaymayo**.
378.5		3610	Top	High point in **Pariashpampa**.
384.5		3370	Bridge	Low point.
390	345	3630	←	Hit main, paved, road in **Pasacancha**. Go L for Caraz, climbing steeply. R descends to Sihuas.
396.5		4090		Climb flattens off. Sihuas visible to R/N.
398.5	346	4200	Pass	**Abra Cahuacona**. Possible to wild camp on either side of the pass; better on the descent. Nevado Champará comes into view before the beginning of a long, long descent.

🚲 **CORDILLERA BLANCA CIRCUIT [cont'd]**

Km	GPS	Alt (m)	Info	Description
407		3900		End of paving.
418		3370		**Tarica**.
418.5		3360	↑	Stay straight. L goes to Quitaracsa.
435.5		2900		**Yanac**, a lovely village on a slope with no motorable streets but the main road. Descend down valley high above the river on a road carved into a steep hillside. The town of La Pampa eventually appears far below.
447.5	347	2410	←	L to Yuracmarca, leaving the main route just after the Km14 marker. Straight descends further, joining the main road in Huarochiri, lower down the Río Santa valley from Yuracmarca.
448.5		2490	↑	Stay straight at a small junction, descending 5km to a river crossing, before continuing to Santa Rosa.
461.5		1850		**Santa Rosa**.
465.5		1650	→	Stay R, descending. L climbs to Pachma Baja.
470	348	1390	←	Go L on main road in **Yuracmarca**. R goes to Chimbote. Lots of fruit for sale.
473		1230		Low point in **Yungaypampa**.
478.5		1310	Tunnel	Tunnel No.1.
482		1370		**Huallanca**.
485		1500	Tunnel	Tunnel No.2 and the start of the many tunnels in spectacular Cañón del Pato.
494		1850		Paving starts.
498		1920	Tunnel	The 36th and final tunnel.
511.5	349	2120	↑	Stay on paving, ignoring the road leading off R to Huata and Pamparomas (see Winchus Loop p210).
520.5	350	2270		**Caraz** (p62), Plaza de Armas.
525.5	351	2270	↑	Stay on main road, when a paved road leads off R for Pueblo Libre and the Winchus Loop.
534	315	2490		**Yungay** (p70), where the road to Llanganuco on the Huascarán Circuit (see p186) begins.
556	306	2640		**Carhuaz** (p64), gateway to Punta Olímpica.
589	303	3060	End	**Huaraz**, Plaza de Armas.

🚲 **CORDILLERA BLANCA CIRCUIT [cont'd]**
Alternative paved route from Recuay via Catac

Km	GPS	Alt (m)	Info	Description
0		3410	↑	**Recuay**, Plaza de Armas. Continue straight.
2.5		3440	↑	Rejoin main road after Recuay.
10	352	3560	←	Turn L onto main street in Catac, for road to Chavín.
11.5		3540		Km0 marker and start of paved road to Chavín.
17	329	3640	↑	Unpaved shortcut from Recuay joins (at 35.5km, see p203).

🚲 **Alternative low route from Chavín to Huari via San Marcos**

0		3150		**Chavín**, Plaza de Armas. Take main, paved, road N.
8	353	2980	←	Junction at start of **San Marcos**. Go L, via the Plaza de Armas.
10.5	354	2950	↑	Go straight. R climbs to Antamina via Huari-pampa – see box p192 **Ruta de los Dinosaurios**.
17.5		2870	↑	Go straight in **Succha** – a dirt road climbs L to Huántar. The low road passes incredible rock slabs – hundreds of metres high and perfectly smooth.
21.5		2720	↑	Continue on the paving, ignoring a dirt road that climbs L to Mallas. Soon cross Puente Jaucan at the narrowest point of the Río Mosna valley.
26.5	355	2620	↑	Stick to the main road in **Pomachaca**, the pyrotechnics capital of the Cordillera. R goes to Llamellín.
31		2800	↑	Keep straight, on the paving. R goes to Chinchas, from where it's about 3 hours walk to the Recuay ruins of Marcajirca.
33.5		2880	↑	Straight. R goes to Cajay.
38	336	3100		**Huari**, Plaza de Armas.

🚲 **Alternative low route from San Luis to Puente Llacma via Pomallucay**

0	338	2980	↑	Go straight/R (at 215.5km, see p205), descending a dirt road towards Pomallucay. L is the main paved road to Acochaca.

🚲 **CORDILLERA BLANCA CIRCUIT [cont'd]**   **Alternative low**
route from San Luis to Puente Llacma via Pomallucay

Km	GPS	Alt (m)	Info	Description
8	356	2780	↑	Straight at junction. R goes to Pomallucay (2.5km away and worth a quick detour to see the church) and Yauya.
12.5		2540	Bridge	Cross main river.
15.5	339	2600	↑	Join main route described at 248.5km (see p205).

LAGUNA PARÓN

Enthusiasts of long, challenging ascents should enjoy this one. Once you turn off the tarmac in the outskirts of Caraz, the climb is incessant – almost 2000m at an average 6% gradient. It's possible to go unloaded on a day trip, but this means arriving at Laguna Parón in the afternoon by which time the peaks are often enshrouded in cloud. Better to cycle to the lake, then camp and go walking in the morning – the views on the hike to Artesonraju Basecamp (see p109) are superb.

The first half of the climb passes quiet villages; flowers and vegetables seen growing in roadside fields are sold in Caraz market and beyond. At 3300m is a control gate manned by Parón villagers where tourists are charged S/.5 entry to the valley; the money goes directly to the Parón community and you're not required to have an additional PNH ticket. Above the gate nothing but zigzags, queñuales and huge rock walls await. The road ends just above Laguna Parón's turquoise waters, with views of Piramide and Chacraraju.

🚲 **LAGUNA PARÓN**   [see Cordillera Blanca Map B, p200]
- **Start & end** Caraz
- **Riding time** 8 hours
- **Paved/Unpaved %** 5/95
- **Distance** 67km/42 miles return
- **Vertical climb** 1950m/6400ft
- **Max altitude** 4200m/13,800ft

Km	GPS	Alt (m)	Info	Description
0	350	2270	Start	**Caraz**, Plaza de Armas. Go N on Jr Sucre, up the E side of the plaza.
0.5		2310	←	L on Jr 28 de Julio, following a 'Tumshukayko' sign.

CYCLE TOURING ROUTES & MAPS

🚲 LAGUNA PARÓN [cont'd]

Km	GPS	Alt (m)	Info	Description
1.5	357	2330	→	R onto unpaved road, signed 'Laguna Parón'. Stick to the main track, heading towards the mountains.
10.5	358	2830	←	L at a fork.
17		3250		**Pueblo Parón**. The control gate is 1.5km further on.
28.5		3970	Bridge	Cross bridge over main river. Soon after is the first possible wild camp of the climb.
33	359	4200	Top	End of motorable road at the Autoridad Nacional de Agua *refugio*, which has been taken over by the Parón community. Ask to camp, though if a caretaker is around you may be allowed to spend the night in a bunk for a small tip.
33.5		4200		End of cycleable path round N shore of **Laguna Parón**. Time to about-turn and cruise back to town.
67	350	2270	End	**Caraz**, Plaza de Armas.

WINCHUS LOOP

This second long excursion from Caraz climbs up more than fifty paved switchbacks into the Cordillera Negra. The reward is twofold: magnificent panoramic views of the northern peaks in the Blanca and the chance to ride past towering *Puya raimondii* (see box p30). These enormous bromeliads are found in the Bosque de Winchus (Forest of Hummingbirds – which flock to the area when the puya are in bloom), at altitudes of 3900m to 4200m.

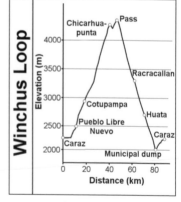

Completing the circuit in a day is a massive undertaking – better to split it into two, with a wild camp at about 3400m or, if acclimatized, near 4300m Chicarhuapunta. Between the two the terrain is so steep that finding a camp spot is extremely difficult. Take water from one of the lower villages as higher up there are no reliable sources in dry season until after the second pass.

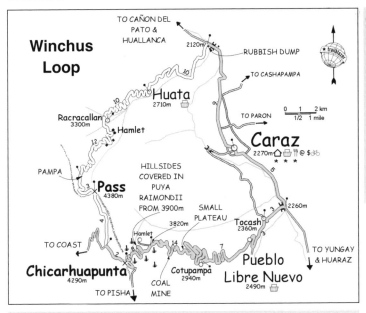

🚲 WINCHUS LOOP

- **Start & end** Caraz
- **Riding time** 2 days
- **Paved/Unpaved %** 55/45
- **Distance** 90km/56 miles
- **Vertical climb** 2500m/8200ft
- **Max altitude** 4380m/14,370ft

Km	GPS	Alt (m)	Info	Description
0	350	2270	Start	**Caraz**, Plaza de Armas. Take main road S, towards Huaraz.
5	351	2270	➜	Go R, signed 'Pueblo Libre'.
5.5		2260	Bridge	Cross new bridge (not yet completed at time of writing – check it has been before leaving Caraz; if not, cross a bridge right by town).
7.5		2360		**Tocash**.
10.5		2490		**Pueblo Libre Nuevo** (Pueblo Libre is slightly lower down, just off the road).
18		2940		Skirt **Cotupampa**. Collect water from the village as there is none for the next section.
34		3900		*Puya raimondii* begin and continue, road-side, to Chicarhuapunta. Soon there are streams – not reliable late in dry season.

CYCLE TOURING ROUTES & MAPS

🚲 WINCHUS LOOP [cont'd]

KM	GPS	ALT (M)	INFO	DESCRIPTION
40		4290	↑	Stick to the paving, when a dirt road goes L to Pisha.
40.5	360	4290	Pass	**Chicarhuapunta** (at Km110 marker). The Pacific comes into view! It's possible to camp near the pass, out of view of the road.
42.5	361	4210	→	Leave paving by turning R onto a dirt road signed 'Huata'.
46	362	4380	Pass	**Pass** with views of the peaks from Champará to Huascarán.
49.5		4160	Camp	Possible campsite with water, but ask permission if there are local people around. Descend on a decent surface, past two hamlets.
60		3370	↑	Continue straight. R descends to a small village.
61.5		3300		**Racracallan**.
71		2710		**Huata**.
80.5	349	2120	→	Turn R on main road, by Huaylas municipal dump.
89.5	350	2270	End	**Caraz**, Plaza de Armas.

❑ Suicide showers

Many showers in Peruvian villages are heated by dodgily-wired electric elements in the shower head. To use, turn the circuit-breaker switch on and open the tap (using a dry or insulated hand if the electrics look really suspect). The higher the flow, the colder the shower – the point where it just starts to buzz is normally the best trade-off between temperature and power. Flip the switch off again at the end.

MOUNTAIN BIKING ROUTES & MAPS

Cass Gilbert

Introduction

Chaki; foot. Nani; trail. Foot trail – or singletrack. It's Quechua, the language of the Incas, and if there's one word you should learn as a mountain biker in Peru, chakinani is it.

Despite pre-dating mountain bikes by several hundred years, the Incas certainly had their singletrack network nailed. Ancient trading routes zigzag their way from the Pacific coastline to the lofty valleys of the Andes mountains and back down into the steamy cauldron of the Amazon basin. Similarly, Inca-trail building skills remain legendary – a million man hours spent positioning great slabs of time-smoothed rock, linking one settlement to the next. None is more famous than the metropolis of Machu Picchu, magnet for all tourists visiting the country. Yet, for the adventure-seeking mountain biker, the more northerly Cordillera Blanca perhaps holds more appeal.

Set at altitudes that touch 4000m, these are trails that whip both muscles and lungs into shape – 15km dirt road climbs answered by relentless chutes of technical singletrack, covering a whole gamut of conditions under tyre. Hurtle down an Incan stairwell, hop a drainage stream, then skittle down a handlebar-width alleyway. A few corners later, dodge round the edge of a quinoa field, squeeze past donkeys loaded wide with eucalyptus, or try and outrun a manic pack of village dogs.

Let's not forget the Blanca's alter ego either, the Cordillera Negra. Facing the imposing majesty of the Blanca's white capped peaks, the snow-free Negra is home to a network of steep, boulder-strewn and exhilarating descents, popularised by a thriving downhill mountain biking scene. Ride here to rub shoulders with local, grass-roots riders. More often than not, you'll see bike frames wrapped from head to toe in old inner tubes for surviving home-grown uplifts – a stack of bikes wedged into the boot of a clapped-out colectivo.

Given the Cordillera Blanca runs some 180km in length, perhaps multi-day rides hold more appeal? For those in search of overnight escapades, uncover a world of quebradas, extending like fingers into these Andean folds, each leading to its own stunning, glacial hike. Aspiring bikepackers can also challenge themselves to the nearby Huayhuash range, hiker-biking their way round in search of the ultimate prize – singletrack that's barely seen a tyre track, amongst some of the finest mountain landscapes in the world.

But whatever you do, don't expect waymarked trails: mountain biking here is an exploratory process, and it's all the richer for it. And wherever you find yourself, you can be sure that it will be about more than just riding your bike – it will be a cultural encounter too. Shepherds tending livestock will doubtless gaze upon your struggles, and perhaps quiz you on your reasons for being here. Tell them you're looking for chakinani, and watch their eyes light up at the word. Despite the best efforts of Columbus and his crew in 1492, Quechua remains the first language of Peru's mountain people. '*Chakinani*', they'll likely repeat with a broad smile, adding yet more creases to their dark, leathery faces. Then they'll tip their hats, bid you safe travels... and point you on towards distant trails.

MOUNTAIN BIKING AGENCIES
Neil Pike

Run by Julio Olaza, the godfather of Huaraz mountain biking, **Mountain Bike Adventures – Peru** (Jr Lucar y Torre 525, ☎ 424259, 🖳 chakinaniperu.com) is the most professional guiding company in town. Julio has unrivalled knowledge of local cross country trails, a fleet of full suspension Specialized Rockhopper bikes, and leads both day trips (S/.130-170, depending on group size and route) and multi-day tours personally. If not at his office, try asking at Olaza's B & B (p57). Bikes are not rented out without a guide.

A more rambunctious alternative, **Riders Huaraz** (Parque del Periodista, 🖳 ridershuarazmtb@hotmail.com) trips are a blast. Excursions in the Blanca or Negra start around S/.150; more technical, downhill-style rides are a speciality. Amiable Antonio rents out older, but well maintained, front suspension bikes for S/.30 a day including helmet and puncture repair kits – he's usually to be found in the adjacent Piccolo restaurant.

❏ **Julio Olaza – Mountain Bike Adventures Peru**

As a young man in the '80s, **Julio Olaza** explored many of the Cordillera Blanca's quebradas on foot. He ran Tasco Bar, a popular hang out for foreign travellers, where in conversation one day he heard mention of 'mountain biking' as the next big craze. Julio was intrigued; so much so that he later managed to get a mountain bike brought out to him from the States. Cordillera explorations took on a new dimension.

Julio spent the early '90s in the US – they were dark years in Peru with the economy in tatters, high inflation and a still-active Sendero Luminoso. On returning with honed biking skills to his native Huaraz, two possible career paths presented: stay safe and open a *lavanderia* (laundrette), or risk starting a mountain biking company. Fortunately for the Peruvian biking scene he chose the latter, opening Peru's first mountain biking agency in 1993.

❏ **Antonio Paredes – Riders Huaraz**
Aged nine, **Antonio Paredes**' interest in mountain biking was piqued upon spotting
a kid pulling wheelies down Jirón Morales in Huaraz. It didn't take long to persuade
his parents to fork out on a steel Goliat bike, or to bloody his face in a first biking
accident. He's progressed somewhat from those days; now running Riders Huaraz
and competing in Peruvian national downhill competitions. A favourite local ride is
'Wilcadrop' at Wilcahuaín, where he can occasionally be found flying down on a full
suspension Santa Cruz Driver 8.

BIKE SETUP

Although there are plenty of flowing trails to be ridden, terrain in the
Cordilleras Blanca and Negra can also be loose and rocky. A mid-travel full suspension rig will help smooth out ancient stairwell descents, but a suspension
fork and large volume, aggressive tyres will be more than sufficient, and better
suited to the long and grinding dirt road climbs. Running a tubeless setup will
undoubtedly help with the thorns that mine the area, just be aware that extra
sealant is not available locally.

Likewise, any spares specific to your bike should also be brought out, to
save wasting time having them sent up from Lima. The same goes with servic-
ing hydraulic brakes – do this beforehand, as options are limited. If you're running a 29er, best bring a spare, as these can only be found in the capital. A
derailleur hanger would be a wise addition to your pack list too.

Routes

GPS ROUTES

GPS tracks for these routes can be downloaded for free from ⌨ blancahuay
huash.com.

PITEC DESCENT   [see p216]

The Pitec Descent is one of the mountain biking staples in the area. It can be
worked into a day ride from Huaraz using dirt roads via Wilcahuaín, Llupa or
Marian (see map p181), or you can catch transport to Pitec from town (see
p120). It also makes the perfect finale back to Huaraz after various forays
around the quebradas, such as those in Quilcayhuanca and Rajucolta. In fact, it's
a trail that's more enjoyable each time you ride it, as you find the flow of the
ride and get to know its quirks.

Starting at 3860m and working its way down to 3200m, the trail is made up
of a series of flowing bouts of singletrack and steppy chutes. Although there are

(continued on p218)

MOUNTAIN BIKING

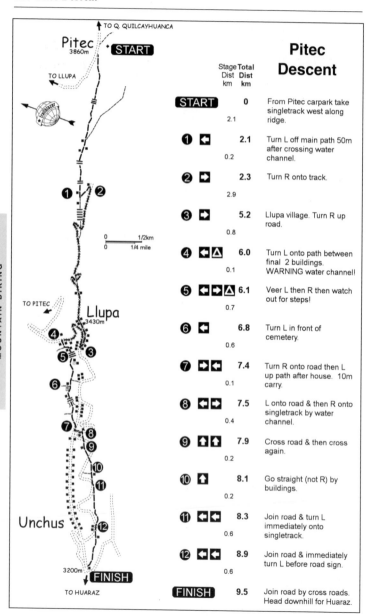

Pitec Descent

Stage Dist km	Total Dist km	
START	0	From Pitec carpark take singletrack west along ridge.
	2.1	
❶ ◀	2.1	Turn L off main path 50m after crossing water channel.
	0.2	
❷ ▶	2.3	Turn R onto track.
	2.9	
❸ ▶	5.2	Llupa village. Turn R up road.
	0.8	
❹ ◀ △	6.0	Turn L onto path between final 2 buildings. WARNING water channel!
	0.1	
❺ ◀ ▶ △	6.1	Veer L then R then watch out for steps!
	0.7	
❻ ◀	6.8	Turn L in front of cemetery.
	0.6	
❼ ▶ ◀	7.4	Turn R onto road then L up path after house. 10m carry.
	0.1	
❽ ◀ ▶	7.5	L onto road & then R onto singletrack by water channel.
	0.4	
❾ ▲ ▲	7.9	Cross road & then cross again.
	0.2	
❿ ▲	8.1	Go straight (not R) by buildings.
	0.2	
⓫ ◀ ◀	8.3	Join road & turn L immediately onto singletrack.
	0.6	
⓬ ◀ ◀	8.9	Join road & immediately turn L before road sign.
	0.6	
FINISH	9.5	Join road by cross roads. Head downhill for Huaraz.

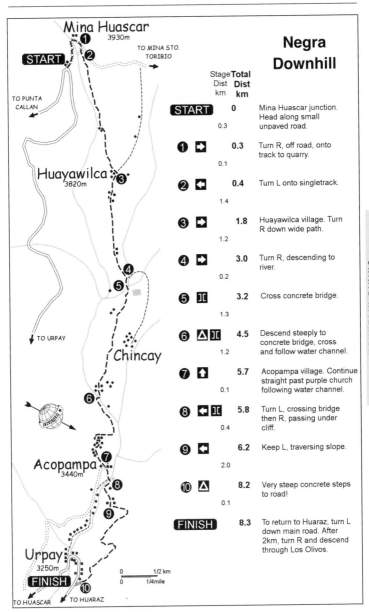

Negra Downhill

		Stage Dist km	Total Dist km	
START			0	Mina Huascar junction. Head along small unpaved road.
		0.3		
❶	➡		0.3	Turn R, off road, onto track to quarry.
		0.1		
❷	⬅		0.4	Turn L onto singletrack.
		1.4		
❸	➡		1.8	Huayawilca village. Turn R down wide path.
		1.2		
❹	➡		3.0	Turn R, descending to river.
		0.2		
❺	�📷		3.2	Cross concrete bridge.
		1.3		
❻	△�📷		4.5	Descend steeply to concrete bridge, cross and follow water channel.
		1.2		
❼	⬆		5.7	Acopampa village. Continue straight past purple church following water channel.
		0.1		
❽	⬅�📷		5.8	Turn L, crossing bridge then R, passing under cliff.
		0.4		
❾	⬅		6.2	Keep L, traversing slope.
		2.0		
❿	△		8.2	Very steep concrete steps to road!
		0.1		
FINISH			8.3	To return to Huaraz, turn L down main road. After 2km, turn R and descend through Los Olivos.

MOUNTAIN BIKING

a few challenging rock gardens and water channels that may require a quick dismount, for the most part it's a fast and flowy trail. Skirting along ancient village walls and squeezing round fields of quinoa, it's a ride that offers great insight into typical mountain life. As close as it is to Huaraz, the pace of life here feels a world away from the hubbub of the city.

Don't forget that locals and their animals use this route, so ride with caution and a smile. The descent from Pitec to Huaraz takes about an hour.

NEGRA DOWNHILL   [see p217]

Although the Cordillera Blanca gets all the press, the Negra's the place to go for fast and furious descents – this is where the local DH boys tend to gather. Most catch a Pira combi (S/.5, from the stop near the stadium), or a taxi (around S/.40), to Mina Huascar, but you can also ride up on dirt or tarmac (see Santo Toribio Circuit p184), working your way up the 1000m climb to really earn your descent.

Although this is a short route in terms of distance, it's a thrilling, white-knuckle affair, with fantastic views out to the Cordillera Blanca across the valley. Much of the route is singletrack, and where it widens, it's still laced with rocks and boulders. Watch out for the steep concrete staircase towards the end of the ride. As ever, we'd recommend walking any parts of the route you're not fully comfortable riding, as there's no medevacing around here...

Allow an hour from Mina Huascar to town.

❏ Bikepacking the Huayhuash

The Cordillera Huayhuash (see p152) makes an epic multi-day bikepack; but it's by no means an easy one. From a mountain biker's perspective, the flowy, rocky and technical trails are hard fought, especially at such high elevations. Many of the climbs are unrideable, so travel light and expect extended hike 'n bikes. Aside from the time taken to manhandle your bike over several high passes, allow for inclement weather to slow progress too.

These challenges aside, the majority of the trail from Quartelhuain to Huayllapa is eminently rideable and laced with some of the finest ribbons of backcountry singletrack you could hope for. Certainly, the experience of riding them is heightened by their sense of context and the magnitude of the mountains around.

The eastern flank of the loop is more bike-friendly than the west, so consider exiting to Cajatambo and catching the 05:30 bus to the coast and then to Huaraz from there. If you do continue round, follow the 4WD track from Huayllapa to Tapush Punta, rather than the more direct trekking route; or consider hiring mules.

It's about 120km from Chiquián to Cajatambo, which can be broken down into four or five days of riding. Cyclists are best off avoiding Siula Punta, tackling the gentler and far more rideable Punta Carnicero instead. Likewise, the dirt road beyond the hot springs at Viconga, following the Río Pumarinri, makes a favourable alternative to the hike 'n' bike over Punta Cuyoc.

CROSS COUNTRY ROUTES NEAR HUARAZ

At the time of writing, the future of mountain biking on hiking trails within Parque Nacional Huascarán is undecided. There's a possibility it will be banned, so please be especially careful when riding within the park, giving way to hikers and dismounting if you encounter mule trains.

Laguna Rajucolta

The 75km-loop to Laguna Rajucolta can either be undertaken as a big day out, or split into a relaxed overnighter by camping below the lake's hydroelectric plant, 32km in. It's a great ride, for three reasons. Firstly, hardly anyone heads out to this part of the Blanca; next up, the singletrack is remote and testing; and lastly it's almost completely rideable – with just one relatively mild 45 minute hike 'n' bike to its name.

To get there, ride out of Huaraz via Rataquena, climbing steeply out of the valley, before picking your way over the ridge towards Quebrada Pariac/Rajucolta. Aim to follow trails on the north side, crisscrossing the river on occasions. Persevere up to the lake on a two track to soak up that magnificent Huantsan view. From there, backtrack out of the park, keeping an eye out for the well-defined trail to the north which leaves from a little west of the entrance gate. After a 45 minute hike, reach a stretch of beautiful pampa, which in turn feeds you into a freeform descent into Jancu.

Jancu is linked to Huaraz by road, but can also be connected with Pitec, via the trail that skirts round the base of Quebrada Shallap – almost all of which is rideable and beautiful singletrack at that (see map p122).

The *Alpenvereinskarte* is useful for the route, and there are plenty of campesinos about to check directions with. In the vicinity of Rataquena we'd recommend riding with a local, as walkers have been victims of robberies in the area (see p53).

Quebrada Quilcayhuanca

Quilcayhuanca lies within striking distance of Huaraz and offers largely rideable singletrack, making for a perfect exploratory trip deeper into the park. It is little travelled – chances are, you won't see a soul – and to the valley junction with Quebrada Cayesh there are no Herculean bike portages to contend with. This junction is a possible campsite with options for stashing a bike amongst scattered boulders if you wish to embark on day hikes. See p123 for hiking details.

Although by taking transport up it's a relatively short out-and-back – 10km each way from the gate (*portón*) at the end of the 4WD track to the valley junction – it's possible to transform into a longer ride by tackling as one long day from Huaraz or combining with Quebradas Shallap, Llaca or Rajucolta. Alternatively base yourself in one of the mountain lodges in the area. Whatever you decide, knit the Pitec Descent into the ride to get yourself back down to town.

MOUNTAIN BIKING

Quebrada Ishinca

Ishinca offers around 11km of singletrack each way, and though there are several stretches where you'll need to push your bike on the climb, the descent back down following a flowing, rockmined trail which wends its way through the millefeuille-like queñual forest makes it more than worthwhile. Whether you head for Collón or Pashpa, the singletrack is almost completely rideable, as long as you're a confident mountain biker; otherwise, there are just short sections where you'll need to dismount. Upon hitting 4WD tracks (above Collón or Pashpa) it's a rough dirt road descent that swooshes down to Paltay. See p116 for more detail.

We recommend making this ride into an overnight loop, either camping at the official site, or travelling light and enjoying a night in the refugio. On the first day, ride out to Taricá before climbing through Honcopampa and Pashpa into the quebrada itself. It's possible to ride down from the refugio to the valley floor at Paltay in around 2 hours, then a further hour on pavement back to Huaraz.

Other downhill rides

Other rides to seek out include **El Cañón** – a whirligig descent that also starts beyond the viewpoint at Rataquena (see warning p219). A downhiller's dream, it's an off-the-saddle affair, a short but intense blast through a giant termite-hill-like landscape. Following a loose and rocky trail that's barely wider than a set of handlebars, it plummets you back down to the south-east corner of Huaraz, by the cemetery.

La Dentista, as it's sometimes known, is a barrage of awkwardly shaped rocks – as large and jagged as a giant's bad teeth – that lies en route to Quebrada Llaca. Before the road dives into the gorge, look out for a trail on the left, which winds its way all the way down to The Lazy Dog Inn, from where you can traverse across to Pitec.

If the idea of an uplift appeals, we'd suggest combining La Dentista with a morning of ice-climbing at Laguna Llaca – if you go with an agency, you should be able to lash your bike on the roof of their vehicle, and tackle the descent when you're done. Be warned: this is a ride for technically proficient mountain bikers only.

MOUNTAIN BIKING

APPENDIX A: SPANISH WORDS & PHRASES

There are two languages spoken in the areas covered by this guide: **Spanish**, which is the main language of Peru, and **Ancash Quechua** (Quechua Ancashino) which is the native language of the indigenous people and is widely spoken in mountain areas, particularly in villages. Many local people are bilingual, but visiting trekkers and cyclists will find Spanish is the more useful to learn, as it's much more common to come across someone who speaks no Quechua, than someone who speaks no Spanish. There are no readily-available Ancash Quechua phrasebooks – the most useful dictionary we are aware of is the Ancash Quechua to Spanish *Diccionario Quechua Ancashino – Castellano*. Those interested in learning Ancash Quechua should enquire about courses at the Centro Cultural in Huaraz. Many of the terms included in the glossary are Quechua – travellers will most often encounter these in place and feature names.

SOME QUECHUA WORDS

Hello/How are you?	*Imanollata kekanky?*	Where are you going?	*Mayta ewanky?*
Goodbye	*Aywalla*	Where are you from?	*Maypitatan kanky?*
Thank you	*Yusulpaaya*		

SPANISH

South American Spanish is an easy language to pronounce, as once some simple rules are learnt, there are almost no irregularities. 'll' is pronounced like a 'y', 'hu' is pronounced 'w'. Unlike in Spain, there is no lisping in South America – the 'c' in 'ce' and 'ci' as well as 'z's are pronounced 's'. 'v' is pronounced like a 'b', 'j' like the 'ch' in a Scottish loch, 'h' at the start of a word is silent if followed by 'a','e','i' or 'o'. ñ is pronounced 'ny', as in 'canyon'.

In general, stress goes on the penultimate syllable unless there's an accent to indicate alternative stress.

The 'tu' form, rather than the more formal 'usted', has been used in the following phrases.

General words and phrases

Hello	*Hola*	How are you?	*¿Cómo estás?*
Good day/good morning	*Buenos días*	What's your name?	*¿Cómo te llamas?*
Good afternoon	*Buenas tardes*	I'm called ...	*Me llamo...*
Good evening	*Buenas noches*	Please	*Por favor*
Goodbye	*Adiós*	impossible	*imposible*
See you	*Hasta luego*	good	*bueno*
Excuse me	*(Con) permiso*	okay	*está bien*
Mr/Sir	*Señor*	bad	*malo*
Madam	*Señora*	beautiful	*bonito/lindo*
Thank you	*Gracias*	it is hot	*hace calor*
Sorry (apologies)	*Discúlpame*	rain	*lluvia*
Yes	*Sí*	wind	*viento*
No	*No*	snow	*nieve*

Where are you going?	*¿Adónde vas?*
I'm going to (Huaraz) via (Punta Olímpica).	*Voy a (Huaraz) por (Punta Olímpica).*
Where are you from?	*¿De dónde eres?*
Where have you come from?	*¿De dónde has venido?*
Which country are you from?	*¿De qué país?*
What's this?	*¿Qué es esto?*
Is there transport to ... from here?	*¿Hay transporte a ... de aquí?*

General words and phrases (cont'd)

Can I stay (the night) here?	*¿Podría pasar la noche aquí?*
Tired?	*¿Cansado/a?*
Do you have children?	*¿Tienes hijos?*
Give me sweets/money.	*Dame caramelos/plata.*
May I..? / Can I...?	*¿Podría...? / ¿Puedo...?*

Where and when

left	*izquierda*	...the house	*..la casa*
right	*derecha*	...the pass	*..el abra/portachuelo, la punta*
here	*aquí/acá*		
there	*ahí/allá*	...the path/trail	*..el camino/sendero*
over there	*por ahí/allá*	...the river	*..el río*
up/down	*arriba/abajo*	...the toilet	*..los baños*
near (to)	*cerca (de)*	...the village	*..el pueblo*
far (away)	*lejos*	...water, food	*..el agua, la comida*
straight ahead	*de frente*	...the singletrack	*..el chakinani*
everywhere	*en todas partes*	When?	*¿Cuándo?*
Where is...?	*¿Dónde está...?*	soon	*pronto*
...the bus/combi/taxi	*..el bus/combi/taxi*	right now	*ahora mismo*
...the campsite	*...el campamento*	later	*luego/más tarde*
...the hotel	*...el hotel*	never	*nunca*

Help!

Help! (urgent)	*¡Socorro!*	I'm cold	*Tengo frío*
Help (assist) me, please	*Ayúdame, por favor*	I'm hungry	*Tengo hambre*
		I'm thirsty	*Tengo sed*
Take me to hospital	*Llévame al hospital*	I'm tired	*Estoy cansado*
It hurts	*Me duele*		

Shopping

Is there...?/Do you have...?	*¿Hay...?*	small/little	*pequeño/a*
(Please) give me...	*(Por favor) dame...*	How much does it cost to...?	*¿Cuánto cuesta para...?*
money	*dinero/plata*		
How much is...?	*¿Cuánto cuesta/es...?*	...hire a guide	*...contratar un guía?*
...that one	*..eso/esa/ese*	...hire mules	*...alquilar mulas?*
more	*más*	...hire a muleteer	*...contratar un arriero?*
less	*menos*		
a little	*un poco/poquito*	...for a day/week/hour	*..por día/semana/hora*
big/large	*grande*		

Trekking gear and accessories

(stove) alcohol	*alcohol*	petrol	*gasolina*
boots	*botas*	roll mat	*colchón*
bottle	*botella*	rucksack	*mochila*
(gas) canister	*bombona (de gas)*	sleeping bag	*bolsa/saco de dormir*
compass	*brújula*	socks	*medias*
first-aid kit	*botiquín*	stove	*estufa*
gaiters	*polainas*	sun cream	*bloqueador/protector solar*
gloves	*guantes*		
(down) jacket	*chaqueta (de plumas)*	tent	*carpa*

Trekking gear and accessories (cont'd)

trekking poles	*bastones*	white gas	*bencina blanca*
trousers	*pantalones*	(Andean) woolly hat	*chullo*

Bike parts & accessories

axle	*eje*
bicycle	*bicicleta/bici*
bottom bracket	*caja de pedalier*
brake pads	*pastillas de freno*
(disc) brakes	*frenos (de disco)*
cable	*cable*
cassette	*cassette/piñon*
chain	*cadena*
chainrings	*platos*
derailleur	*descarrilador*
frame	*cuadro*
gears	*cambios*
handlebars	*manubrio*
headset	*juego dirección*
helmet	*casco*
inner tube	*cámara*
panniers	alforjas
patches	*parches*
pedal	*pedal*
rack	*parrilla*
rim	*aro*
rotor	*rotor*
saddle	*asiento*
spoke	*rayo*
suspension fork	*horquilla de suspensión*
tyre	*cubierta/neumático*
wheel	*rueda*

Bike tools & terms

Allen key	*llave Allen*
glue	*pegamento*
grease	*grasa*
lubricant	*lubricante*
multitool	*herramienta multiuso*
oil	*aceite*
pliers	*alicates*
pump	*inflador*
rubber solution	*solución de goma*
screw	*tornillo*
screwdriver	*destornillador*
spanner	*llave*
tape	*cinta*
tyre levers	*desenllantadores*
a short climb	*una subidita*
an interminable climb	*un subidazo*
consolidated surface	*afirmado*
corrugated	*calamina/serrucho*
descent	*una bajada*
dirt	*tierra*
(steep) gradient	*pendiente (fuerte)*
gravel	*ripio*
mud	*barro*
puncture	*pinchazo*
singletrack (path)	*chakinani*
tarmac (asphalt)	*pista*
ungraded surface	*trocha*

Numerals

1	*uno*	18	*dieciocho*
2	*dos*	19	*diecinueve*
3	*tres*	20	*veinte*
4	*cuatro*	21	*veintiuno*
5	*cinco*	30	*treinta*
6	*seis*	40	*cuarenta*
7	*siete*	50	*cincuenta*
8	*ocho*	60	*sesenta*
9	*nueve*	70	*setenta*
10	*diez*	80	*ochenta*
11	*once*	90	*noventa*
12	*doce*	100	*cien*
13	*trece*	101	*ciento uno*
14	*catorce*	200	*doscientos*
15	*quince*	1000	*mil*
16	*dieciséis*	2000	*dos mil*
17	*diecisiete*	1,000,000	*un millón*

Food and drink

beer	*cerveza*	potato	*papa*
biscuit	*galleta*	raisins	*pasas de uvas*
bread	*pan*	rice	*arroz*
cheese	*queso*	sandwich	*sándwich*
chicken	*pollo*	soup	*sopa*
chocolate	*chocolate*	vegetables	*verduras*
coca	*coca*	water	*agua*
egg	*huevo*	to boil	*hervir*
fish	*pescado*	cold	*frío*
fizzy drink/pop	*gaseosa*	cold food	*comida fría*
fruit	*fruta*	cooked	*cocido*
maize	*maíz/choclo*	to fry	*freír*
meat	*carne*	hot (temperature)	*caliente*
oats (porridge)	*avenas/quaker*	raw	*crudo*
pasta	*fideos*	roast	*asado*
peanuts	*maní*	spicy	*picante*

Food and drink glossary (see also Menu Decoder, p35)

ají	hot pepper from which a spicy sauce is made
almuerzo	lunch
anticucho	beef heart kebabs
causa	mashed yellow-potato dumpling
cena	dinner/evening meal
ceviche	raw fish marinated in citrus juice and spiced with chilli
cevichería	seafood restaurant specializing in traditional Peruvian ceviche
chicha de jora	fermented maize drink, often homemade, popular with campesinos
chicharrones	deep-fried pork or fish
chifa	Chinese restaurant
cuy	guinea pig
desayuno	breakfast
extracto de rana	'frog extract' – a drink which is claimed to have curative and aphrodisiac properties
kiwicha	an edible relative of quinoa
macerado	slightly alcoholic drink served at herbal remedy centres
menú	menu; a basic restaurant selling cheap set-menu food
novoandina	a modern style of Peruvian cuisine
oca	a plant cultivated in Peru for its edible potato-like tubers
pachamanca	traditional Peruvian dish baked in an earthen oven
panadería	bakery
parrillada	barbecue; meat restaurant
pastelería	bakery/cake shop
pisco sour	drink made from pisco (Peruvian grape brandy), lemon and egg white
pollería	chicken restaurant
quinoa	a crop grown for its edible grain-like seeds
refresco	drink made with natural fruit juice and water
recreo campestre	countryside restaurant often serving pachamanca, normally only open weekends
segundo	main course at a menu restaurant, literally 'second'

APPENDIX B: GLOSSARY

ablation valley	a valley formed by a glacier's lateral moraine and the side of the larger valley housing the moraine
abra	high mountain pass
abuelita/o	grandmother/grandfather
acequia	irrigation ditch
aguas termales	thermal/hot springs
alcalde	mayor
alojamiento	accommodation
alpaca	type of domesticated camelid, resembling a long-legged/necked sheep, bred for its wool
alto (de)	high mountain pass
aluvión	flash-flood of mud and gravel, usually sparked by an earthquake
AMS	Acute Mountain Sickness
Ancash	one of Peru's 24 departments; contains the Cordillera Blanca and part of the Huayhuash; its capital is Huaraz
Ancashino/a	a resident of Ancash
andinismo	mountaineering
apacheta	cairn; wayside shrine
apu	gods or spirits of the mountains that protect local people in high areas
arriero	muleteer
ayahuasca	a hallucinogenic drink prepared from the bark of a woody vine
baños	toilets; baths
barranco/a	ravine
basura	rubbish/trash
bencina blanca	white gas
bicicletería	bicycle shop
blanco/a	white
bodega	small shop which also sells alcohol; a luggage compartment on a bus
bofedal	wetland
bus cama	literally 'bed bus' – the most comfortable type of bus
calle	street
Callejón de Conchucos	the series of river valleys to the east of the Cordillera Blanca
Callejón de Huaylas	the Río Santa valley to the west of the Cordillera Blanca
cama	bed
Camino Real	the Inca Royal Road
campesino/a	Peruvian peasant or worker of the land
cancha	small plot of land or block of houses in an Inca town; toasted corn
casa de cambio	bureau de change
caserío	hamlet
casona	large house/mansion, often set around a courtyard
cerro	hill/mountain
chacra	small farm
chakinani	footpath
choza	stone hut with thatched roof
chullo	woollen hat
chullpa	an ancient funerary tower constructed for a noble person
cobrador	conductor (on a bus); collector of money
coca	plant used by Peruvians to ease altitude sickness and for stamina and health; leaves are chewed or made into tea; raw ingredient of cocaine

cocha	lake
colectivo	shared taxi
combi	minibus, smaller than a micro
comunidad campesina	local campesino community
conquistadores	Spanish explorer soldiers who conquered South America in the 16th century
cordillera	mountain range
Cordillera Negra	the snowless range west of the Callejón de Huaylas
correos	post office
Creole	Peruvian-born person of European descent
cruce	crossroads
cuarto	(bed)room – ask for a cuarto in villages with no official hotel
(habitación) doble	twin room
económico	more-upmarket bus companies' cheapest class of bus
encomiendas	bus company cargo service
entrada	entrance/entry
este	east
ferretería	hardware store, often selling bencina blanca
folklórico/a	traditional folk dancing and music
gasolina	petrol/gasoline
grifo	petrol station/gas station
gringo	'foreigner' – used for anyone with whitish skin, rarely an insult
guardaparque	park ranger
habitación	room/bedroom
HACE/HAPE	High Altitude Cerebral/Pulmonary Oedema – rare condition of high altitude sickness caused by ascending too quickly, can be fatal
hospedaje	accommodation/lodging
huayno	form of Peruvian Andean music with high pitched vocals
ichic	small/little
ichu	spiky, golden brown grass that grows in tussocks on the puna
Inca empire	'Tahuantinsuyu' – the largest empire in pre-Columbian America; encompassed Ancash from the mid-15th to mid-16th centuries
janca/janka	mountain range
jatun	big/large
jirca	mountain
jirón	street
lago	lake
laguna	(smaller) lake
llama	South American camelid (relative of the camel), used as pack animals and for their wool
machay	cave
mami(ta)	affectionate term for a woman
manantial	spring (of water)
(habitación) matrimonial	double room (with a double bed)
mercado	market
mestizo	person of mixed American Indian and European blood
micro	minibus, larger than a combi
mina	mine
mirador	viewpoint
mototaxi	auto rickshaw
municipalidad	municipality/town hall/town council
negro/negra	black
nevado	snow-capped mountain

norte	north
oeste	west
Pachamama	goddess revered by Andean Indians, literally 'Earth Mother'
pampa	flat grassy meadow, often boggy
papi	affectionate term for a man
parada	(bus) stop
Parque Nacional Huascarán (PNH)	National Park which contains the majority of the Cordillera Blanca
pasaje	fare/ticket
paso	high mountain pass
peña folklórica	folk-music club
plaza de armas	the main square in many Peruvian towns
portachuelo	high mountain pass
portón	gate/large door; entrance to a quebrada
posta/puesto de salud	health post
pueblo	village
puente	bridge
puna	a high, treeless Andean plateau
punta	high mountain pass
Puya raimondii	the largest species of bromeliad, endemic to Peru
Qhapaq Ñan	the Inca Empire's road network
quebrada	deep, sheer-sided river valley; ravine
Quechua	native South American language spoken primarily in the Andes; Quechua Ancashino is the variety spoken in Ancash
(bosque de) queñuales	polylepis forest
quipu	literally 'talking knots', a recording device of knotted strings used by the Wari and Inca Empires
raju	snow-capped mountain
Recuay	Callejón de Huaylas culture which flourished in 200-600CE
refugio	mountain hut
río	river
ruta	route
selva	jungle
semi cama	literally 'half bed' – a bus that is less luxurious than *cama*, but more comfortable than *económico*
Sendero Luminoso	'Shining Path' – a terrorist group active in much of Peru until 1992
servicios higiénicos (SSHH)	toilets
(habitación) simple	single room
sismo	earthquake
sol(es)	literally 'sun'; the unit of Peruvian currency
soroche	altitude sickness
sur	south
tambo	an inn or rest-house
tarjeta telefónica	telephone card
terminal	(bus) terminal/station
terremoto	earthquake
tienda	shop/store
tranquilo	quiet/peaceful
vicuña	undomesticated camelid living in high areas of the Andes that is related to the llama and alpaca, with very fine wool
Wari	civilization from Ayacucho which ruled Ancash from 600-800CE
winchus	hummingbird
yurac/yuraq	white; '*Yurac Janka*' = Cordillera Blanca

APPENDIX C – GPS WAYPOINTS & ALTITUDES

Each GPS waypoint below was taken on the route at the reference number marked on the map as shown below. This list of GPS waypoints is also available to download for free from ⌨ blancahuayhuash.com and ⌨ www.trailblazer-guides.com.

Map	Wpt	Location	Latitude	Longitude	Alt (m)	Alt (ft)
Alpamayo Basecamp						
1	001	Pomabamba	-8.8205	-77.4608	2960	9710
1	002	Footbridge	-8.8205	-77.4634	2930	9610
1	003	Cross water channel	-8.8158	-77.4746	3100	10170
2	004	Santa Cruz – Alpamayo Circuit joins	-8.8508	-77.5420	3530	11580
2	005	Jancapampa camp	-8.8516	-77.5496	3560	11680
2	006	Leave pampa by walls	-8.8382	-77.5576	3840	12600
3	007	Yanacon	-8.8265	-77.5897	4600	15090
3	008	Bridge at Huillca	-8.8040	-77.6127	4000	13120
3	009	R to Mesapata	-8.8126	-77.6262	4140	13580
3	010	Mesapata	-8.8107	-77.6358	4450	14600
5	011	Gara Gara	-8.8261	-77.6735	4830	15850
5	012	Jancarurish camp	-8.8462	-77.6816	4210	13810
6	013	Ruinapampa camp	-8.8288	-77.7333	4000	13120
6	014	Vientunan	-8.8433	-77.7463	4770	15650
6	015	Osoruri camp	-8.8461	-77.7522	4560	14960
7	016	Paso Osoruri	-8.8577	-77.7554	4860	15950
7	017	Turn-off to Yuraccocha	-8.8667	-77.7740	4420	14500
7	018	Huishcash camp	-8.8671	-77.7780	4300	14110
7	019	Calamina camp	-8.8767	-77.7851	3980	13060
7	020	Hualcayán	-8.8980	-77.8014	3140	10300
3	021	Shortcut to Mesapata	-8.8210	-77.6334	4170	13680
3	022	Wade river	-8.8296	-77.6323	4170	13680
4	023	Viewpoint of Pucacocha	-8.8568	-77.6332	4500	14760
4	024	Laguna Llullacocha	-8.8558	-77.6423	4730	15520
5	025	Alpamayo northern BC	-8.8635	-77.6799	4520	14830
5	026	Bottom of steep moraine	-8.8785	-77.6906	4740	15550
5	027	Santa Cruz Sanctuary viewpoint	-8.8806	-77.6985	5020	16470
7	028	Pass on way to Yuraccocha	-8.8805	-77.7731	4630	15190
7	029	Yuraccocha	-8.8843	-77.7359	4650	15260
8	030	Hit road	-8.9053	-77.8005	2980	9780
8	031	Bridge and river ford	-8.9091	-77.7951	2830	9290
8	032	Leave road at '47.00' sign	-8.9169	-77.7930	2760	9060
8	033	Huancarhuaz	-8.9327	-77.7907	2800	9190
8	034	Hit road in Conay	-8.9491	-77.7823	2900	9510
8/13	035	Cashapampa	-8.9570	-77.7774	2940	9650
Santa Cruz						
9	036	Vaquería trailhead	-9.0107	-77.5312	3680	12070
9	037	Cross bridge	-9.0075	-77.5303	3560	11680
9	038	Yanama route joins	-9.0022	-77.5259	3430	11250
9	039	PNH office	-8.9895	-77.5489	3650	11980
10	040	Paria camp	-8.9515	-77.5625	3800	12470
10	041	Junction to Tuctupampa	-8.9293	-77.5589	4110	13480
10	042	Junction to Tuctupampa	-8.9214	-77.5639	4320	14170
11	043	Punta Unión	-8.9122	-77.5818	4780	15680

Map	Wpt	Location	Latitude	Longitude	Alt (m)	Alt (ft)
Santa Cruz (cont'd)						
11	044	Taullipampa camp	-8.9184	-77.6048	4180	13710
11	045	Junction by boulder shelter	-8.9163	-77.6142	4140	13580
11	046	Junction with mule path from valley	-8.9120	-77.6232	4160	13650
11	047	Arhuaycocha camp	-8.8934	-77.6337	4320	14170
11	048	Arhuaycocha mirador	-8.8895	-77.6326	4440	14570
11	049	Meet main path	-8.9158	-77.6234	4000	13120
12	050	Llamacorral	-8.9458	-77.7016	3800	12470
16	051	Yanama	-9.0213	-77.4713	3390	11120
16	052	Leave road	-9.0302	-77.4782	3470	11390
16	053	Join road in Chalhua	-9.0219	-77.4908	3550	11650
9/16	054	Leave road in Colcabamba	-9.0068	-77.5175	3320	10890
Santa Cruz – Alpamayo Circuit (linking section)						
10	055	Tuctupampa camp	-8.9236	-77.5588	4160	13650
10	056	Alto de Pucaraju	-8.9182	-77.5533	4620	15160
10	057	Cross river	-8.9132	-77.5441	4180	13710
14	058	Junction	-8.9230	-77.5081	3830	12570
14	059	Cross river	-8.9071	-77.5158	3870	12700
14	060	Tupatupa	-8.8843	-77.5207	4360	14300
14	061	Cross river at confluence	-8.8624	-77.5186	3820	12530
2	062	Hit track in Jancapampa meadow	-8.8545	-77.5293	3530	11580
2	063	Leave track in Jancapampa meadow	-8.8541	-77.5399	3530	11580
15	064	Leave track to Lucma to descend to bridge	-8.9070	-77.4865	3640	11940
15	065	Punta Lluchujirca	-8.8828	-77.4734	4170	13680
15	066	Yayno	-8.8857	-77.4557	4100	13450
15	067	Huanchacbamba	-8.8705	-77.4372	3450	11320
Ulta – Yanama						
16	068	Quebrada Ulta trailhead	-9.1308	-77.5364	3950	12960
16	069	Go steeply up through queñuales	-9.1149	-77.5310	4030	13220
16	070	Punta Yanayacu	-9.0906	-77.5252	4840	15880
16	071	Camp by Laguna Ichic Ulta	-9.0782	-77.5206	4510	14800
16	072	Join 4WD track	-9.0454	-77.4943	3540	11610
16	073	Hit Llanganuco road	-9.0419	-77.4916	3530	11580
Laguna 69						
17	074	Trailhead for L69	-9.0468	-77.6095	3930	12890
17	075	Climb zigzags	-9.0255	-77.5993	4150	13620
17	076	By Laguna 68	-9.0189	-77.6013	4370	14340
17	077	Laguna 69	-9.0118	-77.6103	4590	15060
17	078	Pass en route to Refugio Peru	-9.0208	-77.6114	4860	15950
17	079	Refugio Peru	-9.0297	-77.6294	4660	15290
17	080	Cebollapampa camp	-9.0448	-77.6086	3900	12800
Artesonraju Basecamp						
18	081	Refugio building	-8.9992	-77.6848	4200	13780
18	082	Junction to Artesoncocha	-8.9824	-77.6489	4200	13780
18	083	Artesonraju Basecamp	-8.9661	-77.6453	4770	15650
Laguna Lejiacocha						
19	084	Vicos	-9.3282	-77.5535	3020	9910
19	085	Blue water tank	-9.3222	-77.5492	3230	10600
19	086	End of 4WD track	-9.3084	-77.5414	3500	11480
19	087	Clear path begins zigzagging	-9.3050	-77.5336	3570	11710
19	088	Lejiacocha viewpoint	-9.2876	-77.5076	4640	15220

Map	Wpt	Location	Latitude	Longitude	Alt (m)	Alt (ft)
Akilpo – Ishinca						
20	**089**	Pay station in Honcopampa	-9.3624	-77.5229	3420	11220
20	**090**	Junction by last house	-9.3551	-77.5053	3580	11750
20	**091**	Path behind walls	-9.3389	-77.4284	4520	14830
20	**092**	Leave Laguna Akilpo	-9.3441	-77.4234	4710	15450
20	**093**	Paso Urus	-9.3540	-77.4251	5060	16600
20	**094**	Steep section	-9.3554	-77.4246	5000	16400
20	**095**	By small lakes	-9.3585	-77.4239	4880	16010
20	**096**	Refugio Ishinca	-9.3677	-77.4269	4380	14370
Quebrada Ishinca						
20	**097**	Pashpa, Plaza de Armas	-9.3874	-77.4167	4980	16340
20	**098**	Cochapampa	-9.3671	-77.4170	4630	15190
20	**099**	Signed Collón-Pashpa junction	-9.3812	-77.4812	3950	12960
20	**100**	Refugio Vivaque	-9.3736	-77.5216	3670	12040
20	**101**	Viewpoint of Milluacocha	-9.3776	-77.5288	3550	11650
20	**102**	Junction on bend by hut	-9.3819	-77.5180	3410	11190
20	**103**	Road junction to Collón	-9.3954	-77.5266	3280	10760
Wilcacocha						
21	**104**	Turn off 4WD track	-9.5961	-77.5144	3170	10400
21	**105**	Go R onto wide path	-9.6014	-77.5173	3370	11060
21	**106**	Wilcacocha	-9.5974	-77.5317	3720	12210
Laguna Churup						
22	**107**	Llupa, 'Cruce Pitec'	-9.5162	-77.4770	3430	11250
22	**108**	Leave 4WD for last time, going up steps	-9.5114	-77.4633	3620	11880
22/23	**109**	Pitec	-9.5057	-77.4423	3860	12660
22	**110**	Laguna Churup	-9.4865	-77.4309	4470	14670
22	**111**	Laguna Churupita	-9.4794	-77.4250	4600	15090
Laguna Shallap						
22	**112**	First chozas on way into Quebrada Shallap	-9.5121	-77.4263	3870	12700
22	**113**	Laguna Shallap	-9.4948	-77.3601	4280	14040
Quilcayhuanca – Cojup						
23	**114**	Portón de Quilcayhuanca	-9.4977	-77.4161	3840	12600
23	**115**	Nuevo Tambo	-9.4592	-77.3747	3980	13060
23	**116**	Bridge to Quebrada Cayesh	-9.4499	-77.3584	4040	13260
23	**117**	Cross stream at top right of pampa	-9.4285	-77.3515	4210	13810
23	**118**	Camp below Laguna Cuchilla	-9.4181	-77.3565	4540	14900
23	**119**	Cross/recross large side stream	-9.4155	-77.3600	4670	15320
23	**120**	Pass 2 stone circles	-9.4185	-77.3623	4770	15650
23	**121**	Moo lakes	-9.4191	-77.3666	4880	16010
23	**122**	Paso Huapi	-9.4193	-77.3762	5080	16670
23	**123**	Upper of the 2 pampas	-9.4143	-77.3815	4680	15350
23	**124**	Cross bridge over main river	-9.4193	-77.3897	4340	14240
23	**125**	Cross bridge over main river	-9.4466	-77.4148	4170	13680
23	**126**	Portón de Cojup	-9.4799	-77.4483	3830	12570
23	**127**	Marian	-9.5107	-77.5022	3290	10790
23	**128**	Laguna Tullpacocha viewpoint	-9.4241	-77.3475	4300	14110
23	**129**	Laguna Cuchilla viewpoint	-9.4151	-77.3545	4640	15220
23	**130**	Laguna Palcacocha viewpoint	-9.4002	-77.3832	4570	14990

Map	Wpt	Location	Latitude	Longitude	Alt (m)	Alt (ft)
Chacas – Huari						
24	131	Turn R at t-junction in Chacas	-9.1647	-77.3645	3380	11090
24	132	Leave jeep track by PNH sign	-9.1715	-77.3560	3430	11250
24	133	Signed junction and gate	-9.2001	-77.3460	3600	11810
24	134	Puente Taulle	-9.2191	-77.3233	3760	12340
24	135	Campsite by river	-9.2295	-77.2850	4350	14270
24	136	Paso San Bartolomé	-9.2432	-77.2704	4510	14800
25	137	Herder hut where route crosses valley	-9.2665	-77.2597	4230	13880
25	138	Little pampa with corral and gate	-9.3037	-77.2146	3960	12990
25	139	Hit road by Laguna Purhuay	-9.3165	-77.2066	3510	11520
25	140	Hit road in Acopalca	-9.3276	-77.1845	3060	10040
25/26	141	Huari, Parque Vigil	-9.3485	-77.1722	3110	10200
Quebrada Rurichinchay						
26	142	Leave road onto BsAs footpath in Huari	-9.3528	-77.1735	3110	10200
26	143	Yakya – road split	-9.3829	-77.1701	3510	11520
26	144	3660m Pass	-9.3902	-77.1735	3660	12010
26	145	Trailhead by shop in Mallas	-9.4013	-77.1959	3170	10400
26	146	Hit 4WD track in Quebrada Rurichinchay	-9.4030	-77.2116	3220	10560
26	147	Bridge to abandoned mine	-9.3758	-77.2605	3660	12010
26	148	Footbridge over Río Rurichinchay	-9.3669	-77.2693	3810	12500
26	149	Start of grassy ramp	-9.3515	-77.3053	4070	13350
26	150	Viewpoint overlooking Lagunas Rurichinchay	-9.3448	-77.3172	4560	14960
26	151	Hit Mallas-Huántar road by Río Rurichinchay	-9.4090	-77.1969	2990	9810
Quebrada Rurec (Conchucos)						
26	152	Huántar, Plaza de Armas	-9.4520	-77.1766	3350	10990
26	153	Leave road for footpath	-9.4472	-77.1829	3320	10890
26	154	Junction with link to Rurichinchay	-9.4341	-77.2060	3450	11320
26	155	Camp at head of Quebrada Rurec	-9.4249	-77.2749	3870	12700
26	156	Laguna Yuraccocha	-9.4429	-77.2838	4220	13850
26	157	Hit road near Río Rurec	-9.4300	-77.1910	3030	9940
Quebrada Carhuascancha						
27	158	Leave road for footpath via Barrio La Florida	-9.5941	-77.1791	3200	10500
27	159	Hit road to Jato	-9.5920	-77.1855	3410	11190
27	160	Olleros path joins in Chichucancha	-9.5792	-77.2295	3750	12300
27	161	Cross bridge in Huantsanpampa to N side	-9.5572	-77.2518	3970	13030
27	162	Climb up gully, through queñuales	-9.5382	-77.2770	4330	14210
27	163	Begin climb N, up ridge between strata	-9.5379	-77.2825	4380	14370
27	164	Go R/up, just before lake	-9.5284	-77.2840	4440	14570
27	165	Paso Santa Rosa	-9.5110	-77.2834	4780	15680
27	166	Turn L/W, climbing up ichu slopes	-9.4929	-77.2691	4350	14270
27	167	Moraine ridge overlooking Laguna Tumarina	-9.4906	-77.2925	4560	14960
27	168	Laguna Tumagarañon	-9.4833	-77.2995	4430	14530
27	169	Bridge on Tuctopampa	-9.4755	-77.2924	4210	13810
27	170	Laguna Maparaju Baja	-9.4704	-77.2992	4420	14500
27	171	Laguna Jacacocha	-9.4653	-77.2996	4530	14860
27	172	Laguna Cochapatac	-9.4683	-77.2916	4380	14370
27	173	Gate	-9.4796	-77.2533	3950	12960
27	174	Possible bridge to Ichic and Jatun Potrero	-9.4746	-77.2464	3900	12800
27	175	Hit Chavín-Huantar road	-9.4896	-77.1906	3340	10960
27	176	Yurayaco	-9.4912	-77.1783	3250	10660
27	177	Acopara	-9.4893	-77.1632	3160	10370
27	178	Puente Perla near San Marcos	-9.5189	-77.1570	2930	9610

Map	Wpt	Location	Latitude	Longitude	Alt (m)	Alt (ft)
Olleros – Chavín						
28	179	Cross bridge below Olleros	-9.6670	-77.4633	3430	11250
28	180	PNH info sign in Agocancha	-9.6769	-77.4356	3600	11810
28	181	Signposted junction to Quebrada Rurec	-9.6653	-77.4034	3880	12730
29	182	Rejoin 4WD track	-9.6576	-77.3635	4040	13260
29	183	Sacracancha	-9.6478	-77.3417	4030	13220
29	184	Shortcut from Quebrada Rurec joins	-9.6295	-77.3142	4350	14270
29	185	Punta Yanashallash	-9.6077	-77.2859	4680	15350
29	186	Shongo camp	-9.6041	-77.2591	4100	13450
27	187	Shortcut to Jato goes L	-9.5854	-77.2353	3850	12630
Quebrada Rurec (Huaylas)						
28	188	Leave main road on hairpin	-9.6661	-77.4600	3490	11450
28	189	Track	-9.6645	-77.4457	3660	12010
28	190	R, when track splits	-9.6623	-77.4378	3730	12240
28	191	Blue building	-9.6387	-77.3865	3970	13030
29	192	Laguna Tararhua viewpoint	-9.5691	-77.3298	4490	14730
29	193	Bridge over Río Rurec: shortcut to Chavín	-9.6319	-77.3682	4030	13220
29	194	Pass into Quebrada Uquian	-9.6383	-77.3656	4370	14340
29	195	Natural bridge over river in Quebrada Uquian	-9.6240	-77.3197	4210	13810
Quebrada Raria						
30	196	Quebrada Raria trailhead near Carpa	-9.8761	-77.2763	4220	13850
30	197	Lake 4390m	-9.8570	-77.2730	4390	14400
30	198	Punta Raria	-9.8226	-77.2185	4800	15750
30	199	Chozas on ridge	-9.8020	-77.2077	4460	14630
30	200	Taullucro	-9.7719	-77.2153	4180	13710
31	201	Bridge over Río Tiri	-9.7120	-77.1838	3860	12660
31	202	Hit road in Cristo Rey	-9.6596	-77.1877	3430	11250
31	203	Hit main Chavín-Catac road	-9.6492	-77.1983	3430	11250
31	204	Machac	-9.6384	-77.2029	3370	11060
Huayhuash Circuit						
32	205	Quartelhuain camp	-10.1550	-76.9235	4170	13680
32	206	Cacananpunta	-10.1566	-76.9117	4690	15390
32	207	Junction marked by cairn	-10.1572	-76.9099	4590	15060
32	208	Mitucocha camp	-10.1803	-76.8905	4240	13910
32	209	Cross second ridge	-10.1746	-76.9064	4600	15090
32	210	Join alternative day 2 route by roofless hut	-10.1907	-76.8945	4250	13940
33	211	Carhuac	-10.2115	-76.8734	4630	15190
33	212	Trail junction by Artuberto's chozas	-10.2319	-76.8726	4390	14400
33	213	Clifftop mirador overlooking Carhuacocha	-10.2417	-76.8704	4270	14010
33	214	Camp at NE corner of Carhuacocha	-10.2409	-76.8624	4180	13710
33	215	Camp at SE corner of Carhuacocha	-10.2435	-76.8594	4160	13650
33	216	Climb steeply from lakeshore	-10.2041	-76.8929	4260	13980
33	217	Pass into Hidden Valley (don't cross)	-10.2113	-76.8893	4640	15220
33	218	Cross ridge into Hidden Valley	-10.2136	-76.8902	4760	15620
33	219	High point 4870m	-10.2225	-76.8892	4870	15980
33	220	Pass 4810m	-10.2224	-76.8854	4810	15780
33	221	Gap by south shore of Laguna Alcaycocha	-10.2251	-76.8819	4690	15390
33	222	Junction to mirador	-10.2302	-76.8755	4550	14930
33	223	Mirador on side trip	-10.2398	-76.8739	4500	14760
33	224	Pass through wall	-10.2561	-76.8736	4250	13940
34	225	Classic mirador	-10.2850	-76.8646	4550	14930

MAP	WPT	LOCATION	LATITUDE	LONGITUDE	ALT (M)	ALT (FT)

Huayhuash Circuit (cont'd)

MAP	WPT	LOCATION	LATITUDE	LONGITUDE	ALT (M)	ALT (FT)
34	226	Siula Punta	-10.2875	-76.8556	4830	15850
34	227	Cross rock bridge	-10.3099	-76.8490	4660	15290
35	228	Meet mule path	-10.3209	-76.8421	4450	14600
35	229	Huayhuash camp	-10.3279	-76.8432	4350	14270
35	230	Punta Carnicero	-10.2888	-76.8374	4620	15160
35	231	Turn-off to Trapecio Punta from main route	-10.3409	-76.8447	4490	14730
35	232	Portachuelo de Huayhuash	-10.3705	-76.8451	4770	15650
36	233	Viconga gate/cobrador	-10.4124	-76.8492	4520	14830
36	234	Bridge/junction above Viconga camp	-10.4175	-76.8542	4380	14370
36	235	Viconga camp	-10.4187	-76.8578	4360	14300
36	236	Punta Cuyoc	-10.3939	-76.8795	5050	16570
35	237	Junction – R to Cuyoc camp, straight to Huanacpatay	-10.3800	-76.8913	4590	15060
35	238	Cuyoc Camp	-10.3759	-76.8930	4510	14800
35	239	Red scar	-10.3417	-76.8490	4470	14670
35	240	Cross ridge near Barrosococha	-10.3484	-76.8509	4580	15030
35	241	Path reappears/cross stream	-10.3491	-76.8589	4640	15220
35	242	Trapecio Punta	-10.3478	-76.8742	5030	16500
35	243	Start short climb by smaller lake	-10.3563	-76.8755	4810	15780
35	244	Steep descent between large and smaller lake	-10.3655	-76.8785	4810	15780
35	245	Steep scree on way to Paso Jurau	-10.3722	-76.8916	4590	15060
35	246	Paso Jurau	-10.3546	-76.8939	5060	16600
35	247	Reach grassy moraine ridge	-10.3364	-76.8913	4550	14930
35	248	Cutatambo camp	-10.3430	-76.9017	4270	14010
35	249	Sarapococha mirador	-10.3144	-76.9149	4620	15160
35	250	Sarapococha/Laguna Santa Rosa mirador	-10.3172	-76.9092	4560	14960
37	251	Huanacpatay camp	-10.3763	-76.9377	4320	14170
37	252	Junction – go L and cross river	-10.3753	-76.9420	4320	14170
37	253	Huanacpatay/Cutatambo routes join	-10.3586	-76.9583	4000	13120
38	254	Huayllapa cobrador and gate	-10.3572	-76.9969	3600	11810
38	255	Huayllapa	-10.3596	-77.0018	3500	11480
38	256	Lower Huatiaq camp	-10.3316	-76.9962	4270	14010
38	257	Take footpath when track bends R	-10.3063	-76.9971	4640	15220
39	258	Tapush Punta	-10.2913	-76.9992	4790	15720
39	259	Gashpapampa camp	-10.2747	-76.9976	4540	14900
39	260	Cross river in Quebrada Angocancha	-10.2674	-76.9932	4550	14930
39	261	Enter hidden pampa, and turn N	-10.2690	-76.9821	4640	15220
39	262	Yaucha Punta	-10.2673	-76.9770	4850	15910
39	263	Mirador 4900m	-10.2604	-76.9759	4900	16080
39	264	Cerro Huacrish mirador	-10.2461	-76.9766	4790	15720
39	265	Two trails remerge	-10.2412	-76.9697	4250	13940
39	266	Incahuain camp	-10.2360	-76.9661	4060	13320
41	267	Junction – Solteracocha/Rasaqcocha	-10.2379	-76.9430	4120	13520
39	268	Signposted junction – Llamac/water channel	-10.2326	-76.9912	4020	13190
40	269	Pampa Llamac pass	-10.2232	-77.0226	4270	14010
40	270	Paths rejoin just before yellow box	-10.2102	-77.0350	3890	12760
40	271	Llamac	-10.1979	-77.0328	3240	10630
41	272	Gate before climb to Sambuya Punta	-10.2322	-76.9452	4120	13520
41	273	Sambuya Punta	-10.2172	-76.9377	4750	15580
41	274	Rondoy Punta	-10.2140	-76.9368	4750	15580
41	275	Hit road in Rondoy	-10.1828	-76.9340	4010	13160
41	276	Pocpa	-10.1944	-77.0021	3470	11390

CYCLING WAYPOINTS

Huaraz Ruins Loop

Km	Wpt	Lat	Long	Alt (m)	Alt (ft)
0	277	-9.5233	-77.5285	3060	10040
1.7	278	-9.5101	-77.5322	3020	9910
7.5	279	-9.4838	-77.5108	3410	11190
8.4	280	-9.4878	-77.5075	3410	11190
8.9	281	-9.4865	-77.5035	3440	11290
13.8	282	-9.4948	-77.4790	3650	11980
17.2	283	-9.5118	-77.5028	3290	10790
20.2	284	-9.5249	-77.5126	3140	10300

Negra Acclimatization Loop

Km	Wpt	Lat	Long	Alt (m)	Alt (ft)
0	285	-9.5256	-77.5356	3030	9940
0.5	286	-9.5210	-77.5382	3040	9974
1.9	287	-9.5094	-77.5364	3050	10010
5.8	288	-9.4831	-77.5405	3010	9880
9.9	289	-9.4615	-77.5442	3080	10110
14.8	290	-9.4380	-77.5597	3260	10700
19.4	291	-9.4412	-77.5496	2920	9580
25	292	-9.4853	-77.5369	2980	9780
29.4	277	-9.5233	-77.5285	3060	10040

Blanca Acclimatization Loop

Km	Wpt	Lat	Long	Alt (m)	Alt (ft)
0	277	-9.5233	-77.5285	3060	10040
13.8	282	-9.4948	-77.4790	3650	11980
16.8	293	-9.4856	-77.4651	3800	12470
21.3	294	-9.4935	-77.4554	3820	12530
34.8	295	-9.5242	-77.4987	3230	10600
38.7	277	-9.5233	-77.5285	3060	10040

Santo Toribio Circuit

Km	Wpt	Lat	Long	Alt (m)	Alt (ft)
0	296	-9.5270	-77.5358	3030	9940
2.6	297	-9.5255	-77.5454	3180	10430
22.2	298	-9.5553	-77.6007	3930	12890
33.8	299	-9.4910	-77.5841	3990	13090
44.1	300	-9.5077	-77.5437	3160	10370
47.1	296	-9.5270	-77.5358	3030	9940

Laguna Llaca

Km	Wpt	Lat	Long	Alt (m)	Alt (ft)
0	277	-9.5233	-77.5285	3060	10040
1.7	301	-9.5189	-77.5200	3150	10340
5.4	283	-9.5118	-77.5028	3290	10790
8.8	282	-9.4948	-77.4790	3650	11980
11.8	293	-9.4856	-77.4651	3800	12470
23.3	302	-9.4373	-77.4478	4450	14600

Huascarán Circuit

Km	Wpt	Lat	Long	Alt (m)	Alt (ft)
0	303	-9.5295	-77.5292	3060	10040
2.5	278	-9.5101	-77.5322	3020	9910
5.5	292	-9.4853	-77.5369	2980	9780
17	304	-9.3993	-77.5731	2820	9250
25.5	305	-9.3278	-77.6016	2730	8960
33	306	-9.2843	-77.6469	2650	8690
83.5	307	-9.1312	-77.5109	4890	16040

Huascarán Circuit (cont'd)

Km	Wpt	Lat	Long	Alt (m)	Alt (ft)
126	308	-9.1158	-77.3682	2860	9380
130.5	309	-9.0842	-77.3700	2990	9810
154.5	310	-9.0518	-77.4519	4070	13350
164	311	-9.0212	-77.4714	3390	11120
198	312	-9.0511	-77.5909	4710	15450
212.5	313	-9.0485	-77.6103	3930	12890
226.5	314	-9.1054	-77.6886	3400	11160
244	315	-9.1440	-77.7450	2490	8170
266	306	-9.2843	-77.6469	2650	8690
299	303	-9.5295	-77.5292	3060	10040

Huayhuash and Puya Raimondii Loop

Km	Wpt	Lat	Long	Alt (m)	Alt (ft)
0	303	-9.5295	-77.5292	3060	10040
42.5	316	-9.8526	-77.4067	3740	12270
80	317	-10.1221	-77.2931	4110	13480
93.5	318	-10.0861	-77.1941	4260	13980
122	319	-10.1741	-77.1169	2870	9420
130	320	-10.2033	-77.0915	2770	9090
165.5	321	-10.0957	-76.9415	4610	15120
193.5	322	-9.9001	-76.9403	3550	11650
209.5	323	-9.8509	-77.0379	4150	13620
220.5	324	-9.8569	-77.0820	4670	15320
226	325	-9.8349	-77.1157	4880	16010
243.5	326	-9.8818	-77.1860	4820	15810
273	316	-9.8526	-77.4067	3740	12270
315	303	-9.5295	-77.5292	3060	10040

Cordillera Blanca Circuit

Km	Wpt	Lat	Long	Alt (m)	Alt (ft)
0	303	-9.5295	-77.5292	3060	10040
24.5	327	-9.7138	-77.4610	3410	11190
26.5	328	-9.7269	-77.4514	3410	11190
35.5	329	-9.7695	-77.4179	3640	11940
65	330	-9.6893	-77.2546	4470	14670
94.5	331	-9.6104	-77.1823	3220	10560
98	332	-9.5853	-77.1779	3140	10300
120.5	333	-9.4555	-77.1754	3350	10990
133.5	334	-9.4104	-77.1928	3010	9880
143.5	335	-9.3936	-77.1605	3420	11220
151.5	336	-9.3474	-77.1713	3110	10200
188.5	337	-9.1694	-77.2243	4360	14300
215.5	338	-9.0854	-77.3439	2980	9780
223.5	308	-9.1158	-77.3682	2860	9380
228	309	-9.0842	-77.3700	2990	9810
248.5	339	-9.0097	-77.3654	2590	8500
253	340	-8.9888	-77.3768	2460	8070
268.5	341	-8.9416	-77.3372	2800	9190
307	342	-8.8205	-77.4604	2960	9710
334	343	-8.7016	-77.5373	3770	12370
340.5	344	-8.6741	-77.5541	3490	11450
390	345	-8.5943	-77.6567	3630	11910
398.5	346	-8.5717	-77.6805	4200	13780

KM	WPT	LAT	LONG	ALT (M)	ALT (FT)
Cordillera Blanca Circuit (cont'd)					
447.5	347	-8.6799	-77.8912	2410	7910
470	348	-8.7447	-77.8992	1390	4560
511.5	349	-8.9895	-77.8273	2120	6960
520.5	350	-9.0484	-77.8096	2270	7450
525.5	351	-9.0807	-77.7826	2270	7450
534	315	-9.1440	-77.7450	2490	8170
556	306	-9.2843	-77.6469	2650	8690
589	303	-9.5295	-77.5292	3060	10040
Alternative route via Catac					
10	352	-9.8081	-77.4288	3560	11680
17	329	-9.7695	-77.4179	3640	11940
Alternative route via San Marcos					
8	353	-9.5266	-77.1574	2980	9780
10.5	354	-9.5092	-77.1507	2950	9680
26.5	355	-9.3935	-77.1425	2620	8600
38	336	-9.3474	-77.1713	3110	10200

KM	WPT	LAT	LONG	ALT (M)	ALT (FT)
Alternative route via Pomallucay					
0	338	-9.0854	-77.3439	2980	9780
8	356	-9.0688	-77.3527	2780	9120
15.5	339	-9.0097	-77.3654	2590	8500
Laguna Parón					
0	350	-9.0484	-77.8096	2270	7450
1.5	357	-9.0349	-77.8144	2330	7640
10.5	358	-9.0331	-77.7636	2830	9290
33	359	-8.9993	-77.6848	4200	13780
Winchus Loop					
0	350	-9.0484	-77.8096	2270	7450
5	351	-9.0807	-77.7826	2270	7450
40.5	360	-9.1124	-77.8759	4290	14080
42.5	361	-9.1022	-77.8880	4210	13810
46	362	-9.0715	-77.8945	4380	14370
80.5	349	-8.9895	-77.8273	2120	6960
89.5	350	-9.0484	-77.8096	2270	7450

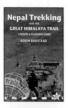

TRAILBLAZER TITLE LIST

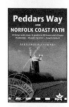

For more information about Trailblazer and our
expanding range of guides, for guidebook updates or
for credit card mail order sales visit our website:

www.trailblazer-guides.com

INDEX

Page references in **bold** type refer to maps
Abbreviations: **L** = Laguna; **N** = Nevado; **Q** = Quebrada

(**Opposite**): Lazing by Arhuaycocha, gazing at Artesonraju; Santa Cruz trek.
(**Overleaf**): Descending to Cutatambo on the Huayhuash Circuit.

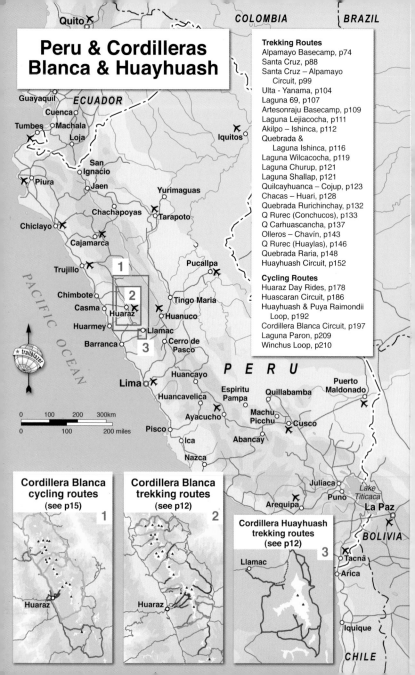

Peru & Cordilleras Blanca & Huayhuash

PACIFIC OCEAN

COLOMBIA   BRAZIL

ECUADOR

Quito

Guayaquil
Cuenca
Tumbes   Machala
    Loja
Piura   San
    Ignacio   Iquitos
    Jaen
Chiclayo   Chachapoyas   Yurimaguas
    Cajamarca   Tarapoto
Trujillo   1
Chimbote   2   Pucallpa
Casma   Huaraz   Tingo Maria
Huarmey   Llamac   Huanuco
Barranca   3   Cerro de
        Pasco

P E R U

0 100 200 300km
0   100   200 miles

Huancayo
Lima   Huancavelica   Espiritu   Quillabamba   Puerto
        Pampa   Maldonado
    Ayacucho   Machu
        Picchu   Cusco
Pisco   Ica   Abancay
    Nazca

Juliaca   Lake
    Titicaca
Arequipa   Puno
    La Paz

BOLIVIA

Tacna
Arica

Iquique

CHILE

Cordillera Blanca cycling routes (see p15)
1

Huaraz

Cordillera Blanca trekking routes (see p12)
2

Huaraz

Cordillera Huayhuash trekking routes (see p12)
3

Llamac